D1495619

Letting the Side Down

BRITISH TRAITORS OF THE SECOND WORLD WAR

Sean Murphy

SUTTON PUBLISHING

First published in 2003 by
Sutton Publishing Limited · Phoenix Mill
Thrupp · Stroud · Gloucestershire · GL5 2BU

British Library Cataloguing in Publication Data
A catalogue record for this book is available from the British Library.

ISBN 0 7509 2936 7

Typeset in 11.5/15pt Photina.
Typesetting and origination by
Sutton Publishing Limited.
Printed and bound in England by
J.H. Haynes & Co. Ltd, Sparkford.

Contents

List of Illustrations

Photographs courtesy of The National Archives.

To the memory of my Mother and Father

Acknowledgements

I would like to express my gratitude to the following people for helping me with my research for this book: Adrian Weale, Bryan Clough, Alan Wharam, Terry Charman, Dr Edgar Flacker, Hugh Alexander, and Julie Ash. I particularly want to thank Dr Robert McKeever, my former tutor in the Department of Politics at Reading University, for his continuing support and general encouragement.

I am also indebted to the staff of the following institutions for their time and assistance during the course of my research: the National Archives (Public Record Office), the British Library, the Imperial War Museum, the Wiener Library, and the BBC Written Archives Centre. Finally, I would like to express my gratitude to my family for their unfailing support, especially Jessica, and my loving sisters Kate and Lizzy.

Foreword

The process of unravelling the full story of the British traitors and renegades of the Second World War has been long and tortuous – and isn't over yet. For nearly fifty years, the dead hand of British official secrecy prevented the whole sordid but fascinating tale from emerging.

But a process which started with John Major's Conservative government, and which has been continued by Tony Blair's Labour administration, has finally allowed many – if not the majority – of the British government's official files on Second World War treason to be released into the public domain.

This can only be a good thing: Britain's Nazi renegades were neither politically nor strategically significant, but their stories serve as a reminder to us that we were lucky to avoid invasion and occupation by Nazi Germany, and that we were lucky that a broader section of British people weren't subjected to the pressures and temptations which caused many of the renegades to change sides.

Sean Murphy has used the latest releases of intelligence documents into The National Archives to peel away yet another layer of the myth, hyperbole and obscurity which has surrounded the renegades, and to explain what caused these people to throw in their lot with Nazi Germany, thus 'letting the side down'. I very much hope you will enjoy reading it as much as I did.

Adrian Weale
Nasiriyah
Iraq
October 2003

Introduction

The popular image of the British public standing shoulder to shoulder with Winston Churchill in 1940 against the might of Hitler's blitzkrieg is an honourable one. Most Britons did support the war. The German invasion of Czechoslovakia in March 1939 in defiance of the Munich Agreement illustrated that Hitler was not to be trusted. The German assault on Denmark, Norway, Belgium and France in May 1940 that broke the deadlock of the 'phoney war' confirmed in the minds of the British public that Germany was a rogue state that had to be halted in its tracks. This general view was reinforced by the determination of Winston Churchill. The view in cabinet that Hitler had to be stopped prevailed over the suggestion of some kind of negotiated peace with Germany.

For a small group of British subjects however Hitler and his Axis partner Italy, and later Japan, could do no wrong. In these people's minds it was Britain that was engaged in an unjust war in which it faced almost certain defeat. The purpose of this book is to provide an account of those British citizens who, by collaborating with the enemy, were in fact 'letting the side down'. In the first section of the book I examine the background activities of various Hitler admirers and sympathisers in pre-war Britain. Many of the 'fellow travellers' of the political right regarded Hitler as a reliable barrier against the spread of Russian communism. It would be wrong to describe this mainly aristocratic clique as 'traitors'. Most were first and foremost patriotic Britons. When war came they remained loyal. This also included the majority of followers of Oswald Mosley's British Union of Fascists.

In the second section of the book I examine the more extreme far-right pro-German sympathisers who continued to support Hitler even after war had started. Many of these individuals had been members of the British Union of Fascists and ended up living in Germany collaborating with the Nazis. Those who did not have an ideological commitment either to fascism or the Nazi Party are also included in this section. These collaborators were motivated by personal or financial gain, greed, fear, blackmail, or some other psychological reason. I have also looked once more at the allegations of collaboration against the Duke of Windsor and P.G. Wodehouse that rear their head from time to time. The notorious Russian 'Cambridge spy ring' that embraced Guy Burgess, Donald Maclean and Kim Philby is not included in this study, partly because the various Soviet spies have been extensively covered elsewhere, but more importantly because Soviet Russia became an ally of Britain following the German invasion of Russia in June 1941.

I have used both extensive primary and secondary sources for this book. More security files are now being released by the government and no doubt further details of British collaborators in the Second World War will emerge over the next few years.

CHAPTER ONE

Hitler's Admirers and Fascism in Britain

On 30 January 1933 Adolf Hitler was appointed Chancellor of Germany. The British Ambassador in Berlin, Sir Horace Rumbold, wrote: 'That Hitlerism will ultimately lead to war is a contingency which cannot be ruled out.'[1] Rumbold had witnessed first hand the rise of National Socialism and believed that with Hitler at the helm Germany would embark on a policy of territorial expansion in Europe. Rumbold sent a five-thousand word memorandum to his masters at the Foreign Office outlining the menacing role of ideology in Nazi foreign policy. His despatches were to become prophetic: 'I should not like to bank on his [Hitler's] desire for peace four or five years hence.'[2] Unlike many of his fellow British diplomats Rumbold had actually read Hitler's vision of 'Lebensraum' expounded in *Mein Kampf*, and was appalled at the anti-Semitism of the Nazis. In London the Army Chiefs of Staff warned the cabinet that German rearmament was under way and that Britain might be forced within a few years to intervene militarily to fulfil her obligations under the Locarno Treaty to prevent German aggression in Europe. In February 1934 the conclusion of a study by the Defence Requirements Committee, set up to take stock of Britain's long-term military position, reported that 'We take Germany as the ultimate potential enemy against whom our long-range defensive policy must be directed.'[3] The views of the military seemed to have been vindicated when Hitler withdrew Germany from the League of Nations in 1933 and two years later introduced conscription.

Not everybody held such negative views of Hitler. The owner of the *Daily Mail* Lord Rothermere wrote a series of articles praising the new German Chancellor. 'The sturdy young Nazis,' he wrote in the *Daily Mail* of 28 November 1933, 'are Europe's guardians against the Communist danger.' Rothermere visited Hitler in Germany and began a correspondence with him. The *Daily Mail*'s special correspondent Ward Price became Hitler's favourite foreign journalist, finding Hitler's fondness for children and dogs 'proof of his good nature'.[4] Lord Londonderry was another Hitler enthusiast. On 12 March 1936 he wrote to *The Times* supporting Hitler's takeover of the Rhineland. He also wrote a book about his visits to Germany, during which he had a two-hour meeting with Hitler.[5]

Many British aristocrats and members of the landed gentry became enthusiasts of the Nazi regime. For these ultra-conservative groups Hitler represented a bulwark against communism. His economic policies promised high employment, and public work schemes such as the building of the autobahns were an indication that Germany was recovering from the Depression years. Hitler's highly charged suspicion of all Jews struck a cord with anti-Semitic groups within British society and there was a steady stream of such pro-German British visitors to Germany during the 1930s. Most saw some virtues in the Nazi totalitarian dictatorship. The Nuremberg Rallies were an opportunity for certain members of London's high society to rub shoulders with Hitler and his henchman. The Mitford sisters Unity and Diana, daughters of Lord Redesdale, were admitted to the Nazi inner circle. When Diana Mitford married the British fascist leader Oswald Mosley in Berlin in October 1936, the couple exchanged rings at the home of Joseph Goebbels and Hitler attended the wedding reception. Another visitor to Germany was Admiral Sir Barry Domville. After joining the Navy in 1892, Domville rose to become Chief of Staff Mediterranean Fleet and Director of Naval Intelligence, before taking up his final position as President of the Royal Naval College at Greenwich. Domville was invited by Hitler to visit the 1936 Nuremberg Rally. After being introduced to Hitler at a tea party he wrote of the German leader: 'This remarkable man was fully alive to the evil potentialities of Judmas, and was determined to remove its influence from European affairs.'[6]

'Judmas' was the name Domville gave to his paranoid obsession with an imaginary conspiracy of Jews and Freemasons. The anti-Semitic Domville took the salute at a military march past in Berlin, and subsequently became a friend of SS chief Heinrich Himmler, whom he accompanied on shooting parties in the Bavarian Alps. Domville later wrote to Himmler and his wife inviting them to visit him if they should come to England.[7] Domville also visited Mussolini in Rome, taking his place besides the Italian dictator at a fascist parade.

It was perhaps rather strange that Domville played down his active interest in politics. In reply to a question from a journalist about his political beliefs, the Admiral declared: 'I am non-party. I hold no political views.'[8] A year earlier the *Berliner Tageblatt* had published an article specially written by Domville for the German press, supporting the German claim for colonies. This gave the Nazis the impression that the sympathetic view of the German cause held by a senior British naval officer would not have been given without British government approval. Domville also wrote the preface to a book designed to show the good side of the Nazi regime by Professor A.P. Laurie entitled *The Case for Germany*. The book was printed by the International Publishing Company of Berlin, a firm under the control of the German Propaganda Ministry.

A further influential fan of Germany was Ernest Tennant, a successful merchant banker. Tennant was a frequent business visitor to Germany, and eventually became a good friend of Von Ribbentrop the former German champagne salesman who later became German Ambassador to London and was subsequently tried for war crimes at the Nuremberg Trials after the war and hanged. Tennant was keen to encourage trade links with Germany and established and financed the Anglo-German Fellowship in 1935.

Perhaps the two most high-profile visitors to Berlin during this period were the former Prime Minister Lloyd George and the former king Edward, Duke of Windsor. Referring to Hitler as 'a great man', Lloyd George told the House of Commons in November 1934 that conservative elements in Britain looked to Germany as a bulwark against communism in Europe. The Germans believed that the ex-king was sympathetic to their fascist views and that had he remained on the throne, Britain and Germany might well have drawn closer together. They were probably correct on the issue of sympathy. The Duke of Windsor took the Hitler salute twice during his visit to Germany, and revealed in 1941 while Governor of the Bahamas his belief that Hitler was the right and logical leader for the German people and that it would be a tragedy if he were overthrown.

The 1930s saw the emergence in Britain of a number of pro-Nazi and anti-Semitic groups. Ernest Tennant was the driving force behind the Anglo-German Fellowship. This group was comprised mainly of businessmen who wanted to maintain commercial contacts with Germany, plus a fair number of British aristocrats who felt a kindred spirit with their Prussian counterparts. It was a powerful lobby which included Lords Airlie, Brocket, Londonderry, Lothian and the Duke of Wellington plus an assortment of MPs and merchant bankers. Large well-known companies were also corporate members of the Fellowship, including ICI, Tate & Lyle, Unilever and Dunlop. The Fellowship served German propaganda purposes in pursuit of consolidating Anglo-German relations. It held glittering gala dinners attended by the German Ambassador, the Duke and Duchess of Brunswick and on at least one occasion by the Foreign Secretary Lord Halifax.

Admiral Sir Barry Domville expanded his pro-Nazi, anti-Semitic philosophy by forming The Link, a group of about four thousand well-connected society figures who were obsessed with the idea of a Jewish take-over of the world, as explained in a document entitled *The Protocols of the Elders of Zion*. *The Protocols*, discovered after the First World War, had fostered the belief that there was a Jewish conspiracy for world domination working in conjunction with leading Russian communists, who just happened to be Jewish. In 1921 *The Times* proved that *The Protocols* were a forgery, concocted by the police in Tsarist Russia to justify their pogroms against the Jews. Domville continued to encourage pro-Nazi sympathies through the activities of The Link. In December 1938, Herr Karlowa, the head of the German Ausland organisation in the United Kingdom, sent a circular letter to five prominent leaders of the Nazi Party in Britain inviting them to a social function organised by The Link. The following passage is taken from the letter: 'I have promised Admiral Domville that we will take part and will see that young ladies attend as dancing partners. We wish to take part in this gathering of The Link and I request you to take energetic steps to see that this is done.'[9]

The Nordic League was a group of race-conscious Britons, including many well-to-do women, who were strongly supportive of Hitler's persecution of the Jews. One of its leading lights was Margaret Bothamley, a colonel's daughter who became a staunch supporter of Nazism in all its forms. Although membership was small, leading figures of the Nordic League were also in touch with other extreme pro-German groups such as the Imperial Fascist League and the National Socialist League, the latter founded by William Joyce, who would eventually become known during the war as Lord Haw-Haw.

Another anti-war movement, the Right Club, was established by Captain Archibald Ramsay in the summer of 1939. Ramsay was a backbench Conservative MP who had represented Peebles and South Midlothian since 1931. He was a Scottish aristocrat who had seen service in the First World War before being badly wounded and invalided out of the Army. Like other extremists, Ramsay became convinced that international communism was controlled by world Jewry. He believed the message conveyed in the forged *Protocols of the Elders of Zion* document, and strongly supported Hitler's persecution of Jews. Only a few days after the infamous Nazi *Kristallnacht* pogrom against the Jewish population of Germany, in which homes, businesses and synagogues were ransacked and some thirty thousand Jews arrested, Ramsay and other pro-German sympathisers had lunch at the German embassy in London.[10] The Right Club membership was made up of establishment figures from the British upper classes, aristocrats and about a dozen Members of Parliament. Captain Ramsay later maintained that the object of the Right Club was to expose the activities of organised Jewry, especially within the Conservative Party. For Ramsay the Jewish conspiracy was forcing Britain into a war in which millions of gentiles would be killed. His patriotic goal was, as he put it, 'to save this country from the strangled tentacles of the Jewish octopus'.[11] The Club's membership was secret and its members listed in the 'Red Book', a sort of right-wing *Who's Who*. There were 135 male members and about 100 'Ladies', all entered in the book in Ramsay's own handwriting. Many of the Club's members were also involved with the Nordic League and The Link.[12]

BRITISH UNION OF FASCISTS

Perhaps the best-known organisation to emerge in the 1930s, containing both pro-German enthusiasts and anti-Semitic elements within its ranks, was the British Union of Fascists (also called the BUF). Various fascist groups had first emerged in Britain during the 1920s, but were considered fringe organisations lacking in any real organisation or leadership. However, the emergence of former Labour cabinet minister Sir Oswald Mosley as a major British fascist and the setting up of the British Union of Fascists party in 1932 sent an uncomfortable message to a British cabinet already concerned by the activities of fascist parties in Italy and Germany. A meeting was called at the Home Office to discuss the potential threat posed by the British Union of Fascists. Representatives of the Metropolitan Police Special Branch and MI5 agreed that Mosley's party and all fascist groups should be put under surveillance in the same way that communist organisations were. The surveillance of British fascists was to reach its peak in 1940 with the internment of Mosley and his core followers, which will be examined in a later chapter.

Oswald Mosley has often been described as a 'brilliant, flamboyant and handsome politician'. He was descended from an aristocratic land-owning Lancashire family that had originally made its money as hatters and clothiers before moving into the property business. Educated at Winchester and Sandhurst Royal Military Academy, the former public schools' fencing champion was commissioned into the 16th Lancers at the outbreak of the First World War, but soon volunteered for the Royal Flying Corps. Mosley was one of the first men to fly over the enemy lines as an observer and he went on to train as a pilot. In 1915 during his pilot training Mosley crashed his plane sustaining severe leg injuries. Before he had fully recovered, and in great pain, he was recalled to his regiment and later saw action at the battle of Loos. After further hospital treatment he was invalided out of the Army with a permanent limp and spent the remainder of the war working as a temporary civil servant at the Ministry of Munitions.

Mosley's fascism was rooted in the First World War. His wartime experiences in the carnage of the trenches made him determined to prevent another conflict and he felt a sense of responsibility to ensure that his friends and contemporaries had not died in vain on the battlefields of France. Filled with an idealistic desire to prevent another European conflict and a determination to build a new postwar 'land fit for heroes', Mosley entered the political arena. In 1918 he was elected as Conservative Member of Parliament for Harrow, then became an independent MP before joining Ramsay McDonald's Labour Party in 1924. He rose to prominence in the Labour Party, serving as Chancellor of the Duchy of Lancaster in the Labour government of 1929–31. But his radical proposals for dealing with the Depression, which involved huge borrowing and a draconian increase in government power were rejected by the Labour Party leadership. As a result, in 1931, Mosley broke with Labour and formed the New Party, to make a stand against what he considered the discredited 'old gang' of the established parties. The New Party performed badly in the 1931 general election. Its meetings were disrupted by political opponents on the left, which on one occasion resulted in Mosley being pelted with stones and chased through the streets of Glasgow.

Mosley's visit to Italy in 1932 had a major effect on him. He respected Mussolini's fascist ideas, which Mosley believed could be adopted to work in Britain. For Mosley the only way for Britain to achieve economic progress and social justice was through the setting up of a corporate state under a one-party regime. Mosley saw the future Britain as 'a society working with the precision and harmony of a human body. Every interest and every individual is subordinate to the overriding purpose of the nation.'[13]

Mosley formed the British Union of Fascists in October 1932. The blueprint for the party's political agenda was Mosley's book *The*

Greater Britain. This fascist handbook urged the establishing of a corporate state through a series of massive public works programmes to solve the unemployment problem, to provide economic protection for home markets, and ensure British non-involvement in all foreign affairs that did not directly affect Britain and her empire. The British Union of Fascists was run along paramilitary lines complete with ranks, Blackshirt uniforms, Roman-type salutes and even a military style private barracks – the so-called Black House in Chelsea. Operating along similar lines to Mussolini's fascists, the purpose of the Blackshirts was to protect Mosley's meetings so that he could argue the fascist position in highly charged speeches without being interrupted by communists and other 'hecklers'. The Blackshirts were armed with truncheons, knuckle-dusters and lead hosepipes and were driven to meetings in armoured cars. Mosley's organisation included a women's section, a Blackshirt Automobile Club and a fascist flying club that included former RAF First World War pilots. Mosley believed that as social conditions worsened in Britain there would be a breakdown in law and order, which could only benefit communists and socialists. Mosley's sense of destiny led him to think that only his well-drilled army of Blackshirts could save Britain from impending economic chaos.

During 1935, Mosley received financial support to the tune of £3,000 a month from Mussolini. Mussolini also made four payments of £5,000 and a special donation of £20,000 to the BUF via a secret London bank account during the mid-1930s.[14] There is no direct proof of financial help from Hitler, although Mosley's wife Diana did try to get money from the Nazis to set up a commercial radio franchise to broadcast programmes from Germany into Britain to boost BUF funds, but the venture never saw the light of day. Prominent figures in British life did offer Mosley philosophical support. These included Henry Williamson, author of *Tarka the Otter*, who attended the Nuremberg Rally in 1935, and the respected British military strategist General 'Boney' Fuller who was a guest at Hitler's birthday celebrations only a few months before the outbreak of war in 1939.

Mosley acknowledged that Lord Nuffield, the owner of the Morris Motors' company, had donated £50,000 to his party. As well as his admiration for Hitler, Lord Rothermere also supported the BUF, writing a series of articles in his newspaper the *Daily Mail* under the headline 'Hurrah for the Blackshirts'. By August 1934, BUF membership had reached 50,000. However, Mosley's hopes were dealt a severe blow by the violence which erupted during the fascist rally at Olympia in June 1934. About twelve thousand people attended the indoor arena, including two thousand Blackshirts. Mosley's speech was continually interrupted by left-wing hecklers, who were violently beaten by Mosley's Blackshirt bodyguards and ejected from the arena. According to Special Branch detectives, knuckle-dusters, razor knives and coshes had been used on members of the public.[15]

The result of the Olympia violence was that wealthy benefactors such as Lord Rothermere and other establishment figures withdrew financial support from the BUF. For many, the Olympia debacle and the wider fascist policy of using violence against political opponents was an uncomfortable reminder of the Nazi Party's murder of its Brownshirt opponents during the infamous 'Night of the Long Knives'. Following the defection of Lord Rothermere, the anti-Semitic section within the BUF believed that a policy specifically attacking Jews would build support in the East End of London, where a large Jewish community of Eastern European origin had developed since the end of the nineteenth century. Anti-Semitic propaganda was well received in the East End, which was then facing large-scale unemployment and housing problems. The BUF attracted working-class support by blaming economic conditions in the East End on Jewish-run businesses, landlords and employers. The BUF did not regard Jews as British, perceiving them as foreigners. Mosley spoke of Jews forming a state within the state and stated that Jews were engaged in social and economic practices which were alien to the British character. At public meetings Mosley accused Jews of being a threat to the nation's economy and of swamping the cultural identity of localities where they had settled.[16]

Mosley's desire to exploit the relative economic success of East End Jews by stirring up feelings of hatred among non-Jews affected by the Depression was similar to the tactics used by Hitler in Germany.

On 11 May 1935 the *Frankfurter Zeitung* published a telegram from Mosley to Julius Streicher, the Nazi Party's notorious 'Jew-baiter'. The telegram thanked Streicher for congratulating Mosley on a recent anti-Semitic speech. Mosley's message read:

> Please accept my very best thanks for your kind telegram which greeted my speech in Leicester. It was received while I was away from London. I value your advice greatly in the midst of our hard struggle. The power of Jewish corruption must be destroyed in all countries before peace and justice can be successfully achieved in Europe. Our struggle to this end is hard, but our victory is certain.[17]

Given Mosley's respect for the totalitarian regime in Germany, it was perhaps no surprise that he renamed his movement the British Union of Fascists and National Socialists in 1935. The BUF rallies in the East End were intended to stir up intense racial hatred. William Joyce described Jews 'as an incredible species of sub-humanity, a type of sub-human creature'.[18] A BUF pamphlet said: 'Not so long ago East London was the home of British stock. The cabinet-maker, polisher and tailor were Englishmen. Today the Englishman in East London is the slave of the Jewish master.'[19]

Opposition to the BUF in the East End was organised by the Communist Party, the Independent Labour Party and the Jewish People's Council against Fascism and Anti-Semitism. Things came to a head in October 1936 when Mosely decided to lead his Blackshirts through the East End to intimidate the Jewish community. When the Blackshirts approached Cable Street, a crowd of some hundred thousand opponents blocked their path. Seven thousand policemen had been assembled to protect the fascists, but after several hours, heavily outnumbered and facing a hail of chair legs, bricks and milk bottles, the police ordered Mosley to change the route of the march and turn westwards. Angry and humiliated, Mosley was forced to abandon the march.

One result of the 'Battle of Cable Street' was police concern about the political violence associated with both the BUF and their communist opponents. This threat to public order posed by political extremism led to the passing of the Public Order Act in 1936, which banned the wearing of political uniforms in public and outlawed paramilitary organisations, which made it difficult for the BUF to defend their outdoor meetings and demonstrations. The police were also given the power to ban marches if they were likely to cause a breach of the peace, and the use of inflammatory language was declared unlawful in public speeches. Following the 'Battle of Cable Street' and the passing of the Public Order Act, the BUF began a gradual decline. At local council elections in 1937 the BUF stood in several parts of the country but did not win a single seat. Its candidates in Manchester, Leeds and Sheffield all finished bottom of the poll, and while it did receive significant votes in the East End, the BUF failed to get any candidates elected. Mussolini withdrew his financial support and Mosley was forced to cut BUF staff members and move his organisation out of the Black House headquarters in Chelsea to more modest accommodation.

ANTI-WAR SENTIMENT

As well as the efforts of fanatical German 'enthusiasts' keen to foster good relations with Hitler, there was also a general sense of pro-German (though not pro-Nazi) sympathy for Germany among the British public during the early 1930s. Britons realised that Germany had been treated harshly under the Versailles treaty that followed the First World War. By the terms of the treaty, Germany lost territory to France, Belgium, Denmark, Lithuania and Poland. Its African colonies were taken away, and German union with Austria was forbidden. The Rhineland was ordered to be permanently demilitarised. Germany was forced to accept sole blame for the war and to pay millions in reparations for damage done to the Allies, even though it was on the verge of bankruptcy with 6 million people unemployed.

After the carnage of the First World War and the effects of the Depression, there was an anti-war sentiment in Britain. The Peace Pledge Union, an anti-war organisation with 150,000 members, urged people never to support the horrors of war again. At Oxford University, undergraduates voted not to go to war under the resolution 'That this House will in no circumstances fight for its King and Country'. In 1933 a by-election took place at Fulham in which a Labour pacifist candidate easily defeated a pro-rearmament government candidate. The Peace Ballot carried out by the League of Nations Union in 1935 which attracted votes from almost 12 million Britons, showed decisive support for Britain remaining a member of the League of Nations and favouring an all-round reduction of armaments by international agreement.[20]

Hitler played on the sense of guilt many in Britain felt about the way Germany had been treated under the punitive terms of the Versailles treaty. It had deprived 20 million Germans in the Saarland, Rhineland, Austria, Sudetenland, Danzig and the Polish Corridor of the right to be part of the fatherland. When Hitler re-occupied the Rhineland in 1936, the Liberal Lord Lothian remarked that German troops had merely entered their own 'back garden'. Hitler's desire to unify Germany with Austria and to incorporate all Germans within Germany, including those in Czechoslovakia, was respected by Neville Chamberlain. The British Prime Minister wanted to resolve differences with Hitler and show him that reasonable territorial claims could be met by negotiation rather than by force. Appeasement failed because in the end Hitler believed that to achieve his aims he would have to pursue a policy of brute force rather than come to terms with Britain and France through negotiation and compromise.

Chamberlain believed Hitler was telling the truth when the German leader had assured him at their historic meeting in Munich in September 1938 that his desire to incorporate the Sudetenland German minority in Czechoslovakia within the Nazi Reich was his last territorial claim in Europe. Six months after the transfer of the Sudetenland from Czechoslovakia to Germany, Hitler entered Prague, effectively destroying Czech sovereignty. The take-over of Prague was a demonstration of blatant aggression. Hitler had broken his promise and seized non-German territory to which he had no legitimate claim.

Following the collapse of the Munich agreement and German occupation of the whole of Czechoslovakia, a strong sense of moral outrage gripped Britain. It now seemed that Hitler's aims were unlimited. Many within the pro-German groups also started to have second thoughts about Hitler. They had no objection to the German leader persecuting communists or German Jews, but they were concerned about Hitler's aggressive foreign policy, and alarmed at the possibility that Germany could pose a threat to Britain's European position. Pro-Germans like the *Daily Mail*'s George Ward Price and the banker Ernest Tennant realised that Hitler's apparent desire to limit his international aims to protecting German minorities was a sham. Tennant had a last-ditch meeting in Germany (with the unofficial blessing of Chamberlain) with his old friend Ribbentrop in an effort to ease international tension. Ribbentrop told Tennant that British statesmen never really understood Hitler and that if Britain wanted war, 'Germany is ready'.[21] Anti-communists were puzzled and angry about the signing of the Nazi–Soviet Pact. So much for Hitler standing as a bulwark against communism! With the approach of war, British fascists and others on the political right had to choose between their sympathy for Nazi ideology and their patriotic duty as British citizens under threat from a foreign power. When the crunch came most remained loyal, with only the extremist German sympathisers such as William Joyce and Margaret Bothamley continuing to support Hitler's aggressive actions.

GERMAN SPIES

Following the outbreak of war, MI5 closely monitored the various British fascist and other extreme pro-German groups, although there is no evidence that members of these factions had any direct dealings with the German Intelligence service. In fact Hitler had hardly any spies operating in Britain in 1940. Until 1937 the German leader regarded Britain as a potential ally, and refused to let the Abwehr Intelligence service establish an espionage organisation there. However, there were a few incidents of British citizens spying on behalf of Germany prior to the Second World War. One case involved a 51-year-old hairdresser from Dundee called Jessie Jordan, the widow of a German soldier who had been killed in the First

World War. The couple had met years earlier in Scotland when Jordan was working as a domestic servant. Jordan remained in Hamburg after the First World War to open a hairdressing salon. Her business began to suffer after the Nazis came to power because she had a large Jewish clientele. In 1937 she decided to move back to Scotland to work as a housekeeper for her brother who had recently been widowed. It appears that she mentioned her new plans to a friend whose husband was in the Abwehr security organisation. The agent whom Jordan visited in a house in Hamburg subsequently recruited her for the spying mission to Scotland. He was already under surveillance by the British Security Service, who in turn followed and continued to monitor Mrs Jordan.

On her return to Dundee she opened a hairdressers shop, which had a fine view of the Firth of Tay and the Tay Railway Bridge. Despite ostensibly returning to Dundee to start a new life, Jordan visited Germany twelve times within eight months, each time being followed by British agents. MI5 obtained a warrant to intercept her mail, and it was discovered that large cash sums were being paid into her bank account. Having given her hairdressing clients her 'special', a 'Viennese Wave', she would leave her shop dressed in old clothes and go on a tour of Scottish east-coast defence stations, carefully marking them off on ordnance maps she had bought. She also visited Aldershot and Southampton on the pretext of taking a nephew to visit relatives. She dropped the boy off with an aunt and continued her mini tour of defence establishments around the United Kingdom.

MI5 discovered that Jordan was also acting as a 'post-box' cover for the Abwehr. Her German spy masters had told her to expect letters from the United States and that she was to forward such letters unopened to addresses in Hamburg and Amsterdam. The discovery of Jordan's postal activities resulted in MI5 alerting the FBI, who eliminated a major German spy network in America. When the police raided Jordan's shop they discovered the defence maps and sketches she had been hoarding. She denied everything in court and even pretended to have forgotten how to speak English fluently, having spent so many years in Germany. But prosecution evidence showed that, although no Mata Hari, her approach was based on giving the appearance of a harmless Scottish housewife, and she obtained information by cracking jokes with barmen across the counters of pubs in the military centres she visited.

Jessie Jordan received four years' penal servitude for 'being in communication with foreign agents between 1 June and 2 March 1938: 'for purposes prejudicial to the purposes and interests of the State.'[22] She later admitted her crimes to MI5 during the war when her case came up for parole.

The interception of letters in the postal system also helped to trap another British traitor. Donald Adams was a racing journalist living in Richmond, Surrey. He had served in the Royal Army Service Corps during the First World War, before being transferred to the Egyptian Labour Corps. After demobilisation in 1921 he remained in Egypt. During this time he associated with a number of local women and lived off immoral earnings. In 1924 he was repatriated from Cairo, and offered his services to MI6 to act as an agent in Palestine. His offer was refused and so he approached the German secret service.

Adams was probably recruited when he worked as a London representative of a German export firm, Burgman of Dresden. His work often took him to Germany and Holland. It was a letter written by Adams acknowledging receipt of £10, which had been sent to him by Messrs Kol & Company, Bankers of Amsterdam, that trapped him. The bank was the conduit for payment to German agents operating in Britain. The information he was providing was poor and easily available from daily newspapers and specialist magazines. Then in June 1939 another letter written by Adams, this time to a cover address in Germany, was intercepted; it gave intricate details of the balloon barrage chain then being built around London. He gave details of the size and number of barrage balloons, how many men it took to inflate and maintain them and their height and manoeuvrability. Adams was arrested and charged that 'He did between November, 1938, and June 30 1939, record information relating to HM Forces which is calculated to be, or might be, directly or indirectly, useful to an enemy'.[23] In September 1939, Adams was sentenced to seven years' imprisonment.

The third espionage case involving a British citizen occurred in the months leading up to the Second World War. It involved an Irish bricklayer named Joseph Kelly who had been working as a labourer erecting the Royal Ordnance Factory at Euxton in Lancashire. Police reported the removal of site plans of the factory after a break-in. Because the theft from the munitions factory occurred at a time of increased IRA activity in mainland Britain, MI5 at first believed that the IRA were acting in conjunction with the Nazis. But at this stage of the IRA's 'English campaign' to bomb Britain into granting a united Ireland, there were no firm links between Irish Republicans and the German Intelligence service. Kelly was a stupid fool who was drawn into espionage through his own greed.

Joseph Kelly was a thirty-year-old married man living in Bolton with his wife and three children. He had previously been in trouble with the law for assaulting the police, breach of the peace, stealing lead and breaking into a warehouse. For these acts he had variously been fined, bound over or placed on probation. He later told police he was first approached outside the factory by an Englishman who offered him money to obtain plans of the site. Kelly was told to go to the German consulate in Liverpool where he offered his services to the Germans. The consul was not expecting Kelly, but took his name and address and said he would get it to the 'right quarter'. Shortly afterwards Kelly received a letter from Holland containing a German visa and a £5 note. He then burgled the factory and took two design plans. The Germans paid him £30 for his work. He hid one plan in his house and took the other with him to Holland. MI5 intercepted the letter Kelly received from Holland because it originated from a cover address used by the Abwehr in the Netherlands. Kelly told his friends in Bolton he was going to Germany to watch a boxing match. Talk among the local boxing fraternity of Kelly's impending visit to Germany revealed that the man he said he was going to watch fight (Paddy Ryan), was at that moment actually in training for a different fight in the north of England. As a result, an acquaintance of Kelly's told the police the Irishman was up to no good. While he was abroad his home in Bolton was searched and the various letters from his 'contact' in Holland recovered. Kelly was followed to Holland where he met a German agent, and then to Cologne where he visited a known Abwehr building. When he returned to England he was watched from the time he disembarked from the boat at Harwich and was eventually arrested at Bolton railway station. When Kelly appeared in court in May 1939 he pleaded guilty to charges under the Official Secrets Act. The prosecution told the court Kelly had entered an office of the munitions factory to obtain plans: 'For a purpose prejudicial to the interests of the State; and attempting to communicate one of these plans, which might be useful to an enemy – in this case the German Espionage Service operating against the United Kingdom'.[24] He received ten years' penal servitude for his crimes and was sent to Dartmoor prison.

After the war had started German spies who were parachuted into Britain or landed by sea, were captured almost immediately. The spies were a mixture of Germans, Danes, Dutch, Swedes, Norwegians and even three Cubans. They were arrested and transferred to Latchmere House, MI5's holding centre for captured enemy agents. Here they were given the choice of either agreeing to work for the British security service or being shot as spies. Most agents were broken under interrogation or agreed to be turned into double agents, but the handful who refused to co-operate were tried and executed under the Treachery Act.[25]

HITLER'S ENGLISHWOMAN

Someone who perhaps most embodied a love of Hitler, a belief in the Nazi cause and a hatred of all things Jewish, was the young daughter of an aristocratic British baron. Lord Redesdale (David Bertram Freeman-Mitford, 2nd Baron Redesdale) was a member of the council of The Link and a keen participant in the Anglo-German Fellowship. His interest in politics clearly rubbed off on his children because three of his daughters became involved in political movements. Unity and Diana (who later married Oswald Mosley), pursued a fascist agenda, while Jessica committed herself to the cause of international socialism.

As a debutante, Unity Mitford's life was an endless round of balls and dinner parties. She was outrageous in her pro-Nazi views, and told anybody who would listen that the Jews had to be got rid of. She met her sister's fiancé Oswald Mosley, who gave her a Blackshirt party emblem, and Unity proudly marched into her local BUF office in Oxford explaining that she knew the party leader personally. She was one of the BUF representatives on the delegation sent to attend the Nazi Nuremberg Rally in 1933. In the summer of 1933 Unity based herself in Munich at a finishing school run by a German baroness. In between taking classes in art, gymnastics and tap-dancing, Unity revealed to her family back in England that she wanted to meet Adolf Hitler. She discovered that the German leader liked to unwind in a small informal Munich inn called the Osteria Bavaria. Unity reserved a nightly table in the restaurant, befriended the doorman and waitresses and waited for Hitler to appear. He soon noticed her and, after enquiring of the restaurant staff who she was, invited Unity to join him for coffee.

What interested Hitler about Unity was her striking looks and confident English manner. He gradually got to know Unity and later her sister Diana, describing them as 'perfect specimens of Aryan womanhood'. Unity could talk to Hitler with an amusing frankness that no German, whether man or woman, would have dared use. She had a good command of German and Hitler probably wanted some light relief from his entourage of 'yes men' and Unity was always on hand to provide it. Unity's friendship with Hitler led to invitations to his flat for tea and to attendance at several high-profile Nazi Party functions. She became a good friend of Joseph and Frau Goebbels and other influential Nazi officials, although some like Heinrich Himmler remained suspicious of the gushing English girl, even suspecting her of being a spy. The young English aristocrat also aroused jealousy among some female relatives of the Nazi leaders.

Unity and Diana attended the Berlin Olympic Games in 1936 as special guests of the Führer. He made them both party members and put his signature on the back of the party badges they wore as a guarantee that their right to them should not be challenged. When Unity was in England she would greet friends with the Nazi salute and the words 'Heil Hitler'. Her car carried a red Nazi pennant on the front off-side wing. While attending a rally in Hyde Park organised by the Labour Party against the British policy of non-intervention in Spain, Unity and some fellow fascists attempted to raise a swastika banner. The crowd set about them and in the scuffle Unity lost her swastika badge. She punched one woman who told her to go back to Germany but Unity had to be rescued by the police when a group of demonstrators tried to throw her in the Serpentine. Hitler personally replaced her lost Nazi party badge.

It is very doubtful whether Unity actually had any influence on Hitler's thinking. She may have given him the impression that important people in England were sympathetic to Germany's aims, but as she was spending almost all of her time in Germany her main conversations with Hitler revolved around art, music and German theatre. Nevertheless, via British diplomatic circles in Europe the titbits Unity gleaned from her conversations with Hitler did reach official ears. After Unity had taken tea with Hitler at his flat in the Prinz Regentenstrasse, Hitler and Goebbels discussed Mussolini's forthcoming German visit. The British Consulate General in Munich sent a message to the British embassy in Berlin on 27 September 1937:

Miss Mitford told Herr Hitler later on that the Duke of Windsor was arriving on the evening of the 25th. Herr Hitler replied 'If Mr Baldwin had not turned out King Edward VIII I might have been receiving him here today instead of Mussolini'.[26]

A year later, on 20 September 1938, the British Consul General in Vienna wired the British Ambassador in Berlin:

Unity Mitford has just been in to see me and has told me that she saw Hitler privately after his Nuremberg speech, when he advised her to leave Germany at once and to tell 'all her English friends' to do the same, as he felt certain there would be war. She says he has now changed his view, but I don't think she has seen him recently. She is staying in Burgenland and said I need not bother to warn her to go, as if war broke out she would of course stay in Germany.[27]

When war did come Unity sent several messages to Hitler asking to see him. He made no reply. She had a permit from the Gestapo to carry a small revolver. Although she had no British fire-arms certificate Unity used to smuggle the weapon in and out of the country. Clearly upset over the declaration of war by Britain against Germany, and hearing nothing from Hitler, Unity went for a walk by herself in the English Garden in Munich. A German friend, concerned at Unity's chronic depression, followed her. The 'friend' saw Unity take a seat, produce the hand gun from her handbag, fire one shot into the ground to see if it was working, before placing the gun against her right temple and pulling the trigger. Unity was rushed to hospital where Hitler, Goebbels and Ribbentrop all sent flowers. Hitler later visited her, paid her medical bills and arranged for her to be transported back to England via Switzerland.

Unity Mitford returned to Britain by cross-Channel ferry, landing at Folkestone on 3 January 1940. Lord and Lady Redesdale were awaiting her arrival in a private ambulance. The British press was quick to criticise what they considered her 'preferential treatment' at the port. The *Daily Mirror* of 26 January wrote: 'the Mitford girl, who has openly been consorting with the King's enemies goes scot free – why? God and the House of Lords only know.' Questions were asked in Parliament about why Unity had not been interned under Defence Regulation 18B. MI5 were also a little puzzled as to why Unity had not been detained in a secure hospital. Some within the security services even doubted whether Mitford had shot herself at all.

In an effort to clarify Unity's physical and mental state the Home Office sent the Chief Constable of Oxford T.E. St Johnstone to interview Lord Redesdale in London. He told the policeman that Unity had been a staunch admirer of Nazi philosophy for many years and was genuinely in love with Hitler himself, though this love was mostly hero worship. Redesdale said Hitler regarded Unity as a very sincere friend but nothing more. Unity's father said he had met Hitler many times and was completely taken in by his apparent desire for peace, but that he had since realised how very insincere all Hitler's statements on this subject had been. When asked about his daughter's present condition Redesdale replied that Unity was physically active and strong and at times would appear mentally normal. Generally she remained listless, could not concentrate and would be quite incapable of organising any activity either for or against the national cause. She would sit and look straight ahead, child-like, while he talked to her. Unity was rarely left alone, being looked after by her mother and two former family servants. She would sit in a bath for hours, once refusing to get out until her father came to High Wycombe from London to help her. She was also incontinent and suffered from a loss of balance.

Chief Constable St Johnstone also studied Unity's medical report which had been prepared by Professor Hugh Cairns, then one of the foremost neurosurgeons in England. His review confirmed that 'The bullet entered the right frontal region, traversed the brain and lodged in the left occipital lobe'. He concluded that 'Unity is incapable of any intellectual activity that would materially assist enemy action in this country'.[28] For this reason St Johnstone recommended against interning Unity.

The controversy surrounding Unity's actions continued after the war. In a session of the House of Commons on 5 December 1945, the MP for Gravesend Garry Allighan asked the Attorney-General whether the government 'proposed to prosecute Miss Unity Mitford, who returned to this country from Germany in 1940 after consorting with the enemy during the war while having the benefit of His Majesty's passport'. The Solicitor-General replied: 'No sir, there is no evidence in the possession of the authorities that would justify criminal proceedings against Miss Mitford.'

Unity Mitford died in the West Highland Cottage Hospital, Oban on 28 May 1948.

CHAPTER TWO

War

In 1939 Oswald Mosley addressed a large crowd at London's Earls Court arena, where he urged Britons to stop the drift to war and repeated his view that Britain had no quarrel with Germany. In Mosley's opinion German expansion in Eastern Europe was of no concern to Britain. He went a step further in maintaining that Britain was about to be dragged into a war by an international Jewish conspiracy working against Germany. After the outbreak of war Mosley campaigned for a peace with Hitler, but also instructed BUF members in the armed forces to obey the orders of their superiors. Most of the smaller fascist and other extreme pro-German groups, such as the Nordic League and The Link, closed down when war was declared, realising that the government would take action against them. The security services knew that secret meetings were held in London attended by Ramsay, Mosley and representatives of the Right Club and the Nordic League including the pro-Nazi Sir Barry Domville. On a visit to the Star and Garter home for ex-servicemen in Richmond, Domville told the elderly residents there was no need to worry because Hitler was going to win the war and bring the Duke of Windsor back as king. It would be to the benefit of everyone once Hitler was in the country, argued the fascist ex-admiral.[1]

In March 1940 Mosley gave a speech at London's fashionable Criterion restaurant to an audience of some five hundred mostly right-wing diners. Once again he argued that the real reason Britain had gone to war with Germany was because the British government was under the control of the Jews. Mosley's mainly wealthy listeners were prepared to accept lingering doubts about the wisdom of fighting Hitler six months after war had been declared. MI5 infiltrated the Criterion lunch as part of its surveillance against the secretive co-operation between hardcore pro-German groups.

THE FIFTH COLUMN SCARE

The German invasions of Denmark, Norway, Belgium, Holland and France in May 1940 led to an almost hysterical suspicion that an organised 'fifth column' of enemy sympathisers and helpers must have been at work in these countries to explain the lightning success of the German blitzkrieg. Sir Neville Bland, the British Ambassador to the Netherlands, sent a report to the new Prime Minister Winston Churchill suggesting that sabotage inside the Dutch government helped the Germans to overrun Holland. He also suggested that even ordinary kitchen maids of German origin were a potential menace to the safety of the Netherlands. In Britain, especially after the disaster at Dunkirk, there was a belief that a similar fifth column inside the country was secretly preparing the way for an invasion. A certain amount of hysteria in the country was directed against people with foreign accents, names or appearances. Members of the public imagined the infiltration of enemy spies everywhere. A man wrote to the War Office in London claiming that coded messages had been left on telegraph poles as a guide for German parachutists. In fact the markings were the work of the local Boy Scouts! Pigeons were also widely suspected of being used to secretly communicate with the enemy and the authorities recruited British birds of prey to intercept homing pigeons released by German agents in Britain. During a police raid on one woman's house, officers found a diary with the entry: 'M.49 destroy British Queen. Install Italian Queen.' It took police six weeks to discover that the woman was a bee-keeper and the diary entry referred to a way of improving the breeding of bees![2]

The press carried scare stories of German agents sabotaging factories, while Mosley's former deputy William Joyce (Lord Haw-Haw) was fast gaining a reputation for detailed knowledge of the intimate goings-on of the British people at war. He supposedly knew on which particular day the village clock in Banstead was running a quarter of an hour slow. There were also the German radio propaganda stations that pretended to be anti-war underground operations run from inside Britain. Such stations were designed to sow confusion and help prepare the way for loyal Britons opposed to 'Churchill's war' to assist the Germans once the invasion had begun.[3]

Churchill was persuaded by MI5 that many foreign nationals living in Britain, as well as refugees from the Low Countries fleeing the German advance, could form part of a potential fifth column. As a result most aliens were rounded up and interned in camps around Britain. In the period May to July 1940, about 22,000 Germans and Austrians and 4,000 Italians were interned.[4] Some of these people had lived in Britain for many years while others were German Jews who had come to Britan to escape persecution by the Nazis.

THE TYLER KENT AFFAIR

The fear of German infiltration in Britain was reinforced by the discovery by MI5 that a cipher clerk at the American embassy called Tyler Kent was intercepting and removing private communications between Winston Churchill, at that time First Lord of the Admiralty, and the American President Franklin D. Roosevelt. In May 1940, America was still neutral but Tyler Kent was an isolationist who did not agree with American diplomats in Europe such as Paris Ambassador William C. Bullitt, who adopted a pro-British and anti-German policy. He also believed that President Roosevelt was being unconstitutional in his efforts to support the Allies against Hitler, by cunningly attempting to manoeuvre the United States into the European war.[5] Kent was anti-Semitic and anti-communist, and was transferred to London in 1939 after spending five years at the American Embassy in Moscow.

At the beginning of 1940, Kent made contact with Anna Wolkoff, a high-class dressmaker and naturalised Britain of Russian parentage. Anna Wolkoff's father, Admiral Wolkoff, had been the Tsar's naval attaché in London at the time of the Russian Revolution and subsequently took a strong anti-communist line. The fiercely anti-Semitic Wolkoff family ran the Russian Tea Rooms in South Kensington that became a meeting place for right-wing political agitators including members of the Right Club. Kent joined the Right Club and told Wolkoff about the sensitive diplomatic files stored at his London flat. Anna in turn introduced Kent to her friend and Member of Parliament Maule Ramsay. Ramsay read some of the Churchill–Roosevelt correspondence. He immediately realised that Roosevelt's public support for American isolationism was a façade, and that he was secretly hoping to get America into the war on the side of Britain. If the correspondence was made public either thorough the press or by Ramsay asking awkward questions in the House of Commons, the documents could embarrass both Roosevelt and Churchill for carrying out such secret communications.

An added complication was the fact that Wolkoff had also passed on some of the intercepted files to a military aide at the Italian embassy in London. Although Italy was neutral, Rome shared certain information with Berlin, and extracts from the Roosevelt–Churchill communication were soon relayed by message to the German Ambassador in Rome. The British government secret Code and Cypher Unit intercepted the Rome message and MI5 realised the damage Kent and Wolkoff had caused to British security. MI5 also had a source of information much closer to home. In true cloak and dagger style a well-bred beautiful ex-cosmetics model turned agent called Joan Miller infiltrated the Right Club. An older MI5 agent named 'Mrs Amos' had introduced her to the Russian Tea Rooms in South Kensington. The older woman had previously been infiltrated into Anna Wolkoff's circle and introduced Joan Miller to Wolkoff as a friend of her son who was serving with the Navy. Curious, Wolkoff asked Joan what job she did and the young agent replied that she had a very boring filing job in the War Office. After the initial introduction to Wolkoff Joan Miller made a habit of calling in at the Tea Rooms, meeting among others Anna Wolkoff's father, the ex-Russian admiral. Joan gradually won the Wolkoffs' confidence by opposing Britain's involvement in the war and her apparent support for the fascist cause. She also invented a pre-war romance with a German officer to add credibility to her position on the war.

As she gained the Wolkoffs' trust Joan became aware of the link between Tyler Kent, Maule Ramsay and the Wolkoff clique. As her friendship with Anna developed Joan found out about Anna's contact at the Italian Embassy.

One day Anna confided in Joan that she had an important message to send to Lord Haw-Haw (William Joyce) in Berlin. The message was just a list of suggested topics for Joyce to include in his Lord Haw-Haw propaganda broadcasts. Wolkoff urged Joyce to avoid mentioning the King in his announcements; to focus more on Churchill's unpopularity by talking about his disastrous Gallipoli campaign in the First World War; to alert listeners to the spread of anti-Semitism; and to add that workers, wives and soldiers were generally all fed up with the war.

Anna told Joan that because her regular contact at the Italian Embassy who would have sent the message to Joyce was ill, she would have to think of another way of getting her note delivered to Joyce (see Chapter Ten). Thinking quickly on her feet, Joan said she believed their mutual friend 'Helen' (another MI5 agent planted in the Kensington Tea Rooms), had a contact in the Romanian Embassy who might be able to help. 'Helen' agreed to assist, and gladly took the letter from Wolkoff. It was sent to Berlin via an MI5 contact in the Romanian Embassy, and shortly afterwards William Joyce confirmed delivery of the message by using a code word in his nightly broadcast.

Joan Miller completed a full report on her surveillance of the Wolkoffs for her boss at MI5 Maxwell Knight (who in later years found fame as 'Uncle Max' the popular presenter of BBC children's programmes). Knight decided that he now had enough evidence to act against Wolkoff, Kent and Ramsay. In fact Kent had been under MI5 surveillance since shortly after arriving in London. En route to England the American had made contact with a naturalised Swedish businessman originally of German stock named Ludwig Matthias. Kent was persuaded to carry a package for Matthias through customs using his diplomatic status. The Swedish police had already alerted Scotland Yard that Matthias was probably a Gestapo agent and when the Swede visited Kent at his West End hotel to retrieve the parcel he had given him for safekeeping, Maxwell Knight's agents followed and identified Kent. The MI5 agents then followed Kent and Matthias as the two men left the hotel together to have dinner in Piccadilly Circus. The reason Maxwell Knight did not move sooner against Kent, or alert the Americans to the clandestine activities of their code expert, was that MI5 wanted to bide its time in the hope of discovering whom else Kent would implicate from among London's pro-German groups, which was exactly what happened.

In the early hours of 20 May, MI5 raided Tyler Kent's flat at 47 Gloucester Place and discovered over a thousand top-secret documents. Police also found the full membership list of the Right Club, which had been entrusted to Kent in a red leather ledger by Maule Ramsay for safe-keeping. The American government waived Kent's diplomatic immunity and he was tried under the Official Secrets Act and sentenced to seven years' imprisonment. Anna Wolkoff received ten years. The arrest and trial of Kent and Wolkoff were the signal for an unprecedented upsurge in the arrest and detention of British fascists. The War Cabinet amended the emergency Defence Regulation 18B, giving the security services new powers to round up and intern all right-wing subversives. The beefed-up defence legislation allowed internment without trial for members of organisations who might be subject to foreign 'influence' or who might 'sympathise' with the system of government of enemy powers. This meant that the security services no longer had to prove that subversive acts had been committed before extremists could be interned.

The British Union of Fascists was proscribed and some eight hundred of its members interned. In normal circumstances imprisonment without trial is anathema to the British people. In fact no evidence existed linking Mosley directly to the Tyler Kent case but Churchill accepted MI5's view that if a German invasion took place Mosley could join the enemy or attempt a coup. Following the retreat from Dunkirk and with Britain facing the threat of an imminent invasion by the Germans, BUF opposition to the war could no longer be tolerated. The government took the view that individual freedom had to be sacrificed for the sake of the country's national security and general morale. The fact that Mosley and Ramsay were 'in communication' meant that the whole spectrum of fascists and anti-Semites was a major concern for the government. MI5's Maxwell Knight described the Right Club as 'carrying on pro-German activities, and secret subversive work, with the object of disorganising the Home Front and hindering the prosecution of the war'.[6] This led to the internment of Ramsay, Sir Barry Domville and most of the neo-fascist fringe extremists who had been meeting secretly since the outbreak of war. An MI5 assessment of Mosley's party justified the security clampdown:

> Under the cover of patriotic slogans such as 'Britain for the British' the movement has become more and more sympathetic with the National Socialist regime in Germany. Its organisation was akin to that of the German National Socialist Party; its leaders visited and talked with the leaders of the Third Reich, and Mosley initiated many of the demagogic tricks of Hitler. For instance, in order to attract adherents to his cause he adopted anti-Semitism, and played on a fear of Communism, and general economic discontent. The outbreak of war found the BUF advocating peace and thus by implication defending the actions of the enemy. Some of its members were so seduced by the ideology of the totalitarian regime that they were prepared to commit offences under the Defence Regulations, and in certain cases showed themselves ready to give assistance to the enemy.[7]

When Mosley appeared before a security advisory committee set up to interrogate fascist internees he suggested that there appeared to be two grounds for detaining BUF members: either because they were traitors, or because their propaganda was undermining civilian morale. The advisory committee's chairman Lord Birkett replied, 'speaking for myself, you can entirely dismiss the first suggestion'. Mosley sent out mixed signals. He admired both the Nazi political system and Hitler's European aims. At the same time as calling for peace with Germany the fascist leader also believed that if Germany were to invade Britain then Britain should fight the Nazis 'with all that is in us'.[8] But he also led a paramilitary organisation modelled on fascist lines, which sang a marching anthem to the tune of the

Nazi 'Horst Wessel' song. Mosley accepted significant financial support from the Italian dictator Mussolini, although he failed in his attempt to get German financial backing for a European commercial radio franchise. Mosley also attempted, with Hitler's help, to secure a radio franchise to transmit programmes from Germany into Britain. Intended to raise funds for the BUF, the business venture never saw the light of day.

The Tyler Kent affair did reveal a conspiracy of sorts. During his advisory committee interrogation, Mosley denied ever having met Ramsay prior to their internment, although MI5 knew the fascist leader had previously visited Ramsay four times at the House of Commons.[9] When questioned by the advisory committee Ramsay related a conversation in which Mosley had invited him to take over Scotland 'in certain circumstances'.[10] Under interrogation Mosley never admitted taking part in the secret meetings with other extremist groups and also denied receiving money from Mussolini on the grounds that he did not know every single source of BUF funding. Mosley told his Special Branch interrogators he believed about only 5 per cent of his followers were possibly acting against the interests of the state.[11] In fact many BUF members fought bravely for king and country during the war including the fiercely anti-Semitic A.K. Chesterton, who served with the British Army in East Africa. One of the earliest casualties of the war was K.G. Day, a Blackshirt serving in the RAF. Altogether about a thousand of Mosley's followers were killed in action during the war.[12] Mosleyites who had recently been evacuated from the beaches at Dunkirk were arrested on their return to Britain. Also interned were BUF veterans of the First World War such as Jim Humphries, holder of the Military Cross and the Croix de Guerre.

BUF NAZI SYMPATHISERS

As MI5 reports indicate, not all BUF members obeyed Mosley's orders to remain within the law, patriotic and loyal to the Crown. There were incidents of subversion carried out by BUF members and pro-German sympathisers.

Alexander Crowle, a Devonport dockyard worker, was arrested for sending details of shipping movements in the Plymouth area to *Action*, the Blackshirt newspaper. Crowle and an accomplice Claude Duvivier, a naturalised British citizen from Belgium, were each sentenced to six months. Rex Freeman, a railway worker and a member of the Stoke Newington branch of the BUF, was prosecuted for printing and distributing sticky-back labels advertising the wavelength of the New British Broadcasting Station, a German propaganda radio organisation transmitting from Berlin. Freeman was sent to prison for five years.[13] His mother Violet, also a Mosleyite, was sentenced to a year in prison for helping her son distribute the propaganda stickers. Olive Baker, a 39-year-old nurse and recent convert to the BUF, also received a five-year jail sentence for distributing postcards advertising the New British Broadcasting Station. While awaiting trial, she slashed her wrists and wrote 'Hail Mosley' and '*Heil Hitler*' in blood on the walls of her prison cell.[14] Elsie Orrin, a Mosleyite from Leyton, was convicted of spreading 'disaffection' among the British Army when she told two soldiers in a London pub that Hitler was a better man and leader than Churchill. Orrin was sentenced to five years' imprisonment. Even Churchill was surprised and uneasy that Orrin was jailed merely for expressing an opinion.[15]

William Craven, an agricultural labourer from Gloucester, was arrested for attempting to 'communicate with the enemy'. Craven was the only child of a Liverpool Corporation worker. His mother died when he was two and after attending elementary school he had drifted in and out of menial work. He taught himself to read and write German though he was never able to speak it fluently as he had a pronounced stammer. Craven first came to the attention of MI5 in 1938 when he started a series of meetings in Liverpool's docks, preaching Nazi and fascist doctrines and distributing BUF propaganda material. His pro-Nazi leanings and belief that he had German ancestry led him to write a letter to the German War Ministry offering his services to the Reich. His letter read:

As a Nordic Aryan proud of my German blood, I believe that the future of the white civilisation is in the hands of Germany united under Adolf Hitler. I therefore desire to place my services and my life at the disposal of the Reich, and to eventually earn the honour of becoming a German citizen, to which end, I am prepared to formally renounce my British nationality, an act which, in spirit, I have already accomplished. Please consider me from this date, as being in your service, for any task, under any circumstances and at any time. *Heil Hitler.*[16]

The letter was intercepted by MI5 and in September 1939 Craven was interned as an 'undesirable' member of the BUF under Regulation 18B. On his release from detention in 1940 Craven approached the Finnish Legation in London to offer his services for the volunteer force being raised to fight the Russians. MI5 believed this was a ruse to get himself to Germany via Finland. Even the BUF found his views extreme and he was ordered by a London official of the party not to attend any branch meetings of the party or to identify himself openly with it.

He then left the BUF, switching his allegiance to the more extreme British National Party, which was formed in 1942 by Edward Godfrey, a wholesale fishmonger from Middlesex. Following his second spell of detention Craven was directed to do agricultural work in Gloucestershire. He enlisted in the Royal Army Service Corps and waited for news of his posting. Instead he received a letter telling him his services were no longer required as he had been interned. The army recruitment agency had run a security check on Craven with MI5, who said that if Craven was allowed to join up, he might engage in activities prejudicial to the security of the state. This led Craven to write a letter to the German Legation in Dublin offering his services, but once again the letter was intercepted by the security service. Its contents followed the same pattern as his earlier letter:

As one who has been, and still is, a friend of Germany, and accepts Adolf Hitler as the leader of Europe, I am deeply grieved over the present situation of the Fatherland. By her refusal to consider the Führer's repeated offers of peace, especially after the consolidations of Europe and the opening of the crusade against Bolshevism,

Britain has lost all moral justification for continuing this fratricidal struggle in the name of justice and humanity. The refusal of Britain to at least withdraw from the conflict and cease to impede Germany in the period following June 1941 and the recent subservient alliance of Churchillian Britain with the America of sycophantic Roosevelt, led me to the decision that there is a higher duty than patriotism, which is the duty of defending our common civilisation against the domination of Asia.[17]

Craven appeared at the Old Bailey and was sentenced to life imprisonment. The trial judge told Craven that the jury had found him guilty of committing an act likely to assist the enemy at a time when hundreds of his fellow countrymen were dying for their country.

There were other cases of pro-German or at least anti-British behaviour. Marie Louise Ingram was a 42-year-old from Southsea who worked in the home of a senior naval officer based at the Navy's Mine Development Department. Ingram was German by birth but had married a sergeant in the RAF and so was exempted from internment. She attempted to recruit BUF member William Swift, a navy dockyard foreman from Portsmouth, into a plot to organise German sympathisers in the event of a German invasion. A Special Branch raid on Ingram's house confirmed her Nazi leanings, uncovering a cache of Nazi flags and photographs. Swift was jailed for fourteen years for attempting to help Ingram 'commit acts calculated to assist an enemy', while Ingram received a ten-year sentence. Charles Max Sakritz, a BUF member with pro-German views from Forest Gate, was sent to prison for a year for defacing a wartime government poster at Upton Park, West Ham. All these offenders were tried under the wartime Defence Regulations legislation that punished anyone who 'communicated information which might be of assistance to an enemy'.

The more extreme members of the Right Club were interned but those whom Special Branch was keen to interview stayed hidden in London safe houses. Shortly after the arrest of Jock Houston, a prominent BUF anti-Semite agitator, his girlfriend Mollie Hiscox and her friend Norah Briscoe were picked up by the police and sent to trial at the Old Bailey. Briscoe, a 41-year-old widow with a young child, had lived in Germany before the war and was very pro-Nazi. Leaving her child to be brought up in Germany, Briscoe returned to England and took a secretarial job in the Ministry of Supply. Mollie Hiscox was a former BUF member who left to join The Link and spent most of her summer holidays in Germany. A Hitler worshipper, Hiscox wrote a letter to the German leader three days before the outbreak of war expressing her unlimited trust in him.[18] Aided by Hiscox, Norah Briscoe planned to do her bit for the German cause by stealing secret documents from her work place. Unfortunately for Briscoe, an MI5 agent acting as an *agent provocateur* befriended Hiscox, and sprung a trap, into which both women fell. Although they had been set up by MI5, both women had clearly intended to supply information to the enemy and were each sent to prison for five years.

There is a certain amount of mystery surrounding the activities of Arthur Albert Tester, another prominent British fascist. Born in 1895 to a British father and German mother, Tester spent his formative years as a businessman in Germany. During this time he specialised in swindling the public by forming bogus companies and enterprises all of which collapsed. He was expelled from France in 1927 on suspicion of conducting espionage on behalf of Germany. The Dutch authorities were keen to interview him concerning forgery and bankruptcy allegations, so he decided to move to England. Although he was technically declared bankrupt in 1930, Tester lived in a large country house in Broadstairs in Kent. He hitched himself to Oswald Mosley's party, becoming a propaganda and press officer for the BUF, and he arranged with Hamburg lawyer Richard Behn to translate into German Oswald Mosley's book *100 Questions Asked and Answered*.

In December 1938, Tester acquired a 250-ton yacht named *Lucinda* and travelled to the Mediterranean with his wife and business associates. Three members of the boat's crew later signed police statements confirming that when they docked at Naples, the fascist flag was hoisted, and Tester donned a BUF uniform (the wearing of fascist uniform in Britain had been banned under the

1936 Public Order Act) and attempted to convert the crew to fascism. Tester also visited local fascists and had a secret meeting with Mussolini in Rome.

In 1939, the *Lucinda* was requisitioned by the British authorities at Port Said. Tester was arrested and deported, saying he was returning to England via Athens. Instead of returning to Britain Tester offered to help the British war effort. He offered to buy up all commercially available meat and other foodstuffs in Greece and Romania, which might otherwise have fallen into enemy hands, and sell it to Britain for a modest profit. He would achieve this through acquiring certain amounts of Greek shipping to transport the goods. The security services discovered that at the same time Tester was doing business indirectly with Germany. Tester had problems settling his debts with creditors and many of his cheques bounced. He claimed to have a fortune tied up in Brazilian coffee, but also boasted having been a British spy during the First World War, and claimed Joseph Goebbels as a close school friend. Tester admitted holding fascist sympathies:

> If sympathy with Germany and Italy and to be a fascist means in the eyes of the British public and or the British authorities a proof of disloyalty, then I am afraid, I must rest under such suspicion. But my foremost and natural feeling is for England, the country of my father.[19]

Despite his avowed love for England, in September 1940 Tester decided to relocate to Bucharest. He obtained visas for his wife and children through Berlin, as it was difficult to obtain Romanian visas for British subjects. While in Bucharest Tester was engaged in buying up and selling Jewish properties on behalf of the Germans. He boasted openly about Germany winning the war, and was strongly suspected of being instrumental in enabling Germany to obtain control of several Romanian petroleum companies.

Tester showed his true colours in an article he wrote in April 1941[20] for the Romanian newspaper *Sera* entitled '*Anglo – Quo Vadis?* by A.A. Tester, personal contact officer of Sir Oswald Mosley, British

Union of Fascists and National Socialists'. In the article, Tester states that 'The German Army will be victorious' and calls for the liberation of Oswald Mosley and peace with the Great German Reich. He argued that Hitler merely wanted to liberate England '. . . from the claws of those Jews who hold power', and called on the British people to '. . . arrest Churchill with his gang of Jewish satellites and make Mosley Prime Minister'.[21]

The United States did not escape Tester's anger. He accused the Jews of taking over the White House, and went on to defame American Jews as 'These corruptors of Nations, their influence, the American people not even realising the Jewish parasites in industry, commerce, banking and the press'. Perhaps predictably, he concluded by stating: 'Only Adolf Hitler has the merit of revealing all the details of Universal Judaism'.[22] The elusive businessman and part-time traitor returned to Athens following the German conquest of Greece, where an MI6 informant spotted him in full Gestapo uniform visiting the offices of the Ionian Bank. He later returned to Romania to co-ordinate a Nazi spy network, but was supposedly killed by Romanian frontier guards. The *Daily Express* correspondent in Bucharest believed that Tester had faked his own death by substituting an unrecognisable body dressed in his clothes.

The most prominent personalities from the main fascist and pro-Nazi groups who were interned continued to argue their political point of view. Maule Ramsay carried out his parliamentary duties from Brixton prison, submitting questions to ministers from his cell. He accused the Jews of refusing to join military units that went into action and asked the Secretary for War how many British Jews had been killed fighting in the front line. Sir Barry Domville kept a diary in prison. On his release from internment he visited comrades still in prison and became even more convinced of the 'Judmas' conspiratorial alliance between Jews and Freemasons. Mosley was imprisoned with his wife Lady Diana. He held key meetings with other fascists while in prison and set up a war charity to raise money for the dependants of internees. At her advisory committee interrogation Lady Mosley's views were more forthcoming than her husband's. She made no secret of her friendship for Hitler, Himmler and Goebbels, and criticised Churchill, whom she had known since childhood, as being interested only in war. Diana later partly revised her view of Hitler admitting that 'He did frightful things'.[23]

Mosley was released from internment in 1943 on health grounds and placed under house arrest. He was suffering from phlebitis. The release was strongly opposed by the TUC and the majority of Labour MPs. The Home Office received 15,000 separate letters, resolutions and petitions in protest at the release of Mosley and other fascists. However, the government no longer considered the fascists a threat to internal security, particularly as the threat of a German invasion had receded. BUF members were still monitored by MI5 and had restrictions placed on their movements. But despite complaints from the Labour Party neither Mosley nor the majority of his supporters had been charged with any criminal offence. After the war, Oswald and Diana Mosley settled in France. Diana stayed on in Paris after the death of her husband in 1980. She remained unrepentant in her fascist views right up to her death in 2003.

TRAITORS EXECUTED FOR THEIR CRIMES

One of the youngest British collaborators of the Second World War was Duncan Scott-Ford. Born Duncan Alexander Croall-Smith, he took the name of his stepfather by deed poll and became Scott-Ford. Originally from a navy family, Scott-Ford entered the Greenwich Naval Training School aged twelve, just three years before joining his first ship HMS *Impregnable*. The fifteen-year-old held the rank of 'Boy 2nd Class', and soon progressed to naval clerk. He acquired knowledge of signalling, ciphering, coding and navigation. When his next ship HMS *Gloucester* paid a visit to the East African port of Dar-es-Salaam, Scott-Ford met a seventeen-year-old German girl called Ingeborg Richter, the daughter of a local car dealer and part-time Nazi Party official. He arranged for Scott-Ford to visit the local German youth centre and gradually the impressionable boy sailor became infatuated with his new German girlfriend. In attempting to impress he may have shown her details of navy codes and the pair corresponded after his ship left Africa. When Scott-Ford's next ship, HMS *Nile*, docked at Alexandria, he became involved with an Egyptian prostitute called Nahid Mohamed. She proved to have very expensive tastes so Scott-Ford altered his Post Office savings bank book and fraudulently withdrew cash to pay for his girlfriend's extravagant lifestyle. He also helped himself to the pay-book of one of his shipmates. Scott-Ford was court-martialled on counts of forgery and embezzlement, sentenced to two years' imprisonment and dismissed from the Navy. He was also suspected of leaking cipher information, though this charge was not made public. He spent six months in prison before returning to live with his mother, who had successfully appealed for his release on the grounds of his impressionable age. His unsatisfactory discharge papers meant it became difficult for him to find work and the reckless ex-sailor turned to drink and developed a grudge against the Navy. In September 1941 he was accepted by the merchant navy as a seaman on board the SS *Finland*. During May 1942 the *Finland* dropped anchor in Lisbon.

Portugal was a neutral country and a magnet for Axis and Allied spies alike. Scott-Ford's case illustrates the technique of enemy agents in Lisbon and other neutral ports in collecting information from British and Allied seamen. In fact Lisbon was probably the worst place for a hard drinking, womanising young man bearing a grudge to find himself in. Predictably, Scott-Ford ended up sampling the fleshpots of cosmopolitan Lisbon. Both the Café Alberto and Cabaret Rasrouage were well-known Nazi spy haunts. Scott-Ford soon found himself in conversation with a Portuguese man named 'Gomez' who was buying rounds of drinks for the visiting British sailors. As he descended into a drunken stupor Scott-Ford confided in Gomez his love for the German girl, Ingeborg Richter, whom he had met a year earlier in East Africa. After sending her three letters, a fourth was returned after the outbreak of war with the words – 'Gone to Germany'. Gomez told his new British 'friend' to return the following evening and he would introduce him to someone who could help him. The man Gomez had in mind was a German called Rithman. He explained to Scott-Ford that as a former sea captain he had often visited Dar-es-Salaam and that he might be able to get a letter to Ingeborg back in Germany. He also promised Scott-Ford 1,000 escudos if the latter could find out why all British ships had orders to be in port on 28 June. When they met as arranged in Estoril the following day, Rithman introduced Scott-Ford to a couple of known German agents, Kuno Weltzien and a 'Captain Henley'. During a four-hour interrogation Scott-Ford was asked about general morale in Britain and how people were standing up to German bombing. Henley handed Scott-Ford the promised 1,000 escudos, persuading him to sign a receipt. He was told to obtain charts showing the positions of British mine fields and to purchase the latest editions of *Jane's Fighting Ships*, *Jane's Aircraft* and *House Flags and Funnels*, as well as to find out where three new battleships were being built. Other instructions included finding out the locations of American troops being deployed in Britain and, bizarrely, why soldiers guarding Gibraltar wore wide, coloured arm-bands. He subsequently received a further 800 escudos and was ordered on his return to Britain to obtain ration cards, clothing coupons and identity cards.

When Scott-Ford's ship arrived back in Liverpool, during a routine security check he was asked if he had been approached by enemy agents while in Lisbon. He admitted he was contacted by German spies but boasted that he had rejected their proposals out of hand. At this stage MI5 were not sure whether Scott-Ford was their man. When he was back in Lisbon a couple of months later he went to the German Embassy but failed to produce any documents. His explanation for this was that his ship's gangways were being closely watched. But he was able to give the Germans details of the five ships that had been sunk in his convoy and the casualties suffered. He also revealed that HMS *Malaya* and HMS *Hermione* were anchored in Gibraltar. He discovered that the British soldiers in Gibralter wore distinctive arm-bands to detect a possible gas attack on the British base. The gas the authorities expected to be used was colourless and odourless, but when it came into contact with water it could be seen and almost detected. The soldiers wore arm-bands as a detector; they changed colour when in contact with this gas.

Although he had gathered some information his German controllers threatened to expose Scott-Ford to the British consul unless he returned with better quality intelligence. On his next visit he was told he would be given £50 to deliver to an agent in

Perthshire, somebody whom the British would never suspect of being a German spy. He never did return because shore leave was cancelled suddenly, and his convoy sailed back to England. Scott-Ford was finally apprehended due to GC and CS cipher intercepts. His German controllers radioed details of their new recruit, code-named 'Rutherford', to Berlin. On his return to England an extensive interrogation of the crew of the SS *Finland* led to Scott-Ford's detection and full confession. A search of his belongings revealed a notebook containing details of the position of ships in the convoy returning from Lisbon to England. He was detained under Regulation 18B of the 1939 Defence Regulations and was subsequently sent to Latchmere House, MI5's wartime holding centre for captured enemy agents. At first he boasted about his espionage activities and believed he was an important figure in the international spy business. He was proud of his ability to collect so much potentially damaging information. He believed that by working for the Germans he would get a good position in the Nazi government once Britain had been invaded. This would allow him the opportunity to be reunited with his beloved Ingeborg, and to achieve his dream of becoming master of his own merchant ship.

Scott-Ford was prosecuted under the Treachery Act of 1940 and appeared at the Old Bailey on 16 October 1942. In court he dropped his arrogant and blustering exterior. He said:

> I had no intention of assisting the enemy. I was frightened by the threats made by the German agents in Lisbon that they would give my receipt for money I had from them to the British consul. My reason for mixing with the German agents was so I might write a letter to Ingeborg Richter in Germany.[24]

Perhaps he failed to grasp the seriousness of the charges against him. He had after all only been paid the equivalent of about £18 for co-operating with the Germans. But as well as giving away detailed information about vital convoy movements, he had also gleaned a lot of military details by touring public houses and talking with fellow seamen. The Germans had also promised him 'glittering prizes' for further information, and it is likely he would have made contact with his German controllers on his return to Lisbon. He was of little value to MI5 because he did not possess important information which might have saved his life (such as the names of others who had passed on convoy details), and he was considered too unreliable for use as a double agent. Scott-Ford was found guilty of aiding the enemy and given the death sentence. His defence council asked for a reprieve on the grounds that he had no political affiliations or interests, and had shown genuine remorse for his crimes. His father had died when he was twelve and the easily led boy had no real home life. No reprieve was forthcoming, and Scott-Ford was hanged at Wandsworth prison on 3 November 1942 by Albert Pierrepoint.

MI5 had no doubts as to the seriousness of Scott-Ford's treachery. The officer in charge of the case wrote: 'There may well be many who will agree that death by hanging is almost too good for a sailor who will encompass the death of thousands of his shipmates without a qualm.'[25]

GEORGE JOHNSON ARMSTRONG

The second British subject to be sentenced to death and executed under the Treachery Act was, like Scott-Ford, a merchant seaman. At his trial on 8 May 1941, George Armstrong was charged with the following offence:

On or about 19th November 1940, being a British subject in the U.S.A., unlawfully did an act which was likely to assist the enemy or to prejudice the public safety, the defence of the Realm, or the efficient prosecution of the war, in that he did write and send a letter to Dr Herbert Scholz German Consul at Boston Massachusetts, U.S.A. offering to place himself at his disposal – contrary to Regulation 2A (1) of the Defence (General) Regulations 1939.[26]

This is the letter that sent Armstrong to the gallows:

Dear Sir,
I am an officer of the British Service, an engineer at recent date attached to the inspection of Aircraft department (A.I.D.) in

England. Latterly I was transferred to the Marine Dept under control of the British Admiralty. My intention is to make German contacts here in the U.S., which may be beneficially used on my return to England. Naturally in the various capacities in which I was employed in England, I have information which would be very valuable in the proper sources. You will no doubt agree with me that it is not advisable to enter into any written discussion upon this subject here at this time, but if you could have someone contact me who was reliable then the matter could be more fully gone into. I was detained by the U.S. Immigration authorities before I could make any such contacts here in the U.S. and have been transferred from East Boston Immigration Station to Deer Island to be held pending deportation proceedings. I feel that the information which I have and the value of someone so placed in England in these times would be greatly appreciated by yourself or those who you would put in contact with me.

PS: My mail is censored by the Immigration Authorities but this letter will not pass through official channels, a direct contact by visit would be the most advisable.[27]

The British security services were aware of Armstrong even before he had written the letter (which was intercepted by the American Immigration Department and passed on to British officials in New York). The merchantman had been spotted making contact with German diplomats and Abwehr representatives in New York. Following his deportation from America Armstrong was arrested when he docked at Cardiff and taken to London for police questioning. He was also interrogated by Lieutenant-Colonel Hinchley-Cooke from MI5. The police asked Armstrong to write a short statement relating to his deportation from America. His handwriting and spelling of certain words were very similar to those in the letter sent to the German consul in Boston. When shown the letter by Hinchley-Cooke, Armstrong was clearly taken aback and surprised that his note had fallen into British hands. He admitted sending the letter. Armstrong probably assumed that the letter was the only concrete evidence of potential treachery. He spun a complex and long-winded explanation to Hinchley-Cooke as to how he had attempted to infiltrate and expose a Nazi spy ring operating in the United States. Armstrong stated that just before the outbreak of war he had met a German named Dr Carl Klein at the Nautical Club in London. It emerged during a conversation that Klein had been a Nazi agent in the Far East during the 1930s. About a year later Armstrong was in New York on shore leave from his ship, *La Brea* and decided to have a drink in an Irish bar called Jimmy O'Dwyer's. Merchant navy officers of all nationalities frequented the popular bar. One evening in the bar, Armstrong met a woman named Alice Hahn who led him to believe she was Polish. She made a point of befriending British merchant navy officers, especially when they were drunk and eager to speak about their convoy adventures in the North Atlantic.

On another occasion while chatting with Alice Hahn, Armstrong discovered she was actually German. She took Armstrong to a fashionable bar on Broadway where merchant navy crews were drinking with Alice's girlfriends. Then the mysterious Dr Klein entered the bar and took Alice to one side for an intense conversation. The couple obviously knew each other. Armstrong went to Boston but was arrested by Immigration officers for missing his ship sailing. While in custody in the civilian holding camp in Deer Island, Armstrong, again by chance, met Dr Klein. Klein and his Russian wife were fighting their deportation from the United States. Dr Klein admitted to Armstrong that he was a German spy but stressed that he had not carried out any spying activities in the United States. He did admit to having placed agents in Great Britain. Armstrong tried to win Klein's confidence by telling the German that because he had missed his ship, on returning to Britain he would be tried for desertion and probably executed, as was the case in the German Navy. The merchantman later stuck to his story that his sole aim was to trap Klein and others into admitting their spying activities so that he could expose them to the British. On one occasion when Klein was taken out of his cell for questioning, Armstrong went through his belongings and discovered a list of British names of people whom he assumed to be Nazi agents. During his MI5 interrogation he was unable to recall any of the 'names'.

Desperately clutching at straws Armstrong said he had written to German Ambassador Scholz to get the consul to visit him at the Immigration Station, where he would again pretend to offer his services to the Germans in order to obtain details of the Nazi's British spy ring. Armstrong said he had also outlined his plans in a letter to the British consul in Boston, at the same time as he had written to Scholz. The only letter with which Hinchley-Cooke confronted him was the incriminating one he had sent to the German Embassy. Armstrong was sent for trial *in camera* at the Old Bailey. He was found guilty and sentenced to death. His appeal on 23 June 1941, at the Court of Appeal, was dismissed. He was hanged at Wandsworth Prison on 10 July 1941.

It may seem a little strange that a man could be tried and sentenced to death on the strength of writing one letter. There appeared to be no other firm evidence against Armstrong. However, his MI5 file reveals an unscrupulous confidence trickster possessing a vivid gift for perverting the truth.

Armstrong was actually born George William Hope and probably used 'Hope' as an alias even after changing his name by deed poll to Armstrong. In 1925, aged nineteen, Armstrong was given one months' hard labour for stealing a bicycle and a raincoat. He committed various petty offences until in 1937 he entered the United States illegally, getting a job as a toolmaker. He was fired from the job for embezzlement and theft and subsequently arrested and deported. On returning to England he worked for the de Havilland Aircraft Company in Edgware but was dismissed for unsatisfactory work. Between December 1938 and February 1939 Armstrong worked for Ratcliffe's Tool Limited in London. He told work colleagues he was also a sergeant in the Royal Auxiliary Airforce. One morning Armstrong's immediate boss received a telegram seemingly from an RAF officer informing him that Armstrong had crashed in Surrey while flying a Blenheim plane. Shortly afterwards Armstrong himself rang his employers from his hospital bed asking for an advance of salary and a loan to pay hospital expenses. Armstrong received £3 from his supportive firm. However, it soon transpired that Armstrong had never been in the

RAF and had not been involved in any plane crash. The firm did not press criminal charges.

Armstrong's next employment was as an engineer on tanker ships owned by Anglo-Saxon British Petroleum. He was soon dismissed for unsatisfactory behaviour. Undaunted, he continued his con-man activities. One day while lodging in a house Armstrong appeared in the uniform of an officer in the mercantile marine. He told a fellow lodger that he could arrange a job for him as a ship's officer on a tanker. In order to arrange the interview Armstrong said he needed £2 payment from the man. Armstrong later arranged for a letter to be delivered to the lodgings addressed to 'Vice Commodore Armstrong'. The letter asked him to attend a conference to discuss the potential appointment of the lodger to the merchant navy. Armstrong asked the man to pay him a further £2 to cover travel expenses to discuss the man's job application at navy headquarters. The lodger alerted the police and Armstrong was arrested. In February 1940 Armstrong was convicted at Willesden Petty Sessions of obtaining money under false pretences. He was jailed for three months. On his release Armstrong embarked on his ill-fated journey to America and ultimately to the gallows.

OSWALD JOB

Job was born of German parents in Bromley, Kent in 1885. His father, who was a naturalised British citizen, ran a bakery business in the East End of London and young Oswald helped in the family firm. Then, in what came as a complete surprise to his parents, Oswald decided to try his luck in Paris and travelled to France to find work. After being engaged as a labourer in a brass foundry he met his future wife and gained further employment in an engineering company.

Job volunteered for military service in 1914 but was rejected on medical grounds because of a rheumatic problem. He remained in France after the war, setting up a machine tools business which he extended to include the manufacture of artificial eyes and wax figures for window displays. When Paris fell to the Germans in June 1940 Job was arrested and sent first to the Fresnes prison and then to the St Denis internment camp for male British subjects in occupied France. Job spent three years in the camp during which time he ingratiated himself with the Germans by working as an interpreter. He managed to escape from the camp, get across the border into Spain and journey on to Portugal before being repatriated back to Britain.

The security services were suspicious of Job almost from the start. He claimed to have passed on messages from the local French Resistance while on temporary release from the St Denis camp. He said he had negotiated his release on the pretext of returning to Paris to settle his business affairs. Job maintained that by gradually extending his leave permit he had managed to devise an escape route out of France. After selling jewellery, clocks and other possessions, he visited his wife at Montaudin and then fled Paris by train to Bayonne and eventually crossed the frontier to Spain where he contacted the British vice-consul at San Sebastian. MI5 were surprised at Job's ability to arrange his own release from the internment camp and to roam around Paris a free man. He maintained he had been able to cross successfully into Spain because he had made a special study of the geography of the country around the frontier from a Michelin map. The interrogator at the British consul noticed that the map was hopelessly inaccurate and soon realised that Job had no knowledge of positions of towns in the area.

When Job returned to England in November 1943 he underwent a routine interrogation at Poole airport. A diamond tie-pin was found under the lapel of his coat and a large solitaire had been concealed in his watch. Job claimed the diamond belonged to his wife and he had brought it with him to augment cash to help his escape. MI5's suspicions were confirmed. Earlier wireless intercepts had revealed that a German agent in Britain (named 'Dragonfly', in fact a double agent controlled by MI5), was expecting the arrival of a courier from Europe carrying items of jewellery to fund payment of a British based Abwehr agent. MI5 passed on instructions that in the event of items of jewellery being discovered the man should be allowed to proceed. Following the formalities at Poole, Job was free to continue on his journey to stay with his brother in London. After a few days under observation in which Job made no attempt to pass on the jewellery, he was interviewed three times by MI5 who continued to question the full details of his dramatic escape from France. Job gave an unconvincing performance but managed to stick to his cover story. On his fourth interrogation he admitted he had won his release from internment by the Germans in return for agreeing to report on bomb damage and general morale in Britain. He said he only accepted the mission as a way of escaping from France. Job also insisted the jewels were his own property. However, when shown the address of his German contact in London, who was expecting delivery of the jewellery, he immediately confessed to everything and admitted to being a German courier. His German controllers had driven him to the Spanish border and he was left to concoct his story of fleeing Paris by train and dramatically mapping his way across the Spanish border.

Following a search of Job's brother's house in Lewisham, police discovered a bunch of keys, which were in fact hollow and contained secret ink crystals. Other materials were found in the handle of his safety razor. The Germans had instructed Job to send letters addressed to British internees in the St Denis camp in the names of their relatives and friends in Britain. Concealed in the letters would be secret messages written in invisible ink about the effects of bomb damage in London and the level of British morale. Job was hardly a typically committed or resourceful spy. The 58-year-old was not very bright, and never mastered the rudiments of the code. This meant that after his return to England he would not have been able to respond to coded messages relayed to him via German broadcasts from Paris.

Job was prosecuted under the Treachery Act and his trial took place *in camera* at the Old Bailey in January 1944. He was found guilty and sentenced to death. In his appeal to the Court of Criminal Appeal Job once again maintained he had accepted the German offer merely as a means of escape and that he had had no intention of spying against Britain. His appeal was refused. While waiting for the date of his execution Job sent a letter to the prison chaplain explaining his plight:

I submit that with my brain unhinged, after the long years of confinement in an internment camp, it is small wonder that a man's powers of reasoning become twisted, or that he is likely to make mistakes.[28]

Oswald Job was hanged at Pentonville Prison on 16 March 1944. The press reports of the case concentrated on the clandestine use of the invisible ink cunningly concealed in an ordinary bunch of keys. The newspapers implied that Job was detained immediately on his arrival in England. MI5's double agent 'Dragonfly' was subsequently closed down to give the Germans the impression that Job had betrayed him. Job's refusal to disclose to the British consul in Spain the real reason behind his 'escape' from internment, and his continual lies to MI5, meant his mission was doomed from the start. He lacked the guile and ingenuity to be a spy and paid with his life.

CHAPTER THREE

Germany's British Broadcasters

Adolf Hitler believed in the use of propaganda as an integral element in seizing and holding on to political power. The German leader had discussed the value of propaganda in *Mein Kampf*, and his maxim was 'the bigger the lie, the more easily it will be believed, provided it is repeated vigorously and often enough'.[1] A week after seizing power in 1933, Hitler set the wheels in motion for the establishment of a Ministry for Public Enlightenment and Propaganda to be run by a national director of propaganda, Dr Paul Joseph Goebbels. On being appointed to his new post, Goebbels remarked: 'Broadcasting is now totally in the hands of the state. We have put an end to endlessly swinging this way and that; we have thus ensured that there will be uniform control.'[2]

German foreign broadcasting expanded rapidly following the 1936 Berlin Olympics. Goebbels utilised German radio broadcasts as a long-range propaganda weapon. A world audience was reached by a huge broadcasting studio complex operating on 100,000 kilowatts from Zeesen, a suburb of Berlin. The German Radio Corporation (Reichsrundfunk) external service broadcast in English to the United States of America, Britain, Ireland and the Far East, as well as transmitting foreign language broadcasts in French, Polish, Spanish, Gaelic and Afrikaans.

Hitler appreciated that he would have to secure British approval if plans to restore Germany to her rightful position as a major European power were to be successful. Britain became an important broadcasting target in Hitler's quest for an Anglo-German alliance against the Soviet Union. As international tensions increased during

1938 and 1939, Hitler hoped to win over the British radio audience by regular English-language transmissions stressing the justice of Germany's territorial claims and reinforcing the message that Germany had no quarrel with the British people. Once war had been declared, German radio attempted to convince its listeners in the United Kingdom that Britain had been dragged into a needless conflict by its 'war mongering' government, as part of an international Jewish conspiracy.

The use of radio propaganda to subvert morale had been tried out during the Battle of France in 1940. During the 'phoney war' period Goebbels established a series of secret stations such as the French separatist Le Voix de Bretagne (The Voice of Brittany) to undermine national morale. The German Propaganda Minister had similar radio stations in mind for Great Britain. As many as one hundred British citizens found themselves working for the English-language service in Berlin. They operated under the auspices of the England Committee, a body within the German Foreign Ministry that monitored diplomatic and propaganda efforts against Britain.

The English radio section of the German broadcasting system was led by Eduard Dietze. The son of a German father and Scottish mother, Dietze was raised in London before returning to Germany on the outbreak of the First World War. In the early 1930s he became the BBC's commentator in Berlin. Between May 1940 and the end of the war, Dietze assembled a mixture of British citizens who for various reasons were prepared to broadcast messages to the United Kingdom. The material provided to the English section was compiled by the Foreign and Propaganda Ministries, often on an *ad hoc* basis involving a fair amount of guesswork about conditions in Britain.[3]

NORMAN BAILLIE-STEWART

Norman Baillie-Stewart was one of the first Britons to join the English language service. Born Norman Baillie Stewart Wright in 1909, he later acquired the name Baillie-Stewart by deed poll. He had already gained notoriety in Britain before the war as the former army officer who had been imprisoned in the Tower of London for passing on military secrets to the Germans. Of all the German sympathisers and collaborators covered in this book, Baillie-Stewart is the only one actually to have betrayed his country *before* the Nazis came to power. After passing out of the Royal Military Academy, Sandhurst, Baillie-Stewart was commissioned into the Seaforth Highlanders. He went to India with his regiment and returned to England in 1932 where he requested a transfer to the Royal Army Service Corps. He claimed his fellow officers generally looked down on him, regarding him with suspicion, even though his father had enjoyed a glittering army career. His army file describes Baillie-Stewart as conceited, bombastic and self-important when dealing with subordinates. As well as being tactless, he resented taking advice, or being corrected. He had the habit of jumping to conclusions and making statements that were later found to be inaccurate.[4] He probably asked to be transferred because he was in debt and could not afford to maintain the extravagant lifestyle, such as playing polo, that was *de rigueur* for an officer in a prestigious Highland regiment.

In July 1932, the British security service SIS received reports that a man claiming to be a serving British officer had attempted to make contact with the German War Office while on a visit to Berlin.[5] Baillie-Stewart's great-grandmother had been German and as a boy he had developed a keen interest in the German Navy, and expressed sympathy for the German fleet defeated at the hands of the British during the Battle of Jutland. The young British officer believed Germany had been harshly punished under the terms of the Treaty of Versailles. While serving with his regiment in India he spent some of his leave in Kenya where he fell in love with a German girl. This gave him greater sympathy for that country and he almost certainly offered his services to the German consulate in Kenya.

Having obtained permission from his commanding officer to visit Germany, Baillie-Stewart headed for the seedy Hotel Stadt Kiel in Berlin. He had developed an interest in the German military and intended to announce himself at army headquarters by 'leaving his cards', the traditional army practice of calling to see fellow soldiers of a foreign military service. Baillie-Stewart later argued that his actions were completely innocent and that somebody had mistakenly alerted London that he was offering himself to Germany as a potential spy. He admitted telephoning the German War Office from a public phone box on Berlin's Unter den Linden and arranging to meet a man whom he had never met before for lunch.

The man who bought Baillie-Stewart the meal was a Major Muller, a serving soldier of Prussian stock, complete with duelling scar down the left side of his cheek. Muller assumed that Baillie-Stewart wanted to sell British military secrets, thinking that the Englishman was in debt. Baillie-Stewart did nothing to deny this was the reason for making contact with Muller or to clarify the original purpose behind meeting the German, and as a result was sucked into a deepening intrigue from which he could not extricate himself. To verify that Baillie-Stewart was a genuine British officer, Muller devised a series of written questions on tanks, armoured cars, automatic rifles and British army logistical organisation. During subsequent meetings with Muller, the calculating (or naïve) Baillie-Stewart readily accepted cash to cover his holiday expenses and to replace a second-hand car he had recently sold in England. Baillie-Stewart later remarked that he had given no information to Muller that the German could not himself have obtained thorough reading openly available British military publications.

It is certain that Baillie-Stewart was followed by MI5 while in Berlin. When leaving Germany by train, a Germanic looking man but who spoke with a Cockney accent joined the Englishman in his railway carriage. On returning to the compartment after lunch, Baillie-Stewart was convinced his case and its contents had been tampered with. Once back in barracks at Aldershot, he discovered from his batman that his room had been searched and somebody had been asking questions at the regimental library about the officer's personal reading material. Baillie-Stewart corresponded with Major Muller by using the pseudonym 'Alphonse Poiret'. Muller's letters were written using the cover name 'Marie Louise', supposedly a young German girl who had fallen for Baillie-Stewart during his Berlin visit. Baillie-Stewart travelled to Rotterdam to continue his liaison with Major Muller. Then suddenly on the evening of 20 January 1933, the young lieutenant was called before his commanding officer and asked to sign a form offering his resignation from the Royal Army Service Corps. Asked for an explanation, Baillie-Stewart's commanding officer ushered him into a room in which he was introduced to a Colonel Syms from the Judge Advocate's Department and a Captain 'B' from MI5. The two men offered Baillie-Stewart a typewritten piece of paper containing charges against him. MI5 knew all about his meetings with Muller, and had intercepted letters with coded messages and containing English bank notes sent by the adoring 'Marie Louise'. They also gave details of army training books removed from the regimental library by the young officer. Requested to explain the reasons behind his actions, Baillie-Stewart dismissed the allegations as absurd and asked for some time to compose his thoughts. The interrogators urged him to come clean and confess to his treachery. In the meantime, his room was thoroughly searched, including stripping the wallpaper from the wall and his clothing being ripped apart. Six days after his arrest Baillie-Stewart was told to pack a few items and prepare to leave for an undisclosed destination pending his court martial.

It dawned on him after a while that the car was headed towards London and he assumed he was being taken to the War Office for further questioning. Baillie-Stewart was surprised and distressed when the car drove into the Tower of London. Some historical images associated with the Tower flashed through his mind; the execution of Anne Boleyn, the Bloody Tower and Traitors' Gate. He was the only inmate in the Tower, a special state prisoner, under the guard of the Coldstream Guards. To begin with the countless sightseers conducted on guided tours of the Tower were not aware of Baillie-Stewart's presence. The press knew he was being detained but not the reason. When Fleet Street did discover the story they were slow to react, fearing accusations of libel or contempt of court. By contrast the American and European newspapers had a field day, filling their columns with endless stories of 'The Officer in the Tower'.

Once the official reason for Baillie-Stewarts's arrest had been made public, and more information on the case emerged, the British press made a meal of the apparent 'spy mystery'. Questions were asked in

Parliament with MPs demanding to know why an officer was being locked up under armed guard in the Tower instead of in an ordinary army barracks. A sentry with rifle and fixed bayonet even stood over the disgraced officer while he shaved! Hundreds of sightseers converged on the Tower to watch and often photograph Baillie-Stewart taking his daily exercise in the Tower grounds watched over by a platoon of Guardsmen. In a sense the wayward officer became one of the first tabloid newspaper celebrities in Britain, selling his story for serialisation in the *Daily Sketch*. Newspapers described him as a greater draw than the Crown Jewels. After nine weeks of confinement in the Tower, Baillie-Stewart's court martial was held at the Duke of York's headquarters in Chelsea with the defendant pleading 'Not guilty' to charges under the Official Secrets Act. The trial received world-wide press coverage, although some of the proceedings dealing with military technicalities were held *in camera*. The prosecution poured over the letters exchanged between Baillie-Stewart and Major Muller, alias 'Marie Louise'. The note which Baillie-Stewart had written to Muller outlining basic details about British tanks and armoured cars was also produced in court, although similar information could easily have been obtained from any good public library.

The incriminating evidence against Baillie-Stewart was that the piece of paper describing British military hardware also bore the Berlin address and telephone number of the German Military Defence Headquarters. MI5 produced a young German woman whom Baillie-Stewart had met and probably seduced on the Harwich to Hook of Holland boat-train. Clearly smitten by the dashing officer, she wrote several letters to him that were subsequently intercepted by MI5, and the woman was persuaded to travel from Germany to give evidence. 'Miss D' told the court that Baillie-Stewart had confided to her that he was on a difficult mission to Holland.

Despite the bizarre stories of coded messages, secret meetings and illicit love letters that emerged from the trial, one thing was absolutely clear. Baillie-Stewart had willingly accepted and received at least £90 in cash from the German War Office. He protested that he never had any intention of giving the German Army information that could be used against Britain, arguing that he had no such information to give. The crucial flaw in Baillie-Stewart's behaviour was his refusal to accept that he was being drawn into the German espionage net for use at a later date. As well as being a potentially useful source of information to Berlin, he had shown in his eccentric behaviour and pro-German sentiment that he was susceptible to corruption and deceit. After sixty-six days in custody and a trial lasting seven days, the court martial found the officer guilty of the charges and he found himself cashiered from the Army and sentenced to a five-year prison term. He later admitted in prison that he had provided the Germans with additional military information. This included the revised billeting arrangements of the Army's Aldershot command; a list of officers thought by Baillie-Stewart to be employed on secret service duties; and sketches of the new 16-ton and 32-ton experimental tanks.

The publicity that surrounded Baillie-Stewart's case was not helped by the climate of international tension that accompanied his trial. As well as military aggression in the Far East with the Japanese invasion of Manchuria, ten days after Baillie-Stewart was escorted to the Tower, Adolf Hitler was appointed German Chancellor. Under the Führer Germany was planning a massive increase in her armed forces, contrary to the terms of the Versailles treaty, as well as embarking on a secret rearmament programme, and Berlin was understandably eager to elicit any military information concerning British military preparedness. Baillie-Stewart's punishment sent a clear signal that Britain was alert to any attempts by foreign powers to corrupt its military personnel. He served his sentence in Wormwood Scrubs and Maidstone prisons. In jail he found himself a marked man, shunned by the other prisoners. He did his 'time' preparing old books for rebinding, his only friend a deaf and dumb man with whom he conversed through sign language. He was finally released from jail in March 1937.

On his release Baillie-Stewart still received massive press coverage as the 'Officer in the Tower'. The *Daily Express* contacted Ballie-Stewart's mother and secured the exclusive world rights for the officer's life story. On his release from Maidstone prison, Baillie-

Stewart carried a letter from the *Daily Express*, saying the newspaper's representatives would meet him at London's Victoria Station. Unknown to the *Express*, the *Daily Mirror* had sent a reporter called Colin Wintle to wait outside the prison all night. When Baillie-Stewart emerged through the prison gate, the *Mirror* man trailed him to Maidstone Station and after boarding the train passed the officer a note inviting him for a drink. By the time the train reached London, Wintle had secured Baillie-Stewart's story, and effectively scooped the *Daily Express*. After arriving at Victoria Station Baillie-Stewart was bundled into a car and pursued by half of Fleet Street in a chase across London.

Baillie-Stewart's notoriety went before him. His photograph had appeared regularly in the newspapers with the result that he was frequently recognised wherever he went. Discharged from the Army and expelled from membership of his London clubs, he also found it increasingly difficult to get a job after leaving prison. He applied to run a public house but was refused a licence because of his prison conviction. He was offered a job on a pig farm but then the farm was closed down on health grounds. He seemed generally unable to settle into civilian life. The remark made to him while in prison by MI5 officer Edward Hinchley-Cooke, also played on his mind. The security man had told Baillie-Stewart: 'If it ever came to a war between England and Germany you will be locked up immediately'.[6]

Taking stock of his position Baillie-Stewart decided to flee the spotlight and start a new life elsewhere. He met a friend who put him in touch with the Austrian Embassy in London and after a short interview the ex-officer was offered a letter of recommendation for a job with the Austrian Tourist Propaganda office in Vienna. Baillie-Stewart wrote to Scotland Yard telling them of his plans to go abroad. For some reason he also wrote to a national newspaper saying that he was going to a country 'where my sympathies lay'[7] and so attracted even more publicity. The tourist office job in Vienna never materialised because it seemed Baillie-Stewart's fame had preceded him to Austria. He secured a couple of temporary jobs and decided to apply to become a naturalised Austrian. Baillie-Stewart's problems only worsened. He managed to get an interview with a senior Austrian policeman, Polizeirat Haslinger, who asked him about his political sympathies. Baillie-Stewart replied that he sympathised with the 'German people', implying that he was pro-Hitler. This was a major mistake because Haslinger was a leading figure in the anti-Nazi movement and was determined not to let his country become engulfed in Hitler's plans to unite Austria and Germany into a 'greater Germany'. Haslinger dismissed Baillie-Stewart but called him back to police headquarters a few days later and accused him of conducting pro-Nazi propaganda and of smuggling weapons into the country for use by the Nazis. Haslinger read Baillie-Stewart a document that stated that he was an 'undesirable' and was to leave Austria within three weeks.

Once his identity had been disclosed and his pro-German views reasserted Baillie-Stewart was almost certainly put under police surveillance. Scotland Yard may also have alerted the Austrian police that the famous British traitor was on his way to Vienna. At some stage in the Viennese capital he met a German agent called 'Edith Shackleton', who claimed to be the sister of the world famous explorer. This encounter probably sealed Baillie-Stewart's fate. When the police expelled the cashiered ex-officer from Austria he went to the British Embassy for help, but on discovering his identity the British diplomats refused to offer any support, even though he was seeking help and protection that he was entitled to expect as a British citizen. Baillie-Stewart decided to travel to Czechoslovakia, less than thirty minutes by train from Vienna. About a fortnight after his arrival, on 12 March 1938, Bratislava radio announced that German troops were marching into Austria. Hitler had achieved his Anschluss.

With the approval of the German consulate in Czechoslovakia the young fascist-inspired Baillie-Stewart returned to Vienna to witness the scenes of jubilation in the streets that accompanied Hitler's march into the Austrian capital. While awaiting the result of his application for German citizenship, Baillie-Stewart belatedly started his job at the Austrian Tourist Board. One night while listening to an English language radio service broadcast from Berlin, he heard an announcer speaking in what he considered to be a wildly exaggerated Oxford accent. It especially amused and annoyed him when the presenter ended his announcement with the signing off phrase 'Hearty Cheerios'. Perplexed by what he perceived as an assault on the spoken English language by the strange-sounding announcer, Baillie-Stewart wrote to the Vienna section of the German Propaganda Ministry declaring that he could do better! Much to his surprise he was invited by the radio station controller to make a voice test recording. He heard nothing about the result of his 'audition' for some weeks and then received a telegram out of the blue requesting him to travel to Berlin for a three-week trial period as a radio announcer. While settling into his new job, war was declared and his application for German citizenship approved.

To take up German nationality before the outbreak of war in 1939 was perhaps fortuitous for Baillie-Stewart because it meant that he would not face the same questions concerning his nationality and allegiance that would determine William Joyce's fate in 1945. The two renegade broadcasters clearly never hit it off. When William Joyce arrived in Berlin on the eve of war and shortly afterwards secured his first job broadcasting for the Germans, he was introduced to his fellow Englishman. Obviously feeling a little insecure at the sudden appearance of Joyce, Baillie-Stewart's opening remark to him was: 'I suppose you've come to take our jobs away'.[8] On one occasion Joyce asked Baillie-Stewart if he would mind if he (Joyce) took his place on his early morning broadcast. This suited Baillie-Stewart so he agreed to let Joyce fill in for him on this and one other occasion. When Joyce suggested that he could take his place for a third broadcasting shift, Baillie-Stewart said he was happy on that occasion to do the programme himself, to which Joyce replied: 'What? Are you going to take *my* broadcast?'[9]

Baillie-Stewart resented the popularity that Joyce enjoyed with Goebbels and other leading Nazis. During this period Joyce was at the height of his notoriety as the famous broadcaster 'Lord Haw-Haw'. If the Germans had invaded Britain Joyce was earmarked for a leading position in the pro-Nazi British government. In contrast Baillie-Stewart was requested by Berlin University to draw up a list of British historic buildings and other places of interest, which were to be spared during a German invasion. This task in itself indicated Baillie-Stewart's lower position in the pecking order of collaborators.

After a regular stint of news reading Baillie-Stewart soon fell out with officials at the Propaganda Ministry. He criticised the style and content of some of the broadcasts. One script he was asked to read stated that the German flag had been 'hissed' (instead of hoisted) at Danzig. After the German battleship *Graf Spee* was sunk by the Royal Navy at the Battle of the River Plate, the German press carried a story that Britain had used gas shells against the German vessel. When it was suggested that this information be included in a propaganda broadcast, Baillie-Stewart objected on the grounds that the story was ridiculous. He said the British Navy would have no need to use gas shells against a ship, particularly one on the open sea, where the wind would simply blow the gas away. Baillie-Stewart's views on this incident reached radio controller Dr Hetzler via a Gestapo informant. The British broadcaster was warned that he had made a *Staatsfeindliche Aüsserung*, a criticism of the state, which meant he was considered 'politically unreliable'. He was told his broadcasts would cease. The Propaganda Ministry had clearly dismissed Baillie-Stewart for being disruptive. The Gestapo file on him included the remarks he had made about the *Graf Spee* and his earlier 'indiscretion' in Vienna where he tried to help Jewish friends leave the country. These problems were soon overcome because the Foreign Minstry wanted Baillie-Stewart to work for them, and he became caught up in the struggle between the Foreign and Propaganda Ministries. In the German Foreign Office he worked on translating propaganda material, including a famous leaflet dropped from the skies urging the British Army in France to surrender prior to the Dunkirk evacuation. He also lectured in English at Berlin University. One of his young Berlin students later sent a letter of support for Baillie-Stewart to Bow Street Magistrates Court when he was prosecuted after the war for collaborating with the enemy. It read:

He opened up his mother country before our eyes, told us about its people in a favourable way for the English, their way of living, their honesty and high principles of life. We learned about England

and Germany as brother nations which, only through rather unlucky and unfavourable circumstances, had to go to war with one another.[10]

Baillie-Stewart continued to argue with his bosses in the German Foreign Ministry. On one occasion he telephoned an official on important business who simply put the phone down on him because at that moment Hitler was speaking on the radio. Baillie-Stewart rang the official straight back and asked him what the result would be if every German stopped working just because Hitler was speaking, especially when the speeches were repeated on the radio several times a day. For this impertinence Baillie-Stewart was summoned to see Dr Hesse the head of the England Committee, who reminded the Englishman where he was, and warned him that the Gestapo would not take kindly to his actions. Taking the hint, the ex-officer requested permission to return to Austria on health grounds. He had contracted pernicious anaemia and hepatitis. The increased Allied bombing of Berlin in 1944 also left Baillie-Stewart in no doubt that he should leave the city, especially when his house was almost flattened, and he succeeded in obtaining a transfer to the German Foreign Office in Vienna.

After the war Baillie-Stewart was arrested at an Austrian village named Alt Aussee by the advancing American forces. He was dressed in the traditional alpine lederhosen costume consisting of short leather trousers, a grey and green short jacket, and feathered hat. He was forced to wear these garments travelling back to England and was still wearing the lederhosen at his trial at the Old Bailey.

JOHN AMERY

What set John Amery apart from other pro-Nazi sympathisers was the fact that his father Leopold S. Amery was a well-known senior British politician and member of Winston Churchill's War Cabinet. The Amery family had to endure the embarrassment of listening to John's highly charged speeches broadcast from Berlin, but it was his father who was forced to publicly acknowledge the damaging fact that his son was a traitor. Before entering the political arena, Leopold Amery had enjoyed a glittering career in newspapers. He turned down the editorship of both the *Observer* and *The Times*, deciding instead to become a Conservative MP. After serving as Parliamentary Under-secretary at the Colonial Office, Amery was promoted to the cabinet as First Lord of the Admiralty. In 1924 he found himself in Stanley Baldwin's government as Colonial Secretary, a job which entailed overseeing the vast expanse of the British empire. Leopold Amery had begun a lifelong friendship with Winston Churchill at Harrow School, and when Churchill was recalled from the political wilderness in May 1940 to form his wartime government, he invited Amery to join the cabinet as Secretary of State for India.

Given his privileged background, John Amery seemed destined to emulate the success of his distinguished father. What transpired was the complete opposite. Amery was a reckless child, prone to extreme temper tantrums, panic attacks and prolonged bouts of bedwetting. His very experienced nanny told Amery's mother: 'This is a very hard child; I don't know quite how to deal with him.'[11]

Amery's kindergarten teacher was also concerned about the apparently wayward boy:

Even at his admission I got the impression that he was an extremely abnormal boy. He always wanted to do the exact opposite of what he was asked to do. This differed from the ordinary forms of rebellious spirit shown by healthy children. It was constant and persistent and gave the impression of being a fixed attitude of an abnormal type. He was really unteachable and only learned to read after great pain and effort of all concerned. He showed no interest and had a tendency to shut himself [*sic*] and live inside himself.[12]

In 1925 John was sent to Harrow where his father had achieved noted academic success. Things seemed to go from bad to worse for Amery as one of his tutors later recalled:

In the whole of my experience as a schoolmaster, I found him, without doubt, the most difficult boy I ever had to manage. He was certainly abnormal in that he seemed unable in those days to distinguish right from wrong. He seemed to think he could be a law unto himself and that every rule and regulation that bound others did not apply to him.[13]

Amery absconded from Harrow and, armed with his father's revolver and wallet, headed for France but was apprehended before he could leave the country. As a temporary measure his parents decided to remove him from Harrow and place him in the hands of a private tutor. This seemed to have paid off because Amery was offered a place at Oxford. To the dismay of his parents Amery decided against pursuing his studies, preferring a career in the film business.

After initial training in the rudiments of film production he soon had aspirations to become a film director. He soon tired of this idea, especially after a film he had secured the finance to make, ground to a halt in Africa, leaving a stranded film crew to clear up the mess. Amery owed money everywhere and his eternally patient father was forced to pay off angry creditors. Amery also developed a passion for fast cars and unsuitable women. In July 1932 he appeared at Bow Street Magistrates Court charged with causing an obstruction with his car in central London for which he received a £5 fine. In total, Amery managed to accumulate seventy-four motoring offences, and in an early episode of 'road rage' attacked a driver who had driven across his path, violently smashing the driver's windscreen in the process.

Amery was sexually obsessed from an early age. He had homosexual encounters and a fixation with prostitutes. Aged seventeen he contracted syphilis, then a notoriously difficult disease to cure. Perhaps a bigger shock for his father was John's announcement that he intended to marry Una Wing, an actress with convictions for soliciting in the West End of London. Amery was still under twenty-one and so not permitted to marry in England without his parents' consent. In an attempt to separate John from his would-be bride, Leopold Amery secured a job for his son with the Shanghai department of the Reuters news organisation. Amery initially agreed with this plan but then thwarted his family's attempts to block the wedding by marrying Una Wing at the Greek Orthodox Church in Athens.

The marriage soon broke down. While it lasted Una claimed that Amery continued to pay prostitutes, and even invited his wife to join in group-sex bondage sessions. Amery also prostituted himself, partly for sexual satisfaction, and also to ease his deteriorating financial position. However, in 1936 Amery was declared bankrupt, with liabilities of over £5,000. His father was again forced to bail him out of trouble when his reckless son paid for some diamond jewellery for Una Wing with a cheque that bounced. The police pursued Amery to Paris, resulting in him appearing in court on fraud charges. Leopold Amery settled the outstanding bill for the jewellery.

In the wake of his bankruptcy and eager for a fresh start, Amery left England to travel around Europe. During a visit to France he met and fell under the influence of Jacques Doriot. Doriot was a former senior French communist who was expelled from the party in 1934 following disagreements with directives issued by the Comintern in Moscow. Instead Doriot, rather like his British contemporary Mosley, turned to the right, forming his fascist and anti-Semitic group, the Parti Populaire Français. His party adopted paramilitary style uniforms and paraded through the streets of Paris waving military flags and banners. The impressionable Amery was clearly influenced by Doriot and travelled with him on visits to Germany, Italy, Austria and Czechoslovakia. Even before he had met Doriot, Amery was predisposed to fascism. Like many of his upper-class contemporaries in England during the 1930s he was strongly opposed to communism and because many Bolsheviks were Jewish, Amery believed Bolshevism and Jewry were the same thing. His strong anti-Semitism may have stemmed from his early business setbacks. Leopold Amery later wrote of his son:

His failure in the film world, and his unfortunate experience with money-lenders similarly inclined him to accept current Nazi and Fascist doctrine of the Jews as the prime instigators of Communism as well as the evils of international high finance.[14]

Not surprisingly, Amery was drawn towards the nationalist rather than the republican cause during the Spanish Civil War. He claimed to have served with pro-Franco Italian forces, but was more likely involved as a go-between for the French Cagoulards (the hooded cloaks), an anti-communist group, and fascist contacts in Spain. He was probably also involved in some smuggling scams and possibly a gun-running operation between France and Italy. In April 1940 Amery was back in France and arranged to meet his father in Paris. Amery senior urged his son to join the Army or contribute in some other way to the war effort. (John Amery's brother Julian later joined Special Operations Executive where he helped train Albanian partisans.) Amery told his father he would also consider the idea of joining up but first had to return to the south of France to clear up some business matters. He probably had no intention of returning to England, partly because he did not want to fight but possibly because he sensed that more important developments were about to take place in mainland Europe. Amery's hunch proved correct when in May 1940 the Germans launched an invasion of France and Belgium. When France collapsed he found himself in the unoccupied zone, where by the terms of the Armistice outgoing visas were not granted to British subjects of military age. Amery lived a quiet life in the Vichy zone. As a British subject trapped in a foreign country he was entitled to a small relief grant that he collected from the American consulate in Nice. He was actually allowed £20 a month instead of the usual £10. This may have been due to his father's intercession, especially when Amery claimed to have contracted tuberculosis and to need extra money for medical bills.

The German invasion of the Soviet Union in June 1941 galvanised Amery into action. It made him even more determined to fight Soviet communism in anyway possible. He contacted the Italian Minister of Justice in Vichy offering his services to fascist Italy. This drew no response. He also approached the Finnish representative in Paris with a view to volunteering to fight in Finland's war against the Russians. Again he drew a blank. Whether these were just 'stunts' designed to draw attention to himself is not clear. What may have had the desired effect was a letter Amery wrote to the *Petit*

Dauphin, a French newspaper, in March 1942. In it he protested against the bombing of the Renault works at Boulogne-Billancourt by the RAF. He also penned other anti-British articles for the French press. With the security services monitoring both the French press and letters sent home by British residents in the unoccupied zone, news of Amery's articles soon reached MI5. From July 1942 they kept a file on Amery's activities. The file was to grow substantially during the next few years.

Amery's criticisms of his own government in the press also attracted attention from the Germans. Nazi agents in the unoccupied zone were also aware of his friendship with Jacques Doriot and other pro-fascist collaborators. In August 1942 a local German official visited Amery and invited him to Berlin to discuss possible employment in propaganda work. Amery met Dr Fritz Hesse, the chairman of the England Committee, and it was agreed that he would make a series of radio broadcasts to the British people. The England Committee was a section within the German Foreign Ministry established by von Ribbentrop in November 1939. The committee met every Friday from 1940 until the end of the war and its role was to co-ordinate the surveillance of all aspects of British affairs. It monitored the British press and reported on proceeedings in the House of Commons. Other German government departments were allowed to send representatives to England Committee meetings including the Propaganda Ministry, and representatives from the Wehrmacht and Luftwaffe. The England Committee was staffed by Germans who had gained first-hand experience of the British 'way of life'. Its chairman was Dr Fritz Hesse, who had previously worked for the German news agency at the German Embassy in London between 1933 and the outbreak of war. Part of the committee's function was to advise von Ribbentrop of the circumstances that might lead Britain to seek some sort of peace with the Third Reich. This was the reason why Amery was such a good 'catch' in Berlin, and prompted Dr Reinhard Haferkorn of the German Foreign Ministry to remark later: 'I might say that it caused rather a sensation in Berlin when it was known that the son of a British Cabinet minister had volunteered to work for the Germans.'[15]

The platform the Germans handed to Amery enabled the Englishman to express his view that Britain should unite with Germany against the common Soviet threat. As he later explained to MI5:

> It came as a very great shock to me when I heard that England and Soviet Russia had become allies. So much so that I thought that the people responsible in London were acting in a manner that no longer coincided with British imperial interests.[16]

As well as hoping to gain propaganda value in using Amery, the Germans had another motive for getting the cabinet minister's son behind the microphone. As Adrian Weale suggests, towards the end of 1942 the tide of war was beginning to turn in favour of the Allies. The seemingly indestructible German Army was in serious trouble in Russia and had suffered a setback at the hands of the British at El Alamein. The British and American forces landing in North Africa ('Operation Torch'), sent the message that Germany could not sustain a war on two fronts. Berlin wanted to open negotiations to neutralise Britain and America. If they could be persuaded to make peace, then Germany would have a free hand to defeat the increasing threat of Soviet communism. German Foreign Minister von Ribbentrop saw an opportunity to use Amery to float the idea that Germany was once again ready to come to terms with Britain. Put simply, if Britain would agree to accept the German position in Europe, Germany would pledge non-interference in the British empire. Amery was happy to pursue this policy particularly as he had stated to Dr Hesse at the beginning of his negotiations with the Germans that

> I was not interested in a German victory as such, that what interested me was a just peace where we could all get together against the real enemies of civilisation, and that the British Empire as it was, intact, must be a part of this and not a dependant of such a regroupment.[17]

During his stay in Berlin Amery and his companion Jeanine Barde were invited to stay at the Hotel Kaiserhof as guests of the Foreign

Ministry. Instead of being paid a salary Amery received very generous living expenses. He gained a tremendous sense of self-importance, believing himself to be an indispensable cog in the Nazi propaganda machine. He could also indulge himself in the fleshpots and seedy drinking dens of wartime Berlin. Amery's opening radio broadcast on 19 November 1942 set the tone for his subsequent speeches and fascist writings:

Listeners will wonder what an Englishman is doing on the German radio tonight. . . . I come forward tonight without any political label, without any bias, but just simply as an Englishman to say to you: A crime is being committed against civilisation. Not only the priceless heritage of our fathers, of our seamen, of our Empire builders is being thrown away in a war that serves no British interests but our alliance with the Soviets![18]

Amery's anti-Semitism was also very much in evidence in his broadcasts:

There is not one, not one single great daily newspaper in London that is not Jewish controlled, not one news reel, it's so easy to check it at Somerset House. You are being lied to, your patriotism, your love for our England is being exploited by people who for the most part hardly have the right to pretend to be English.[19]

Amery made seven radio broadcasts from Berlin. Simply because of who he was, the speeches were widely reported in the British press. But his words had no real effect on British listeners. His radio delivery was poor; one listener described Amery's talks as 'Screeching, incoherent rodomontades'.[20] He recorded three further talks but these were never broadcast, partly because there was no response from the British government. The speech containing German peace feelers to Britain also fell on deaf ears:

Ask yourselves just one question only: Is this war really necessary? Who are these men who are urging you to go on and on? Who are these men who persistently undermine any possibility of coming to reasonable terms with Germany? There is more than enough room in the world for Germany and Britain. Your leaders say Germany seeks world domination. Did it ever enter your mind that this is but another trick of that long-planned strategy of Jewish propaganda, expected to thwart Germany's commanding position on the Continent, to which she is after all entitled? Whereas Germany never – and you know this – denied Britain her Imperial position. It is up to you to say the word, to come slowly, gradually, but irresistibly back to common sense.[21]

Amery complained bitterly to Dr Hesse that there was little point in him appealing for Anglo-German co-operation while in the very next studio Lord Haw-Haw was antagonising and alienating the same listening British public with his jeering anti-British invective. Referring specifically to William Joyce and Norman Baillie-Stewart, Amery said:

These people had come to Germany on or before the declaration of war. Also they had adopted German nationality and considered themselves Germans, in consequence their views and outlook widely differed from mine. . . . It was in my view quite insane to carry on as they did calling the British 'the enemy' and so forth as was their custom, if we wished to get together.[22]

While John Amery's broadcasts made no impression on British listeners, in an ironic twist, his father Leo was contributing to the BBC's German language service from London, regularly broadcasting on the 'German Workers' programme. Perhaps a more important irony was the fact that Leo Amery was part-Jewish, his mother coming from a Hungarian Jewish family.[23]

After the failure of his Berlin broadcasts, Amery returned to Paris with Jeanine Barde. His seemingly unlimited German expense account ensured that the couple stayed at the best hotels, so it was no surprise when Amery and his entourage spent Christmas in the swish Hotel Bristol. He met up with his fascist French mentor Jaques Doriot, and discussed with him the idea of creating an anti-Bolshevik legion, recruited from British soldiers held in German POW camps, to fight against the Soviets on the Eastern Front (see next chapter).

Amery returned to Berlin in February 1943 to start work on his book *England Faces Europe*, a work designed to consolidate the views expressed in his earlier radio broadcasts. He continued his exotic lifestyle including marathon drinking sessions. One morning he discovered his lover Jeanine Barde dead in bed beside him. According to Reinhard Spitzy, a high-ranking Nazi official who became friendly with the couple after meeting them on a train, Spitzy later met a very drunk Amery in early 1944 at the Foreign Press club in Berlin. By then, according to Spitzy, Amery 'was no longer capable of anything and had turned totally to drink'.[24] Amery believed he had killed Jeanine by accident. She had complained of a headache, and he mistakenly gave her one of the poison capsules he had intended to use on himself if captured by the enemy. An autopsy revealed that Barde had actually died through choking on her own vomit following a particularly heavy drinking session.[25] Within a week of Jeanine's death, Amery had found a new mistress, named Michelle Thomas, whom he met on a train journey from Paris to Bordeaux.

Amery continued to work for the German propaganda machine but was rather limited in what he could offer. He was initially given the job of news editor for the English broadcasting section, Radio National but he was too much of a loose cannon to hold down a responsible position in a radio station. In an attempt to put him to some further use, Dr Hesse sent Amery on public speaking engagements around Europe. Amery visited Norway (where, appropriately, he met President Vidkum Quisling), Belgium, Italy, Serbia and France. During these trips he was happy to show off his wild reckless behaviour, although Hesse at the German Foreign Ministry had deep reservations, recalling that

During his stays in France and Italy Amery caused constant trouble to the German authorities by his drunken habits and general activities. No one took him seriously. But I have no complete information in this respect because it was Plack (a Foreign Office functionary), who had charge of him, and in fact I was not interested. The only thing that worried me was the bills I had to pay.[26]

While professing his supposed British patriotism Amery continued to denounce the British government. In a speech delivered at the Paris Gaumont Palace in May 1944, he explained:

Do not expect to see an Englishman speak badly of his country; I remain strongly attached to my native land. If I am speaking here today, it is because I detest those who have thrown England into this war, the people responsible for the murder of women, children and the aged, who have covered the English flag with mud and blood. We others who are Nationalists, we will never forgive Churchill and his clique for these murders.[27]

After the Allied invasion of Europe in June 1944, Amery's value to the Germans decreased. He was effectively a spent force, required only to make the occasional radio broadcast. With Berlin under intense Allied bombing (his beloved Hotel Kaiserhof was almost in ruins), and finding himself at a loose end, Amery accepted Mussolini's invitation to visit him at his Lake Garda headquarters. The by then deluded dictator asked him for help in his efforts to broker a peace between Germany and the Western Allies. At this stage even Amery realised that the war was lost, although he did manage to deliver a few propaganda messages on Mussolini's radio network in northern Italy. In early April 1945 British and American forces began their final assault on Italy. While Mussolini and his mistress Clara Petacci were arrested and executed by communist partisans, Amery and his companion Michelle Thomas were more fortunate. They were arrested in Milan by Italian partisans who handed them over to the British Intelligence Corps.

OTHER BRITISH BROADCASTERS

Long before he had completely fallen out with his German master, Baillie-Stewart's replacement as a newsreader on the English section was seventeen-year-old James Clark. The young man was the son of Frances Dorothy Eckersley, the ex-wife of former BBC chief engineer and Mosley supporter Peter Eckersley. Mrs Eckersley was herself drawn to the fascist cause being described by MI5 as 'a strongly pro-German fascist and a fanatical admirer of Hitler'.[28] A member of the extremist organisations The Link and the Right Club, Mrs Eckersley was a frequent visitor to the Salzburg Festival and Nuremberg Rallies. She also lunched with Unity Mitford at the Osteria Bavaria restaurant in the hope of seeing Hitler, and she was later responsible for introducing her pre-war fascist colleagues William and Margaret Joyce to contacts in the German broadcasting organisation.

Eckersley took her son James on regular trips to attend Nazi rallies at Nuremberg. The young schoolboy was electrified by the Nazis' display of bugles, cymbals and trumpets, set among a torchlight procession of marching fanatics. James was sent to the Humbolt School in Berlin-Tegel in July 1939 and his mother joined him there just before the outbreak of war. Mrs Eckersley thought the 'Polish business' would blow over so she remained in Berlin. Her husband tried to send her money via Spain but this never arrived, so to finance their stay in Berlin both took work broadcasting German propaganda. Dr Erik Schirmer, a Foreign Ministry contact Eckersley had met in Nuremberg, telephoned her offering 20 Reichsmarks a day to work as an announcer. She worked as a continuity announcer, while young James was employed to read the English news.

As the war became prolonged, mother and son became disillusioned with the Nazi regime. James was suffering from nervous exhaustion and was plagued by self-doubt. He also found it difficult to accept Japan as an 'ally' when the Japanese entered the war on the side of the Germans in 1941. The young Eckersley later admitted that the German air raids on London had brought him to his senses and he began to feel a certain pride in being an Englishman and a corresponding hatred of the Germans, although he was not able to express such thoughts in wartime Berlin. He was also concerned about his mother. Frances sustained a fall at work in January 1943, causing concussion and she became too ill to continue broadcasting. The couple survived on a small monthly sickness payment and supplemented their income by selling their cigarette ration on the black market.

By the last year of the war, when both James and his mother refused to do any more work, they were arrested by the Gestapo and put into internment camps. Frances Eckersley said later:

> The reason I worked for the Germans was for the money. When I began I no more thought I was working for the Germans than anything. I was only doing it to get money to support myself.[29]

When it had become obvious to listeners that James Eckersley's broadcasts were that of a raw youth, he was replaced by the more mature voice of 'Jack Trevor'. Trevor was born Anthony Cedric Sebastian Steane in London in 1893 and after attending Westminster School and New College, Oxford, served as a captain with the Manchester Regiment during the First World War. He later became an actor under the stage name of Jack Trevor and acted in silent movies in Germany, usually playing the part of a British aristocrat or other upper-class English stereotypes. When war broke out Trevor maintained he was arrested by the Gestapo and beaten up for refusing to give the Hitler salute, losing several teeth in the process. He came to the attention of Goebbels (probably through the propaganda maestro's affair with film actress Lida Baarova, whom Trevor knew), who ordered him to read English news broadcasts and to appear in anti-British propaganda films. Facing further threats from the Gestapo to his family and himself, Trevor agreed to work for Goebbels. In one film recalling the life of Paul Kruger, the President of the Transvaal, Trevor played the part of a British officer fighting against the Boer farmers. A scene depicting Trevor, and the actor playing the part of General Kitchener, discussing ways of waging war on the Boers more ruthlessly and without the humane methods which had been previously used, was later used by MI5 as evidence of Trevor's collaboration with the Nazis. William L. Shirer, the American journalist who became famous for his wartime broadcasts from Berlin, met Jack Trevor during his time in the German capital. His impression of the actor turned propaganda announcer was not favourable:

His own burning passion is hatred of the Jews. Last winter, it used to be a common sight to see him stand in the snow, with a mighty blizzard blowing, and rave to an SS guard outside the studio about the urgent necessity of liquidating all Jews everywhere.[30]

One British citizen who broadcast on the English section was already well placed within the Nazi bureaucracy long before the outbreak of war. Vivian Stranders was born in London in 1881. The son of a professor at the Guildhall School of Music, Stranders was educated at London University before moving to Germany to work as a language teacher. He returned to England to teach and also joined the Territorial Army. During the First World War he served as a captain in the Royal Flying Corps.

At the end of the war he took a job as a military interpreter to the Allied Reparations Commission in Kiel.[31] Stranders believed, like many Englishmen, that Germany had been harshly treated under the terms of the Versailles treaty, having to pay vast reparations to France and other countries. He saw for himself first hand a country on its knees, and was driven to help Germany in any way he could. As Adrian Weale points out, given Stranders' later activities in Berlin, it is possible that he was recruited by the German secret service when he first went to work in Germany. Stranders was attached to the 'Inter Allied Aeronautical Commission of Control' in Berlin, the body set up to check that the Germans observed the various clauses of the Treaty of Versailles.

After being demobbed in 1921, Stranders established an import company in Dusseldorf trading in motor-cycles and aeroplane components. He married a local girl, Charlotte Hulsberg, and the family business flourished, mainly because a motor-cycle engine was the only type permitted to power light aircraft under the terms of Versailles. But his business suffered in the declining economic climate of galloping inflation and Stranders agreed to take a job as an adviser to the Heinkel Aviation Company. The Germans were keen to find ways around limitations on rearmament and needed military and commercial expertise. Through his membership of the Dusseldorf Aeronautical Club Stranders had commercial contacts in

Britain and France. He made frequent visits to the Bristol aircraft factory at Filton and was instrumental in getting engine parts sent from Britain and France to Sweden, from where they would be quietly shipped into Germany.

In 1926 Stranders was recruited as a spy by a German civil servant called Major Weber and encouraged to press his business contacts in Paris about the type of machine guns, tanks and aircraft being ordered by the French government. Unknown to Stranders, his frequent business trips to London and Paris were monitored by the British and French Intelligence services. MI5 set a trap for him but he cancelled a British visit at the last moment travelling instead to Paris. There he was arrested by the French Deuxième Bureau for espionage and supplying prohibited engineering material to the Germans. Stranders appeared in a closed court in Paris and was given a two-year prison sentence and a fine. After his release from prison Stranders returned to live in Germany and became a journalist. Settling in the old town of Weimar he soon became well known to local National Socialists as an Englishman strongly opposed to the terms of Versailles and sympathetic to the Nazi cause. He became editor of a war veterans' publication called *Steel Helmet*, and also published a book called *The Industrial Espionage of the Entente*, arguing that the Allied Control Commission on war reparations was no more than a cover for England and France to extract all the industrial and commercial know-how they could from Germany.

In 1933 Stranders became a naturalised German citizen. He attended Nazi rallies and offered full support to Hitler by joining the party and proudly wearing his Nazi party badge. He took a teaching job at Bonn University eventually being made a professor in 1936. MI5 continued to monitor the former RAF officer and his passport was placed on a Foreign Office blacklist. He was also stripped of his captain's rank in the RAF reserve. Ironically, Stranders was later made an SS-Sturmbannführer (major), for his role as a Waffen-SS expert in British affairs.

Margaret Bothamley was a leading member of the Ealing Branch of the pre-war pro-Nazi group The Link. She was a popular hostess on London's fascist scene, holding cocktail parties for fellow extremists at her flat at 67 Cromwell Road, Kensington. A few weeks before the outbreak of war, Bothamley decided to follow her Nazi sympathies and travelled to Germany via Austria. She exhibited an eccentric conflict of loyalties being staunchly pro-Hitler while decorating her Berlin flat with portraits of the King and Queen and the royal princesses.

Bothamley was born in 1897. She married a German citizen, Adolf Bleibtreu in Weimar, but the marriage did not last because she decided to travel around Austria, Czechoslovakia and Hungary for long periods without her husband. Bothamley was convinced that the Treaty of Versailles was creating economic chaos, which would lead to a Russian-inspired communist revolution, starting in Germany before spreading to Britain. When it was Hitler who benefited from Germany's economic problems, Bothamley quickly rallied to his side. She, like others, could see no wrong in the saviour of Germany and European democracy. She accused the Jews of having too much influence in the British press, which they used to work up public opinion against the German people.

In August 1939 Bothamley travelled with over a hundred fellow British pro-Nazi members of The Link to attend the Salzburg music festival. She stayed behind in Berlin for a few days and when war was declared, being unable to leave Germany, was interned. Luckily for Bothamley the Germans had heard about talks she had given in the 1930s to the Anglo-German Fellowship in which she had warned of the communist menace. She was summoned to the German Propaganda Ministry and reluctantly volunteered to make some broadcasts. After the war she said she had been troubled doing the broadcasts but believed she had no choice given what she saw as the clear danger presented by Soviet communism. As Bothamley explained at her trial: 'I felt like a mother who saw her children in danger and could only warn them by calling to them from a house which was not on speaking terms with mine.'[32]

Another prominent female broadcaster was Margaret Joyce, wife of the infamous William Joyce. Margaret was just as fascist and pro-German in her thinking as her husband. Before the war she had been an active member of the BUF in Carlisle and met and fell in love with her future husband while he was on a series of speaking engagements in the north of England. The couple married in 1937. After arriving in Berlin with her husband just a few days before the outbreak of war, a chance meeting with their old friend Frances Eckersley led to the Joyces being interviewed by the German Foreign Ministry.

Although Margaret Joyce made the occasional broadcast for the Germans shortly after the war had begun, it was not until 1942 that she broadcast under her real name. The vehicle for her propaganda broadcasts was a weekly programme called *Tuesday Talk for Women* in which she addressed the economic conditions in Britain and Germany from a woman's point of view. She spoke about the wide choice and reasonable price of fashionable women's clothes available to the Berlin housewife, contrasting this with the lack of affordable fashions on offer in British shops. Margaret promised that even Christmas would be more comfortable in Berlin:

> The Germans, whom the British press pretends to pity so much, will have their children with them for Christmas, and even the poorest will have their Christmas tree, extra coal and little luxuries.[33]

The roster of female broadcasters was completed by Pearl Joyce Vardon, Suzanne Louise Provost-Booth and the somewhat anomalous Susan Hilton. Vardon was born in Jersey in the Channel Islands in 1915. Following the Nazi occupation of the Islands, Pearl gave up her teaching job to work for better pay at the German Todt organisation. This was the German construction company that built communication lines and defensive structures on the island. She met a German officer through a friend whose boarding house had been requisitioned by the Germans. When her boyfriend was posted back to Germany Pearl was desperate to go with him. The Germans agreed to pay for her transportation to Berlin with the proviso that Vardon agree to make some announcements on Nazi radio. She accepted and was soon heard doing continuity links between music programmes before progressing to a programme called *For the Forces and their Kin*, which featured her reading out letters written by British POWs to their friends and relatives in Britain. She received payment of 450 Reichsmarks per month. Her German colleagues described Vardon as 'very pro-Nazi' and a woman who 'simply hated all things English and loved all things German and everything to do with Germany'.[34]

Suzanne Louise Provost-Booth was living in France when it was overrun by the Germans in 1940. Born in London in 1890, she acquired British citizenship by marrying into the famous Booth's gin family. Her daughter was married to the brother-in-law of the Conservative Minister R.A. Butler. The treacherous but well connected Provost-Booth worked as a Gestapo collaborator in Paris before relocating to Berlin after the D-Day invasion to continue her work for the German war effort, this time in broadcasting. Using the radio pseudonym 'Mrs Evans', she gave a newspaper interview after the war in which she described herself as

quite harmless of course . . . I used to read the Japanese news in English every afternoon. Then I took part in dear Margaret Bothamley's sketches – poor dear Margaret, such a dear, but a silly old thing, quite harmless, too . . . I had to say in this sketch, I do hate Adolf Hitler, my dear, and Margaret would explain how good Hitler was, and then I'd say, 'Now I'm beginning to understand. I think England should side with Adolf Hitler'. That's all.[35]

Perhaps the odd one out among the female broadcasters was Susan Hilton. During the war she worked mainly for Irland–Redaktion, the radio station which broadcast Nazi propaganda to neutral Ireland.[36] Born and raised in India of British parents, Hilton was disgusted at the way the British colonial administration treated Mahatma Gandhi and his supporters. She also hated her time at boarding school in England and developed an aversion to the class divisions so rife in British society. She subsequently joined the BUF, working on its newspaper *Voice of the People*, her fascist links leading to her being put under police surveillance. Following the death of her young baby, she decided to leave England to join her husband, a mining engineer working in Burma. A German destroyer in the Indian Ocean sank the passenger ship on which she was travelling, and Hilton and other survivors were transferred to a Norwegian vessel doubling as a prison ship. This ship was also torpedoed (this time by the British) off the French coast, and Hilton found herself taken to Paris in December 1940.

Having had her British passport confiscated by the Germans, Hilton approached the Irish Embassy which, realising her predicament, gave her a certificate saying she had Irish nationality. The German Embassy, admitting that military action by their Navy had caused Hilton to be 'shipwrecked', gave her food coupons plus a small living allowance. When a German official suggested to Hilton that she tell the story of her maritime experiences on the German-controlled Paris Radio, she jumped at the chance and was paid 500 francs for recording an extended interview. She was desperate to raise enough cash to continue her voyage to join her husband in Burma. When her money ran out Hilton asked to be interned but the Germans refused because she was registered as 'Irish'. Her only lifeline was a suggestion by a member of the German overseas propaganda organisation that she work for the Nazis abroad, either in Portuguese East Africa or the United States. The life of an under-cover spy did not appeal to Hilton but reluctantly she accepted a position in the Propaganda Ministry in Berlin. She worked for the Büro Concordia on both the Radio Caledonia and Christian Peace Movement stations, broadcasting under the name of Ann Tower.

Following a meeting with the Irish Minister in Berlin, it was agreed that the Irish certificate she had been issued with in Paris was invalid and that she had no claim to Irish nationality. This was ironic, given that she also worked for the Germans' Irish service. She went on to write an article for a Nazi overseas magazine describing the Sinn Fein uprising in Ireland. It was translated into Dutch, Danish, Hungarian and Arabic. Her article was based completely on the use of German library books available to her, but she was described on the cover of the magazine as both an author and an actual participant in the 1916 Irish revolt! The Germans eventually equipped Hilton with the standard 'Foreigner's Passport' issued to all the British collaborators in Germany. During her period in Berlin Susan Hilton became increasingly dependent on alcohol. This meant she could be more easily controlled by Doctor Hetzler and her other German bosses. She once committed the cardinal error of broadcasting while under the influence of drink, and was swiftly taken off the air. Instead she was sent on a fact-finding trip around Germany to prepare material for inclusion in a propaganda programme about the religious freedoms enjoyed by the Roman Catholic Church in Germany, and of how worship continued undaunted by the damage caused by the relentless Allied bombing of German cities.

As her drinking increased Hilton was considered a security risk and was closely monitored by the Gestapo. Her movement in Germany restricted, she was transferred to Vienna to work for German Radio's *Voice of the People* programme. Hilton approached the Turkish consulate in Vienna, attempting to obtain special papers to leave for a neutral country. Betrayed to the Gestapo, Hilton was imprisoned in Vienna and sentenced to death for espionage. Her arrest came just a few days after the abortive attempt by a group of army officers to assassinate Hitler, so all foreigners were considered to be potential conspirators in the plot. She was subsequently removed to a civilian internment camp at Meckenbeuren near Lake Constance to await her fate.

Another British citizen to find himself stranded in Germany, although in more suspicious circumstances, was William James Edward Percival. A freelance air correspondent from St Helens in Lancashire, Percival travelled to Berlin and Cologne in late August 1939 to research and write an article on the German aviation industry. As Europe hovered on the verge of war, Percival was invited by the press department of the German Foreign Office to visit the Polish–German frontier where atrocities were supposed to have taken place. Reports flooded into Berlin that the Poles were committing outrages against local German civilians. The German propaganda machine was working all-out to give the impression in the British media that the Poles were acting aggressively against their German neighbours.

Percival sent despatches to the *Daily Sketch* in London confirming the truth of the German allegations but offering no hard evidence to support their claims. On 1 September Percival broadcast a short statement about his visit to the frontier on Berlin's English Short Wave Radio service, saying he was the last English journalist remaining in Berlin, and claiming to have seen German refugees from Poland who had been badly treated. Percival insisted he had been given a written undertaking by the Germans stating that he would be sent to a neutral country in the event of war breaking out between Germany and Britain. He said the Germans had broken their promise, and detained him as a spy, even after he had attempted to leave Berlin to return to England with the British diplomatic contingent. He further claimed to have been taken to the notorious Gestapo headquarters at Albrechtstrasse and given a severe beating by SS guards, which resulted in a temporary loss of hearing. He gained his release by agreeing to correct news item scripts written by William Joyce. After Dr Boehmer of the Propaganda Ministry asked him to write a personal report on the English News Service, Percival says he was re-arrested and sent first to a jail in Cologne and then to the civilian internment camp at Wulzburg. In November 1941 he was transferred to the camp at Tost where P.G. Woodhouse and other British civilians had been sent after falling into German hands.

The Germans still attempted to bully Percival into working for them, either as a radio broadcaster or as a spy based in Lisbon. He said he refused all their offers, only eventually agreeing to work on *The Camp* British prisoner of war propaganda magazine because the Germans had threatened his girlfriend Elfriede Gabel if he didn't co-operate. He said the Germans also agreed to send him to Berlin for medical treatment on his ears, damaged by SS interrogation, and he was subsequently booked into Berlin's smart Adlon Hotel by the German Foreign Press Office. During his stay in Berlin Percival met John Amery who, he asserted, tried to persuade him, without success, to write recruitment propaganda material for the British Free Corps. In return Amery promised him a good position in the British government that would be formed following a German victory. For some reason the Germans allowed Percival to travel to Bayreuth to research a book he was writing on Wagner. During the visit he stayed with Frau Winifred Wagner and also met and wrote an article about Franz Lehar. Percival argued that he was trying to occupy his time with writing about the arts and that his contribution to *The Camp* magazine was purely neutral and that in fact he had worked hard behind the scenes to omit as much overt German propaganda from the POW journal as possible. When in early 1944 he refused to do any more work for the Germans, Percival was sent to the Laufen internment camp in Bavaria.

Subsequent MI5 investigations after the war discovered a multitude of holes in Percival's account of his wartime actions. Eye-witness accounts by other civilians detained at the Tost internment camp all pointed to Percival being a German stool pigeon. He was often seen in the company of German personnel and received more medical attention than any other internee. He told one fellow prisoner that when war broke out, the departing British Ambassador Sir Neville Henderson offered him the opportunity to leave Berlin, but he had refused because he preferred to stay behind and play golf! He told another fellow inmate that his hearing problems had been caused by the amount of time he had spent close to the constant noise of aeroplane engines during his years as an aviation correspondent (this in contrast to the story he recounted to MI5 after the war that his hearing had been impaired by the beating he had suffered at the hands of the Berlin Gestapo). Percival's altruistic fears for his girlfriend's safety were also unfounded. He admitted working for the Germans in 1942 and 1943 only because they made threats against his lover Elfriede Gabel. MI5 enquiries confirmed that he never actually met Gabel until mid-1943, by which time he had carried out the bulk of his collaboration with the enemy. It also later emerged that, in May 1944, he had been given the chance of repatriation back to Britain from the Wulzburg civilian internment camp. He declined the offer. Clearly, Percival's account of a man trapped in Germany in circumstances beyond his control, and being forced to co-operate with the enemy, was, at closer scrutiny, completely false. He would seem to have been a model 'collaborator'.

Working alongside Percival on *The Camp* was a Londoner named Arthur Perry. A shadowy figure on the international espionage scene during the 1930s, Perry worked for the League of Nations Governing Commission responsible for administering the Saar region, the disputed area bordering France and Germany, which was returned to Germany after a plebiscite in 1935. He then worked as a translator for a cocoa importer in Hamburg, before joining Royal Dutch Shell Oil in The Hague in 1939. As a travelling businessman Perry had every opportunity to trade in economic and political information. He was on holiday in the Balkans when war broke out and immediately approached the British consulate in Bucharest offering to work as a spy for the security service. London believed he was operating as an *agent provocateur* in the service of the Germans so declined his offer. Shortly afterwards he claimed to have been arrested by the Gestapo in Vienna and after interrogation under torture was put into the civilian internment camp at Tost. Perry arrived at Tost with five trunks of luggage; the other British internees immediately suspected him of being in league with the Germans and nicknamed him 'The Snooper'. Despite later denying all connection with the Nazis, his colleagues at Royal Dutch Shell remembered him as being very pro-German and proud to wear a swastika in his buttonhole. He was often on the telephone to 'friends' in Berlin, and bragged about the farcical shortcomings of SIS in the Netherlands that were finally exposed by the 'Venlo incident' of November 1939 when two British Intelligence officers were kidnapped under bizarre circumsances by Nazi agents on the Dutch–German border. Of little use to the Germans in Tost, Perry was sent to Berlin to continue work on pro-German publications and the Foreign Ministry's language service.

There was a high turnover of broadcasting staff within the English radio section. One new arrival in Berlin was Ralph Powell, nephew of Lord Baden-Powell the founder of the Boy Scouts movement. Powell had married a German and settled in Holland where he became a language teacher. Once Holland was overrun Powell was interned by the Germans but gained his freedom in exchange for accepting employment as a translator and newsreader in the Foreign Ministry. He maintained that he was forced to work for the Germans by threats of reprisals against his German wife and family.

Another British citizen, John Alexander Ward, had relocated to Germany after the First World War, working as a translator in Frankfurt. In 1939, Ward was interned by the Germans, but realising his pro-Nazi sentiments they employed him to broadcast propaganda to Allied troops based in North Africa. He also worked for the supposedly neutral, but German run, Radio Metropole on which he gave 'defeatist' talks under the name of 'Private Donald Hodgson' of 3rd Battalion, the Gloucestershire Regiment (his former army unit). After the war, Ward told MI5 that he had spent half his life in Germany and both his wives had been German. He had made no attempt to obtain German nationality and expressed the desire to return to England in order to bring his son up as a British subject. Like other renegade broadcasters Ward had enjoyed many of the advantages of living as a German, but as conditions deteriorated in the 'fatherland' Ward was quick to reassert his affection for Britain.

Gerald Hewitt was the son of a distinguished Knight of the Realm, Edgar Percy Hewitt. The young Hewitt studied at Cambridge but left at the end of his first year to teach English in France. He only spent a few months in England over the next twenty years, although in 1935 he was issued with an updated British passport while living in Paris. Apart from teaching, Hewitt wrote anti-Semitic articles for French magazines and submitted similar items for inclusion in *Action*, the British Union of Fascists' weekly journal. He lived in the French capital with his elderly mother until the German invasion in 1940 after which they relocated to Nice. In the following year they were anxious to return to Paris and it was suggested that he could indeed return if he would agree to do propaganda work for the Germans. Hewitt later told MI5 that he accepted the German offer as long as the propaganda was anti-communist and not anti-French or anti-British. He readily agreed to collaborate with the Germans because he needed money for food, rent and luxuries obtainable only on the black market.

Hewitt was taken to Berlin to be wined and dined by officials from the propaganda branch of the Foreign Office. He was also introduced to, among others, Rudolf Hess, John Amery and William Joyce. After some radio production training in Berlin, Hewitt returned to France to work for the Nazi controlled Paris Radio, where he was paid 1,000

Reichsmarks a month to supply propaganda scripts and make sound recordings under the name of 'Smith'. In a letter to his mother he described Hitler as 'the greatest man of all time'.[37] Hewitt later denied his broadcasting activities but at the end of the war MI5 discovered several recording discs at the Paris Radio station containing his voice. In one of his recordings he said: 'Do all of the English approve of the weekly – one almost says daily – massacres of French civilians by the French and above all the American aviators?'[38]

The Allied landing in North Africa in 1942, plus the destruction of the sixth German Army at Stalingrad, shook Hewitt's faith in the cause of his German masters and he began to look for a way out of his treasonous activities. He turned for help to an old pupil from his pre-war teaching days, Henri Mazaud. The Frenchman was an active Resistance figure, and Hewitt offered to give away some French collaborators to the Resistance movement in exchange for his own safety. Mazaud refused Hewitt's offer, and when it became obvious after D-Day that the Allies would soon be in Paris, Hewitt left the city with the Germans. Fearing he would become trapped in Berlin, he tried unsuccessfully to enter Switzerland. The Swiss handed him over to the British.

BÜRO CONCORDIA

As well as its general overseas services, German broadcasting also operated a secret organisation named Büro Concordia.[39] Its purpose was to give the impression that pro-German underground 'pirate' radio stations were being operated at various locations actually inside Britain. The stations purported to be staffed by groups of patriotic Britons who considered it their duty to oppose the government's war against Germany. The message of these 'patriots' was that the war was not serving British needs but was instead subordinated to American and Russian interests. The voices of the best-known renegade British broadcasters such as William Joyce and Norman Baillie-Stewart could not be employed on the new clandestine radio stations because they would have been recognised, thereby exploding the pretence that the programmes originated inside Britain. Similarly, although some German nationals were employed to speak in English on the Reichsrundfunk's main overseas stations, German voices could not be used on supposedly 'British' based stations. Instead, new voices had to be found and the Germans began to cast their net. There were three main secret stations.

The New British Broadcasting Station began transmitting in February 1940 and used as its opening theme tune, 'Loch Lomond', and always closed with 'God Save the King'. Rather strangely, the British government allowed the programmes to be listed alongside those of the BBC in British newspapers, whereas anyone discovered placing advertising 'stickyback' posters for the new stations in a public place faced prosecution for aiding the enemy.

The first voice to be heard on the New British Broadcasting Station was that of Kenneth Vincent Lander. The Oxford-educated Londoner was a frequent visitor to Germany in the 1930s, studying at Munich University. He then took a job teaching languages at the Hermann Lietz Schule at Schloss Bieberstein near Fulda. Lander gradually became attracted to National Socialism and decided to seek German naturalisation, but his application was turned down. When war was declared Lander was initially left alone to continue his teaching job but, perhaps inevitably, was contacted by the Reichsrundfunk and summoned to Berlin. The Germans told Lander they were trying to bring about a change of attitude among English people towards Germany and that Lander could contribute to this aim. As he later commented:

The material which I broadcast consisted partly of notes from the German News Service which I was given to construct a small talk from in criticism, from a British point of view, of the British Government's policy, the idea being that they were not acting in British interests, and speeches already prepared which I was given to broadcast.[40]

Lander was paid 600 Reichsmarks per month for his broadcasting duties. The Germans considered him to be politically reliable hence he was not punished when he refused to be transferred to the British Free Corps.

Lewis Barrington ('Barry') Payne Jones from Birmingham was another pro-Nazi sympathiser who left England in the summer of 1939 to start a teaching job at the Berlitz School in Cologne. He had gone on many exchange trips to Germany while a schoolboy, and the impact of Hitler drew him into the fascist camp. Jones later became a committee member of the Birmingham district branch of The Link and regularly received German propaganda from an active Nazi Party member based in Munich called H.R. Hoffman. In April 1939, Jones wrote to Hoffman offering his services to the Reich.[41] As he was a fluent German speaker, Jones suggested that he could work as a translator or interpreter. In his letter Jones stated that he would be prepared to travel to any part of Germany with only two weeks' notice and to undertake any post Hoffman thought appropriate. Hoffman acknowledged the letter, telling Jones he would hear something soon. In the meantime Jones took up an appointment at the Berlitz School.

When war came the 25-year-old was not interned, which was unusual considering his age. He may have become a naturalised German by then, as he had met and married a local girl named Gretel Becker. He was twice interviewed by the Gestapo but declined to work for them until June 1942 when the Berlitz School was damaged by Allied bombing. By then his wife was pregnant so Jones had to make ends meet somehow. He eagerly volunteered to broadcast for the Germans' European stations' English service based in Berlin, Luxembourg and Hilversum, earning about 1,000 Reichsmarks per month. Jones was a willing collaborator. In August 1942 he wrote to his brother in England: 'On 1 August I was promoted here to Berlin, where I am doing very well. Indeed you needn't brag about all the money you are earning; you're not the only one: I have never earned so much money in my life as now.'[42] MI5, who were monitoring his mail, wrote in Jones's file: 'His ordinary correspondence with his parents reveals him a spoilt smugly self-satisfied, semi-educated prig.'[43]

Another early contributor to the New British Broadcasting Station was Leonard Banning. Like so many collaborators Banning was a member of the BUF during the early 1930s and continued to write for Mosley's propaganda machine even after leaving Britain to take up a teaching post in Germany. Banning broadcast under the aliases 'John Brown' or 'William Brown'. He wrote and performed a programme called *Between Ourselves*, a series of talks which suggested to listeners that they were being misled by the leaders in Britain. Banning also found time to pen recruitment literature for the British Free Corps. One of Banning's colleagues described him as the 'driving force' behind the NBBS.[44]

The third major recruit to the New British Broadcasting Station was Kenneth James Gilbert. Born in India in 1917, Gilbert had fascist sympathies and was living in Kent when the war started but quickly moved to the Channel Islands to escape military service. Gilbert portrayed himself as a conscientious objector but his alleged peace-loving sentiments aside, he was known to Kent police as a man of 'violent disposition and a heavy drinker'.[45] When the Channel Islands were occupied by German troops in 1940, Gilbert approached the Germans and volunteered to do anything he could 'to help bring about peace'.[46] The Germans sent him to Berlin where, following an interview with William Joyce, Gilbert began broadcasting for the New British Broadcasting Station (NBBS) under the alias 'Kenneth James'. Gilbert's violent streak surfaced when he became involved in a fight with an SS guard for failing to produce his identity card. As a result Gilbert was sent to a forced labour camp. He later told MI5 that the real reason for his imprisonment was because he had tried to resign from the Concordia organisation. The controller of the English section at Concordia was Dr Erich Hetzler, a fanatical Nazi and a member of Ribbentrop's personal staff. Hetzler made an example of Gilbert, and after five months' of beatings at the hands of 'privileged prisoners' in the labour camp, the terrified Gilbert reluctantly agreed to return to work at the NBBS.[47]

Another recruit at Concordia, Signalman William Colledge, described the climate of fear that pervaded the radio station following Gilbert's return: 'We had all worked under the shadow of the threat of the concentration camp but now seeing James, everyone was terrified.'[48] Colledge (cover name 'Winter'), had been captured while serving with the North Somerset Yeomanry in North

Africa. He co-operated with his captors, even agreeing to spy on his fellow prisoners. Brought to Berlin to meet Dr Hetzler, Colledge volunteered to broadcast for Concordia but lacked the vocal skills required and was used instead to prepare news bulletins.

Rifleman Ronald Spillman of the King's Royal Rifle Corps was captured in Crete and soon volunteered to work for the NBBS. His initial zeal for collaboration rapidly wore off:

At the beginning I was sincere and really believed I was doing the right thing from the humanitarian angle. Later on, when I did come to my senses it was too late to back out. I know I should have backed out. I fully realised it, whatever the consequences would have been. I stopped on because for one reason I didn't think the station was having any effect on the English public, another reason was that I was engaged to the girl I met.[49]

A second part of the Büro Concordia operation was the Workers' Challenge. This station claimed to be run by a group of socialist workers who believed that the British working class was being exploited and betrayed in the interests of capitalism. Workers' Challenge urged workers to get rid of Churchill and his political cronies by organising anti-war strikes at arms factories and other vital industries. Its no-nonsense approach was designed to encourage 'ordinary' workers to reflect on how the war was being waged. The station's message included such lines as:

Organise a real working-class meeting, a march, and a demonstration; get the banners out. Churchill means hunger and war. Down with Churchill. Up with the workers' Britain. No bloodshed for capitalism. Let the bosses fight for their profit. Kick 'em out of Westminster into the Thames.[50]

The Minister of Labour, Sir Ernest Bevin, also came in for criticism: 'Just think of that bloody rat sitting in his office, drawing his dough and telling us that we ought to work eighty-four blinking hours a week.' As well as the blunt approach, Workers' Challenge also employed some ripe language for its intended down to earth 'home' audience. Words used included 'bugger', 'bastard', 'sod' and probably the first use of 'fuck' over the radio airwaves.[51] The station conveyed a picture of desperate men being thwarted by the authorities at every turn: 'You'll probably 'ear us tomorrow night at the same hour, but it's getting 'ard, the police always on our 'eels nowadays.'[52]

The speakers on the station were mainly soldiers recruited in German POW camps. William Henry Humphrey Griffiths, a Welsh Guardsman, was captured at Boulogne in May 1940 and incarcerated in the POW camp at Thorn in Poland. Speaking in a rough working-class accent, Griffiths became the station's most prominent announcer. Griffiths later claimed that he had been threatened with death if he refused to co-operate. He may have tried to wriggle out of the required task by deliberately having to do several 'takes' on his recorded speeches, but eventually Dr Hetzler and William Joyce were entirely satisfied with his 'audition'. Griffiths was joined at the microphone by a Sergeant MacDonald and later by Donald Alexander Fraser Grant, who broadcast under the alias of 'Jock Palmer'.

Fraser Grant was born in the village of Alness in Ross and Cromarty. He left school at sixteen to help run the family provision store, before leaving home to take a job with the Gestetner copying company in Newcastle. In 1934 he relocated to London to work as a travelling salesman selling vacuum cleaners. A fierce anti-communist, he joined the South Kensington branch of Mosley's fascist movement, and then switched his allegiance to the more extreme Imperial Fascists League, before finally gaining membership of the The Link. Fraser Grant made several trips to Germany as part of the Weltklub Union, an exchange organisation established to foster peace and understanding between nations. He went on an exchange trip to stay with a German family in Magdeburg where he found himself stranded when war broke out. Interned by the Germans, he was sent to Hanover and given a job in a typewriter factory.

On hearing of Fraser Grant's German sympathies, Dr Hetzler summoned him to Berlin and invited him to contribute to Workers Challenge and to the newly planned Scottish station, Radio

Caledonia, a propaganda station intended to stir up Scottish nationalism, particularly in the mining industry and the Clydeside dockyards. The station transmitted daily at 18:00 using 'Auld Lang Syne' as its signature tune. It urged the Scots to withdraw from the war and in return promised home rule for Scotland when Germany had defeated the Allies. Fraser Grant was motivated by money and negotiated a pay deal of 600 Reichsmarks per month, five times more than he was getting working in the typewriter factory. After the war he maintained that he only agreed to work on Caledonia because he didn't believe the war really concerned Scottish interests. His actions were a classic case of combining a well-paid job with fascist ideology from the relative security of a Berlin studio.

The final broadcasting arm of the Büro Concordia was the Christian Peace Movement. It transmitted a daily half-hour programme using as its signature tune 'O God Our Help in Ages Past'. The station delivered a long-running sermon of peace to all Christians and pacifists. Its insidious preaching may have struck a cord with pacifist groups in Britain such as the Peace Pledge Union. One broadcast item in August 1940 asked British Christians why Germany's peace offers had been refused:

> Do we really want to carry on the war? – Are we so enthusiastic as all that about it? – Is it necessary? – Those of us who have lost relations or friends in the forces know all too well the sorrow of being parted, that suspense of hearing nothing for weeks, perhaps months, and of not knowing whether they are alive or dead.[53]

The scripts were written by Pte Cyril Hoskins, captured after Dunkirk and recruited by William Joyce from the POW camp at Thorn in Poland. The main speaker on the station was Reginald Arthur Humphries, a seaman in the Royal Navy, being announced on the radio as a 'Father Donovan, who through personal experience is fully aware of the political and religious situation and what it means to everyone'.[54] Posing as a man of the cloth, the sanctimonious Humphries delivered pseudo-sermons with a political edge. The Christian Peace Movement was a short-lived Concordia station, running for less than two years before being closed by the Germans because radio reception in Britain was poor. During the summer of 1943 a new station called Radio National took to the airwaves. It was managed by the German Foreign Ministry and indirectly linked to recruitment to the British Free Corps, which is examined in the next chapter. Radio National's chief announcers were British POWs like Roy Courlander, Frank Maton and Roy Purdy.

Roy Nicholas Courlander was born in London, the illegitimate son of a British woman who subsequently married a Lithuanian businessman called Leonard Courlander. Roy Courlander attended boarding school in England before joining his parents on their plantation on a South Sea island in the New Hebrides. At the beginning of the war, Courlander signed up with the New Zealand Expeditionary Force and saw action in North Africa and Greece where he was captured in 1941. He was sent to a POW camp at Marburg and because his New Zealand pay book had no place of birth stamped on it, Courlander passed himself off as a 'White Russian', pretending to have been born in Riga and expressing pro-German views. He acted as camp interpreter at Stalag XVIIIa and ingratiated himself sufficiently with the Germans to warrant being sent to Berlin, where he met John Amery and William Joyce. He volunteered to make some broadcasts for Radio National. Courlander was given clearance to travel as a civilian in Berlin and divided his time between the radio station and the recruitment of renegades for the British Free Corps at the Genshagen 'holiday camp' (see Chapter Five).

The other pro-fascist who divided his time between broadcasting for Radio National and helping to indoctrinate volunteers for the British Free Corps was Francis 'Frank' Paul Maton. His fanatical fascist views were put to use following his capture in Crete in 1941 and transfer to Stalag IVa. At Radio National he broadcast under the name 'Manxman', but later assumed the name 'Frank MacCarthy' on joining the Free Corps. Working alongside Courlander and Maton was Raymond Davies Hughes from Mold in North Wales, an RAF air gunner who had been shot down over the Baltic coast in August 1943. After interrogation at the Luftwaffe holding centre at Dulag Luft, Hughes claimed to have been taken to the German capital to meet Amery and Baillie-Stewart, who intimidated him into co-operating. As well as receiving a monthly salary of 350 Reichsmarks from the German Foreign Ministry, the RAF man also worked for Radio Metropole, the station which broadcast to places as diverse as North Africa and Wales! Hughes was paid a further 600 Reichsmarks a month for making propaganda speeches to the United Kingdom in the Welsh language. His career as a radio announcer was curtailed because of poor scripts, a lack of style and bad punctuation. He wasn't helped by the coaching he received at the microphone by Margaret Joyce, herself considered wooden and unconvincing as a broadcaster.

Another voice heard on Radio Metropole was that of Henry Wicks. A member of the BUF and Nordic League, Wicks gained some notoriety before the war for a series of press attacks and court action against his former employers the Sun Life Assurance Company of Canada. Wicks believed corrupt practices were being carried out by Sun Life, who had dismissed him for dishonesty. He brought an action for libel but the verdict went against him and he was ordered to pay costs. His next move was a letter libelling a solicitor named Gurney who was employed by the Sun Life Company. This letter led to his prosecution and conviction at the Central Criminal Court in 1936 where he was sentenced to twelve months' imprisonment. When he came out of prison Wicks applied for his discharge from bankruptcy but the Registrar described him as 'an unscrupulous and dangerous man, though of undoubted ability', and refused the application.[55]

In the summer of 1939 Wicks fled to Berlin on the grounds that the financial frame-ups to which he had been subjected meant he would never get a fair hearing in England. The press highlighted his case, labelling him 'An English refugee in Berlin'. Wicks blamed his situation on the Jews, telling the press: 'Owing to the rule of Jewish terror in London, it is not possible to speak freely or to open the eyes of the English people about things which are going on.'[56] The Nazis naturally welcomed an anti-Semite fleeing supposed persecution in Britain and let Wicks and his family stay at the house of a German interpreter called Doctor Carl Schmidt. When war was declared he was interned at the civilian camp at Tost where fellow prisoners described him as embittered and blatantly anti-British. He was often physically assaulted for his views and eventually volunteered to return to Berlin. He readily agreed to broadcast for the Germans and during his time at Radio Metropole he wrote and performed scripts and acted in adaptations of plays by Shaw and Galsworthy. After the war he trotted out the usual story, that he had had every intention of sabotaging the German radio service, and would never have worked for it willingly. Wicks' adoptive daughter Margaret also made broadcasts, which she did with the encouragement of her German husband. The MI5 dossier on Wicks described him as someone who had not committed deliberate treason to help achieve a German victory. He was just an unscrupulous egotist who was hell bent on venting his personal grievances against those in Britain whom he believed had set out to ruin him. His visit to Berlin gave him the chance to air his views through the Nazi propaganda machine. He effectively used the Nazis for his own ends and they in turn used him for theirs.

Sergeant Arthur Chapple exhibited all the signs of a typical renegade. He always maintained that he was a lifelong socialist and anti-fascist, despite volunteering to broadcast from Berlin and join the British Free Corps. The Yorkshireman's first job was working as a reporter on the *Wakefield Times*. He then joined the Royal Army Service Corps and was attached to the NAAFI organisation. He was captured in France in 1940 and interned at Stalag XXa at Thorn. While imprisoned at Thorn, Chapple met William Joyce and volunteered to write for *The Camp*. He was also used to seek out potential Free Corps recruits among captured British POWs at the German administered Genshagen 'holiday camp' in Berlin. Chapple's ridiculous rationale for taking part in Radio National was that he believed himself to have been deliberately selected by the Germans because of his anti-fascist views, in order to give the propaganda broadcasts political balance. He did not of course admit to holding anti-fascist views when he subsequently agreed to join the British Free Corps.

One of the few radio announcers to broadcast under his real name was Edward Salvin Bowlby. He was born in Ireland in 1911 and later moved to England where he joined the BUF and worked as a cinema manager in Stockport. On the outbreak of war Bowlby, then living in Budapest where he hoped to start a language school, was arrested by the Germans and placed in the civilian internment camp at Tost in Silesia. His strongly anti-Semitic views led to his release and he was first offered translating work in the Foreign Ministry and then a broadcasting post on the Concordia service by Norman Baillie-Stewart.

Roy Walter Purdy was born in Dagenham, Essex in 1918. Before the war he was an active member of the Ilford branch of the BUF. In 1939 he joined the merchant navy as an engineer before being transferred to the Royal Navy with the rank of sub-lieutenant. In June 1940, his boat the *Van Dyck* was sunk off the Norwegian coast and Purdy was taken prisoner and transferred to five different POW camps before ending up at the Marlag/Milag Nord camp for navy personnel in northern Germany. Purdy was unpopular with his fellow prisoners because of his obvious lying. He said that his sister was about to be married to a lord and would then be presented at Court. He was always boasting about his pre-war days in the BUF and the merits of fascism. After three years in captivity Purdy decided to assist the Germans. The suspicions of his fellow prisoners were first aroused when he acquired a copy of William Joyce's book *Twilight over England*. On being sent to Berlin Purdy met Joyce (who autographed his book), and promised to make ten radio broadcasts in exchange for being allowed to escape to a neutral country. Purdy worked for Radio National calling himself 'Pointer' and 'Ronald Wallace'. Another POW, Sqn Ldr George Robert Carpenter, who had been shot down over Holland, was taken to Berlin to broadcast alongside Purdy. The RAF man refused point-blank to collaborate with the Nazis, and later recalled Purdy as a man worthy of the traitor tag. The first time Carpenter saw Purdy, the merchant seaman was sitting in a radio booth in the Berlin offices of Radio National. His opening broadcast was: 'This is British Radio National – the only radio station run by Englishmen.'[57] Purdy then went on to appeal to mothers in Britain to refuse to let their sons fight: 'Did you bring up your sons to die on the beaches?' Purdy boasted to

Carpenter that he was the golden voice of German broadcasting and was much in demand by all the propaganda stations. One of his more odious broadcasts for Radio National was made in August 1943 and was entitled 'The Conduct of Jews in Public'.

I must apologise if what I have to say offends you, but it has to be said. Next time you travel by train or bus and one of your companions is obviously a Jew, I want you to observe his actions. You can hardly mistake their dominant characteristics – their coarse, greasy hair, their greasy foreheads, their negroid lips – but their actions betray their race more than their appearance. They enter the carriage with a swagger and will stand in the centre of the compartment and gaze with sensuous eyes at the occupants. They will edge near to the young and obviously unattached female. When they are seated, their eyes usually roam in the direction of our womenfolk. When the train is full, they will remain seated, jeering and laughing. On the streets their behaviour is the same. They will not allow the free passage of fellow pedestrians. To pass these monuments of all that is disgusting one must get into the road. They abuse every bit of hospitality we have shown them. There is only one way to rid ourselves of this ill-mannered race. We must escort them to the chosen land and give the Arabs a chance to educate them.[58]

The opportunity to deliver such obnoxious broadcasts to a British radio audience (however small), gave Purdy, the boy from Essex who had left school at sixteen and had always felt inferior among the other Royal Navy officers, an inflated sense of importance. Like the other British renegades, Purdy was living in relative luxury in Berlin. He was issued with a German identity card under the assumed name of 'Ronald Wallace' with date and place of birth given as 11 December 1914 in Buenos Aires, and was allowed to travel freely in the German capital. He met and fell in love with a young German woman called Margarete Weitemeier who soon fell pregnant.

The time Purdy had spent in various POW camps did not go unnoticed by the Germans. They decided to test his loyalty by sending him on a 'spying' mission to one of the most high profile officer camps in Germany, Oflag 4C, situated near Leipzig, and perhaps better known as Colditz Castle. A series of breakouts from the supposedly escape-proof prison had embarrassed the German High Command. From the moment Purdy arrived at the British wing of the prison his fellow inmates had their doubts about him. Julius Green, a captain who travelled from camp to camp carrying out dental surgery, remembered Purdy from their time in the Marlag internment camp and asked him what he had been doing during his stay in Berlin. Purdy replied that he had escaped from the Genshagen camp and gone to live with a German girl who had been his sister's pen pal before the war. He said that when the girl's flat was destroyed in a bombing raid he had tried to obtain official evacuee papers but was arrested by the Gestapo.

Suspicion of Purdy among the Colditz internees increased over the next few days. First, an escape tunnel, which had recently been dug by the prisoners, was shown to Purdy and shortly afterwards mysteriously 'discovered' by the Germans. Then a concealed cupboard containing foreign currency and false documents was revealed along with a miniature radio, the first to be found in a German POW camp. As the 'coincidences' began to mount up fingers started to point at Purdy. A band of officers considered hanging him after holding a court martial. The following day Purdy was interrogated by the camp security committee and then by a senior British officer, Lt Col. Cecil Merritt VC, a Canadian hero of the raid on Dieppe. Purdy could not provide a convincing account for the time he had already spent in Germany. Under constant questioning he eventually admitted he was a traitor broadcasting for the Nazis, and that he had been living on good rations with a woman in Berlin. He said he had only pretended to work for the Nazis to provide a cover for his real purpose of sabotaging the German war effort by throwing Molotov cocktails into official buildings during the air-raids on Berlin and stealing sensitive documents from the German Admiralty. Following his 'confession' a senior British officer went to the commandant and told him that unless Purdy was removed from the prison he could not answer for his safety.

His cover blown, and so of no further use to the Germans in Colditz, Purdy was taken into protective custody and then returned to Berlin. When the Germans found out and confronted him with his boasts in Colditz – that he had secretly sabotaged the Reich – the merchant seaman later claimed he was given the option of either working for the SS propaganda unit, Standarte Kurt Eggers, or being executed. He wrote pro-Nazi leaflets and translated for the Germans until March 1945. According to his subsequent interrogation by MI5 after the war, Purdy said that he continued to try to sabotage the German war effort by dropping sugar into a petrol tank used to refuel German military vehicles.[59] With the war coming to an end, Purdy made a desperate attempt to obtain German citizenship and marry his girlfriend Margarete who by now had given birth to their son, Stephen. After Purdy's request for citizenship was refused by the Gestapo, he made his escape through Italy and finally gave himself up to the Americans. He never saw Margarete or his son again.

One of the more high-profile traitors to be employed by Radio National was Benson Railton Metcalf Freeman. Although he never actually spoke on German radio, Freeman was one of the brains behind the scenes, dreaming up scripts and other production ideas. Freeman was the classic English upper-class fascist. Born in Newbury in Berkshire, Freeman was the son of a Royal Navy commander. He followed his father into the services, graduating from the Royal Military Academy at Sandhurst in 1924 before being commissioned into the King's Own Royal Regiment. He soon developed a fascination for flying, indeed, many future British fascists took a keen interest in aviation during the 1920s and '30s. Oswald Mosley was himself an accomplished aviator, having proven his bravery in the skies over France with the Royal Flying Corps during the First World War. Following the successful completion of his pilot training Freeman transferred to the RAF as a flying officer. He eventually became a flight instructor and test pilot before retiring from the service in 1931 to run a farm in Gloucestershire. Along with many others of his social class, Freeman became obsessed with the threat of communism. As he was later to explain:

I have been bitterly opposed to the appalling menace of Soviet Communism for a long time. I have studied Moscow propaganda for about 15 years and its hideous exploitation by World Jewry and I am more than dismayed at the fearful fate that awaits this country and western Europe and eventually the world when this menace overpowers them.[60]

It was perhaps no surprise that Freeman joined the BUF in 1937 and he remained a committed fascist. When war came he resumed his role of training new pilots but seemed reluctant to get involved in action himself. When he was given orders to fly with his squadron from Croydon to France his group came under attack from a flight of German Messerschmitts and Freeman's plane was forced to crash-land in a field. The fascist officer was interrogated at the Luftwaffe transit camp Dulag Luft at Oberursel near Frankfurt. The camp had a similar function to the British Free Corps indoctrination base at Luckenwalde, namely using stool pigeons and intimidation to induce captured airmen to reveal important technical information. Freeman's German captors soon realised that he held anti-Soviet and pro-Nazi views, and they hoped he would agree to work for them perhaps as an informer in the camp or as a radio propaganda announcer in Berlin. Freeman had no intention of betraying his fellow officers, so his usefulness to the Germans at Dulag Luft was minimal. He also refused to write articles for *The Camp* magazine. Freeman was unpopular in the camp because he was a bore, obsessed with the menace of communism, as well as being a traitor. He was eventually removed from the camp and called to a meeting in Berlin with the German Foreign Ministry's Dr Hesse. Here, Freeman prophetically stated that Germany had made a major error in invading Russia and that despite its initial successes against the Red Army, the Wehrmacht advance would eventually be driven back and defeated.

Clearly obsessed with the Russian threat, Freeman decided to accept Hesse's invitation to write anti-Soviet radio scripts for the 'Germany calling' service, working under the assumed name of 'Royston'. At one stage he shared an office with Norman Baillie-

Stewart whom he believed 'had all the outward characteristics of an English officer and gentleman but was just about the weakest moral specimen I ever met'.[61]

This description aside, Freeman and his double-barrelled colleague were in many ways very similar. Both men were upper-class, Sandhurst-educated officers, holding arrogant and forthright views. Baillie-Stewart had already fallen out with his German superiors over the policy and content of radio broadcasts, and Freeman also ended up rowing with the wrong people, in particularly Dr Hesse, about the effectiveness of the Foreign Ministry's anti-Soviet propaganda. Both Britons failed to realise that they were simply puppets in the hands of an arrogant totalitarian regime which, at the time, believed it had the world at its feet. Frustrated with his radio script-writing role, Freeman began looking for a fresh challenge. It arose when he met SS-Standartenführer Gunther D'Alquen, commander of the Kurt Eggers Regiment, a propaganda unit responsible for, among other things, providing Waffen-SS war correspondents.[62] The two men held similar views on the nature of the Soviet threat and Freeman readily agreed to join the SS, holding the rank of Untersturmführer (second lieutenant). Less than a year after joining the SS, Freeman's unit was evacuated southwards in the face of the Russian advance on Berlin. In the chaos that surrounded the German collapse Freeman was given the opportunity to flee to neutral Switzerland. But the eccentric flying officer was determind to return to England, and handed himself over to the American forces in the Lenggries area in early May 1945. Freeman never considered himself a traitor. As he put it: 'My conviction is that the war could have ended long ago if Churchill, certain other leaders in this country, and the Jewish financiers had been willing to fight the Bolshevik menace along with Germany.'[63]

CHAPTER FOUR

William Joyce

At the end of September 1939 the character known as Lord Haw-Haw was the best-known voice heard on British radio. He received massive newspaper coverage and was even the subject of a London theatre revue. But far from being the mainstay of the British musical comedy scene, the voice of Lord Haw-Haw belonged to the most famous and committed of all the German collaborators – William Joyce. Joyce's broadcasts from Berlin had a tremendous impact on morale in war-torn Britain. Haw-Haw's sneering and jeering struck at the heart of a British radio audience hungry for news about the war. Joyce was to pay the ultimate price for his treachery and he remains, along with Guy Fawkes, Britain's most notorious traitor.

Joyce was born on 24 April 1906 in Brooklyn, New York. His parents Michael and Gertrude Joyce were immigrants from Great Britain. Michael Joyce came originally from County Galway in Ireland, but had become a naturalised American citizen in 1894. In 1909 the Joyces left America and settled in County Mayo. William Joyce's education was in Catholic schools in Ireland. After attending convent school he entered the Jesuit-run St Ignatius Loyola College in Galway. Apart from doing well in Latin, French and German, William asserted himself as a tough, argumentative character. After getting into a fist fight with another boy William sustained a broken nose. At first he did not report his injury. Consequently it was not treated properly and his voice acquired the nasal twang that was later to become a distinctive feature of his broadcasts from Berlin.

During the Irish Troubles the Joyce family remained staunchly loyal to the British Crown. In the bloody Irish civil war William acted as an informer against the Republicans. There was no doubting his burning patriotism as he passed information to the British irregular forces (the infamous 'Black and Tans'). Following the Anglo-Irish Treaty and the establishment of the Irish Free State in 1921, the Joyce family, fearing retribution by IRA sympathisers, moved to England. The young Joyce lied about his age and enlisted in the British Army. After serving four months his true age came to light when he contracted rheumatic fever and he was discharged. Joyce still saw an attraction in military service and in 1922 approached the London University Training Corps. He viewed the Corps as his first step towards gaining a commission in the regular army. In his application letter to the Corps Joyce reinforced his loyalty to the British Crown but also added:

I must now mention a point which I hope will not give rise to difficulties. I was born in America, but of British parents. I left America when two years of age, have not returned since, and do not propose to return. . . . I am in no way connected with the United States of America against which, as against all other nations, I am prepared to draw the sword in British interests.[1]

Michael Joyce supported his son's application in a letter to the University authorities: 'With regard to my son William. He was born in America. I was born in Ireland, his mother was born in England. We are all British and not American subjects.'[2] Michael Joyce had lied to help his son. By English law it was the father's nationality which passed to the child. Michael Joyce had renounced his British citizenship when he became a naturalised American citizen in 1894. This meant that William was definitely an American. Some years earlier Michael Joyce had told William's younger brother Quentin that all the family were American citizens, but swore him to secrecy on the subject. For some reason which has never been identified Michael Joyce drilled it into all his children that they were 'British'. Although American born, perhaps Joyce actually believed he was British. His patriotism was never in doubt in the early years as he pledged himself to king and country and often sang the national anthem at fascist meetings.

In 1923 Joyce embarked on a course of academic study eventually graduating from London University with a first class honours degree in English. He also married and had two children but the marriage was dissolved in 1936. During the early 1920s Joyce developed a political rather than military career. He joined a group called the British Fascisti Limited, which was modelled on Italian fascism. They were easily identified as they wore a black handkerchief in their breast pocket and a badge that read, 'For King and Country'. The British Fascisti was comprised of reactionary conservatives alarmed at possible communist infiltration of the embryonic Labour Party and socialist revolution in Britain. The group also had paramilitary aspirations that helped attract Joyce to its ranks. In October 1924, a meeting was held by the conservative-supported candidate for Lambeth North. Fearing that 'Reds' would attempt to disrupt the meeting, the British Fascisti sent a protection squad to the meeting led by Joyce, then an eighteen-year-old undergraduate. Heckling turned to violence and in the ensuing fight Joyce was slashed across the right cheek with a razor. Left with a permanent scar, Joyce claimed that his assailant had been a 'Jewish Communist', although this was never proven. This experience may have have contributed to Joyce's 'near hysterical loathing' of Jews.[3] The incident also showed that Joyce would not hesitate to use strong-arm tactics should the need arise. He faced assault charges following a fracas at a Blackshirt meeting at Worthing in 1934, but was found not guilty. He also appeared twice in the dock, in 1938 and 1939, charged with physically attacking hecklers at a street meeting of his newly formed National Socialist League. Once again magistrates dismissed the case against him.

Away from street provocations, Joyce continued his academic studies, embarking on a master's degree. It came to nothing because he later alleged that his 'Jewish' tutor had stolen his research notes. The tutor wasn't Jewish. He then applied to join the Foreign Office and though he had the academic credentials for the job, he was rejected at his first interview. Joyce blamed the 'old boy network' for preventing someone from his background from being selected for a job he knew he could do.

Politically Joyce flirted with the Conservative Party but his extreme nationalism and increasingly anti-Semitic views did not fit the party mould. He left the Conservatives in 1930 and found his political home in Sir Oswald Mosley's newly formed British Union of Fascists. People were immediately struck by the brilliance of Joyce's oratory. The author Cecil Roberts described an after dinner speech given by the firebrand fascist at the Park Lane Hotel:

> Thin, pale, intense, he had not been speaking many minutes before we were electrified by this man. I have been a connoisseur of speech-making for a quarter of a century, but never before, in any country, had I met a personality so terrifying in its dynamic force, so vituperative, so vitriolic. The words poured from him in a corrosive spate.[4]

Joyce gave up his job as a teacher at the Victoria Tutorial College to become full-time Propaganda Director of the BUF, at a salary of £300 a year. In anticipation of travelling with Mosley to Germany to visit Hitler, Joyce applied for a British passport. Filling in his application form Joyce declared that he was a British subject by birth having been born in Galway. At that time a birth certificate was not required to support a passport application; it only required a public official to endorse an application. Joyce asked an accountant at his bank in Belgravia to vouch for him and the banker had no reason to doubt that Joyce was born in Ireland. Joyce had enormous satisfaction in obtaining his passport (although Mosley did not invite him on his German trip). However, describing himself as a British citizen was to have drastic consequences for Joyce.

Joyce and Mosley were never kindred spirits. Politically Joyce felt Mosley was not strongly committed to anti-Semitism. He also felt the leader (or, as Joyce referred to him, 'the bleeder') had pushed him into standing in an unwinnable constituency during the London County Council elections of March 1937. Joyce polled only 14 per cent of the votes compared to the Labour Party's 63 per cent. Writing in his memoirs Mosley described Joyce dismissively as 'intensely vain; a quite common foible in very small men, as Bacon shows in his essay on the diminutive. It was a shock to his vanity that I dropped him.'[5]

Mosley eventually ditched Joyce on financial grounds. The BUF could not afford to pay a full-time staff of a hundred and forty and the number was reduced to thirty. Joyce took the news badly and promptly left the BUF to form his own party, the British National Socialist League. It was a small organisation comprised mainly of BUF defectors. Joyce produced a booklet for the organisation entitled *National Socialism Now*. His views became increasingly pro-Nazi as he hailed Hitler's success against 'international Jewish finance'.

The inaugural meeting of the National Socialist League was held in Joyce's house at 28 Fawcett Street in Fulham. Among those present was Christian Bauer, a German news correspondent with strong links with the Nazi Party. After he was excluded from Britain Bauer remained in regular contact with Joyce. MI5 were tapping Joyce's telephone and reading his correspondence. A letter Joyce wrote to Bauer on 11 April 1939 was intercepted by MI5, and contained the line, 'The constant campaign of slander and vilification against Germany makes me sick. I am at least determined that I am not going to fight for Jewry.'[6]

In 1937 Joyce married Margaret Cairns White, a committed fascist speaker and party organiser from Manchester. She had first heard Joyce speak at a meeting in Dumfries in 1935 and travelled to hear him at other fascist gatherings. As the countdown to the Second World War began, Joyce's following declined and membership of the National Socialist League became restricted to friends, family and assorted misfits. Joyce had to make a choice. He could not join a British fight against Hitler. Instead he called for a pact with Germany on the basis that, 'Britain and Germany, particularly with the assistance of Italy, can form against Bolshevism and international finance, twin Jewish manifestations, a bulwark much too strong to invite attack'.[7]

During the Munich crisis an MI5 report alleged that during a meeting of the right-wing group, the British Council Against European Commitments, Joyce was reported to have said: 'If there is a war with Germany I will be shot rather than take any part in it on behalf of Britain.'[8] MI5 surveillance on Joyce intensified as he maintained contact with the known Nazi agent named Christian Bauer. This led to MI5 recommending to the Home Office that if war broke out with Germany, Joyce should be detained.

On 24 August 1939 Joyce renewed his passport for a further year, once again falsely stating that he was British by birth. Christian Bauer sent a message to Joyce offering him employment and German citizenship should he decide to travel to Berlin. At a party for National Socialist League members, Joyce announced to the assembled gathering his and Margaret's intention of leaving for Germany. According to the testimony of his close colleague John Macnab, Joyce asserted:

I am determined to throw in my lot with Germany and become a German and if I do return to England, it will simply be for the purpose of putting my affairs in order and then returning to the land I have chosen.[9]

On the same day that Joyce renewed his passport he received a telephone call from an MI5 agent. The caller suggested that Joyce leave the country as he was about to be interned as a Nazi sympathiser under the Defence Regulations. The man who telephoned was Maxwell Knight who had known Joyce since the early 1920s when both men were prominent members of the British Fascisti Party. The reason Knight tipped off Joyce is not known. He may have attempted to recruit Joyce as a useful MI5 contact in Germany. Alternatively he may have feared being compromised by Joyce over their mutual fascist background. Either way, Joyce took the hint and he and Margaret went to Victoria Station where they embarked for Berlin.

The couple arrived at Berlin's Friedrichstrasse station on Sunday 27 August 1939. Almost immediately Joyce began to seek employment. The Nazi official Bauer's offer of a job and German citizenship came to nothing, but a chance meeting with prominent British fascist Frances Eckersley in a Berlin hotel led to a contact within the German Foreign Office. Momentarily the Joyces lost their

nerve and decided it might be more sensible to return to London.
But it was too late. They only had enough currency to get as far as
the German border, but with war imminent, and Joyce fearing being
stranded as a refugee on the continent, the couple had no choice but
to remain in Berlin. Mrs Eckersley's contact led Joyce to a meeting
with Walter Kamm, head of the English language section of the
Reichsrundfunk (the German Radio Corporation).

At first Kamm was unimpressed with Joyce's radio voice test,
considering his voice to be rather nasal. By chance a sound
engineer who had studied in England happened to be monitoring
the audition. He believed Joyce had vocal characteristics that could
be successfully exploited on the air. Less than three weeks after
arriving in Berlin Joyce was contracted as an 'editor and speaker'
for German radio.

The nickname 'Haw-Haw' was first used by a journalist compiling
the Jonah Barrington column in the *Daily Express*. On 14 September
1939, Barrington referred in his column to a Berlin radio
announcer: 'He speaks English of the haw, haw, dammit-get-out-of-
my-way variety, and his strong suite is gentlemanly indignation.'
Barrington added the prefix 'Lord' to the name a few days later. For
a time the name Lord Haw-Haw therefore referred to all English
language announcers broadcasting to Britain. Those included as
'Haw-Haw' were Norman Baillie-Stewart and Jack Trevor. During
the period of the 'phoney war' Joyce's rasping voice and distinctive
signature call sign 'Germany Calling, Germany Calling', made a
major impact on the listening British public. In Whitehall the
Ministry of Information asked the BBC to find out the size of Joyce's
listening audience. The report established that by the spring of 1940
one-sixth of the adult population or 6 million people were regular
listeners, half or 18 million people were occasional listeners and only
one third or 11 million never listened. There were approximately 23
million regular listeners to the BBC's own news programmes.[10]
Propaganda chief Goebbels' diary entry for 6 January 1940 echoed
Joyce's popularity in Britain. 'Our English radio broadcasts are being
taken with deadly seriousness in England. Lord Haw-Haw's name is
on everybody's lips.'[11]

By the time Germany had defeated much of continental Europe and was threatening to cross the English Channel, Joyce was able to cite examples of German military superiority in contrast to a whole catalogue of British military disasters. Far from being the joke figure he had seemed during the phoney war, 'Lord Haw-Haw's' exaggerated boasts and claims suddenly sounded less amusing. In one broadcast he recalled Britain's past glory and its renowned military capabilities prior to the war, before placing the blame for its sudden decline on the current government.

. . . She [England] was regarded by millions of neutral people as the greatest fighting power in the world . . . and the shattering of this illusion is perhaps the most profound moral shock that England's friends have had to bear in this tragic conflict, needlessly prolonged through her government's choice.[12]

Joyce also suggested that with Britain appearing to be close to defeat, the public could no longer trust its incompetent government. Commenting on the hurried evacuation of the British Expeditionary Force from Dunkirk, Joyce said:

As the bloody and battered fragments of what was once the British Expeditionary Force drift back in wreckage to the shores of England it is not impossible that the public will turn savagely upon the men who have so cruelly and unscrupulously deceived it. At any rate the bitterest of disillusionment will now blend with the fear of invasion which not even the strongest nation could bear. And the fault is very largely that of the warmongers who educated the people to believe that it would be an easy matter to deal with Hitler.[13]

Joyce reserved his bitterest attacks for Neville Chamberlain's successor, Winston Churchill:

Is it not a little amusing to think of the trumpetings and flourishings with which Churchill became Prime Minister of

Britain. He was the man to frighten Hitler. He was the providential leader who was going to lead Britain to victory. Look at him today – unclean and miserable figure that he is – and contrast his contemptible appearance with the bright hopes that his propagandists aroused in the minds of people foolish enough to believe that this darling of Jewish finance could really set the might of National Socialist Germany alight. The old world is tumbling about the ears of the reactionaries who sought to destroy the new. When Germany declared herself independent of their caprice and threw off the shackles of gold they resolved upon her destruction – but thanks to God and the Führer – it is not Germany that is confronted with destruction today.[14]

People listened to German radio and especially Haw-Haw because they were hungry for news of the war. At the start of hostilities war news was often reported by German radio before the same information was released in Britain. Commenting on the war in France, Lord Haw-Haw announced in May 1940 that the Germans had taken Amiens and Arras. The BBC reported the same news some twelve hours later. This led some people to believe that there was usually a 'grain of truth' in Joyce's broadcasts. He eventually revealed his own identity over the airwaves on 2 April 1941:

I, William Joyce, will merely say that I left England because I would not fight for Jewry against the Fuehrer and National Socialism, and because I believe most ardently, as I do today, that victory with a perpetuation of the old system would be an incomparably greater evil for England than defeat coupled with a possibility of building something new, something really nationalist, something truly socialist.[15]

Apart from constant criticism of the government's conduct of the war an important aspect of Lord Haw-Haw's influence was his ability to play on ordinary people's fear of the unknown. He was successful in spreading rumours that unsettled his British listeners, although most of the rumours were without any foundation.

Nevertheless his announcements did have an adverse effect on public morale. He referred to local conditions in Britain in a way that suggested that he had received his information from German agents on the spot. In fact Haw-Haw gleaned most of his information from reading British newspapers obtained in neutral countries – which is why he could focus on local news events such as the reliability of British public clocks: 'We know about Banstead, even that the clock is a quarter of an hour slow today.'[16] He also seemed to possess inside information on local factory conditions. A drop in production at a Midlands munitions factory followed Haw-Haw's announcement that the factory was soon to be bombed – adding the chilling post-script, 'Don't trouble to finish the new paint shed, you won't need it.'[17] An example of one of the many letters written by both individuals and organisations to the Ministry of Information came from a sweet factory in Surrey. The confectionery firm British Fondants Ltd wrote to the Ministry claiming some of its employees had heard Haw-Haw say: 'They have not yet hit the British Fondants factory but they will do so and the time they have selected is at 5-15pm when the girls are leaving work.'[18] A Home Intelligence Report from Bristol stated with some alarm that:

> The effect of Haw-Haw is considered in this region to be extremely insidious, and this danger is underestimated by the BBC and the Government, who do not fully appreciate to what extent this propaganda is believed.[19]

Similar concern was expressed in Scotland.

> Haw-Haw broadcasts are being fairly well listened to and discussed by Clydeside workers. . . . Haw-Haw is considered by many of them to be a very good speaker who very often hits the nail on the head and is only condemned for his exaggeration.[20]

Following the end of the London Blitz in May 1941, the impact of Lord Haw-Haw's broadcasts gradually diminished. By this stage Joyce and his wife Margaret had received their naturalisation papers as German citizens. The famous American broadcaster William L. Shirer asked Joyce if he was at all concerned about being regarded as a traitor in Britain:

> He argues that he has renounced his British nationality and become a German citizen, and that he is no more a traitor than thousands of Britons and Americans who renounced their citizenship to become comrades in the Soviet Union, or than those Germans who gave up their nationality after 1848 and fled to the United States. This doesn't satisfy me, but it does him. He kept talking about 'we' and 'us' and I asked him which people he meant. 'We Germans, of course,' he snapped.[21]

Apart from presenting his nightly broadcasts to Britain Joyce was commissioned by the German Foreign Ministry to write a book outlining his political philosophy. The Germans regarded such a book as having useful propaganda value, particularly if it was circulated in neutral countries such as the United States. It was also intended for release in Britain following the completion of the German invasion. When the invasion failed to materialise, Joyce's book was given to British POWs to read. Entitled *Twilight over England*, it consisted of Joyce's well-worn tirade against capitalism, international Jewish finance and the British government; anti-communist or anti-Bolshevik remarks were removed to avoid giving offence after the German–Soviet Pact. The book rehearsed the conventional pre-war fascist argument that the British public had been forced into a war with Germany by incompetent politicians and influential Jews: 'The decision to attack Germany was arbitrarily taken by a handful of men who were responsible only to the City of London and its Jewish lending houses. No acts of despotism could be more complete.'[22]

The setting up of the Büro Concordia stations which purported to broadcast from inside Britain posed the problem of finding new radio voices. Although Joyce's voice could not be used on the Concordia network, he was heavily involved in writing scripts for the new stations. Following the distribution of *Twilight over England* among POWs, Joyce was invited to visit Stalag XXa at Thorn in East Prussia to scout for potential recruits. He offered would-be radio broadcasters private accommodation in Berlin, the opportunity to wear civilian clothes, and receive a salary. Joyce managed to recruit a handful of men in this way (he was more successful in signing men up than John Amery had been during his abortive visit to the St Denis internment camp).

Joyce was less successful in his attempt to persuade Tom Cowen, a private in the Pioneer Corps, to join his band of misfits. When Joyce appeared one day at Stalag IIId POW camp at Lichterfelde near Berlin, he interviewed five men including Cowen. The soldier recalled Joyce's line of questioning:

> He then asked me what I would say about the German system if I was allowed to speak over the wireless. I said, as a British soldier it is not my duty to speak on the German wireless, and if I did speak I shall probably get into trouble. He said, 'You will not have any trouble about that, England can't possibly win the war.'[23]

The Germans were nevertheless proud of Joyce's achievements and in 1944 he was awarded the Kriegsverdienstkreuz 1st Class (War Merit Cross), a civilian decoration bestowed on to public servants for their work on behalf of the war effort

With the tide of war turning in the Allies' favour Hitler created the Volkssturm, the German counterpart of the Home Guard, consisting mainly of young boys and old men. Joyce was conscripted into the Propaganda Ministry's own unit. By February 1945 the Allied bombing of Berlin forced the Reichsrundfunk to evacuate to the town of Apen situated near the Dutch border. In early April Goebbels ordered that 'the Joyces are at all costs to be kept out of Allied hands'.[24] One option was to ship the Joyces by U-boat to neutral Ireland. Joyce was in favour of this but he realised that with the war lost it would be impracticable to evade the Royal Navy and the RAF, which by then had complete control of the air and sea-lanes around Germany. A more immediately feasible measure was the transporting of the Joyces to Hamburg where William Joyce was given new identity papers in the name of Wilhelm Hansen, a schoolteacher born in southern Ireland.

On 30 April 1945, Lord Haw-Haw made his final broadcast. His voice sounded tired and his speech was slurred – in fact he was so drunk the broadcast was never transmitted. His final words before the microphone were:

Germany will live because the people of Germany have in them the secret of life, endurance and will of purpose. And therefore I ask you in these last words – you will not hear from me again for a few months, I say 'Es lebe Deutschland, Heil Hitler and farewell'.[25]

Soon afterwards the Joyces went into hiding in the town of Flensburg on the German–Danish border. A plan to smuggle them into neutral Sweden came to nothing as escape routes were blocked by the advancing Allied forces. On 7 May Germany capitulated and British soldiers occupied Flensburg. Joyce was out walking alone in the woods when he spotted two English officers gathering firewood. Joyce spoke to the men first in French, before saying in English, 'There are a few more pieces over here.' Immediately one of the officers, Lt Perry of the Royal Armoured Corps, challenged him. 'You wouldn't happen to be William Joyce would you?' Joyce reached in his pocket for his false papers and the officer, thinking he was about to produce a gun, shot Joyce in the thigh. By a strange irony Lt Perry was a German Jew. (His original name was Pinschewer when he fled Germany for England in 1935.) Perry searched Joyce, looking for a weapon. Instead he found two passports, one in the name of Wilhelm Hansen and the other bearing the name William Joyce. Margaret Joyce was arrested shortly afterwards. Two days after his arrest Joyce was visited in his hospital bed at Luneberg by Capt. William Scardon, the former Scotland Yard detective who had been commissioned into the Army Intelligence Corps. Joyce agreed to dictate to Scardon a full statement of his activities, including the rationale behind his decision to go to Germany and broadcast to Britain:

I was actuated not by the desire for personal gain material or otherwise but solely by political conviction. I was brought up as an extreme conservative with strong imperialist ideas but very early in my career, namely in 1923, became attracted to fascism and subsequently to National Socialism. Between the years 1923 and 1939 I persued [sic] vigorous political activities in England, at times as a conservative but mainly as a fascist or National Socialist. I was very greatly impressed by constructive work which Hitler had done for Germany and was of the opinion that throughout Europe as also in Britain, there must come a reform on the lines of National Socialist doctrine.[26]

Among Joyce's papers Scardon found a birth certificate that seemed to confirm that the suspect had been born in New York in 1906. Joyce also claimed to have taken out German nationality in September 1940. On 16 June Joyce was flown back to England accompanied by former police Commander Leonard Burt. As the aeroplane approached the English coast, one of the guards asked Joyce for his autograph. He wrote, 'We are about to pass over the white chalk cliffs of England's bulwark. It is a sacred moment in my life, and I can only say whatever my fate may be, God bless old England on the lee.'[27]

CHAPTER FIVE

The British Free Corps

As well as addressing his fellow countrymen on German radio, John Amery also suggested the formation of an anti-Bolshevik legion, recruited from among captured British prisoners of war to fight on the Eastern Front. For propaganda purposes the band of British volunteers would be put in German uniform and posted to the front where they would be photographed alongside regular SS units. Amery believed that once captured British soldiers realised that their comrades were apparently engaged against the Soviets, they too would volunteer, which would itself set off a new wave of recruitment within the POW camps. Amery presented the idea to Dr Fritz Hesse of the England Committee, the Foreign Office advisory body of German experts familiar with British culture which had been established in 1940 by Von Ribbentrop to monitor propaganda activities against Britain. Although Hesse had appreciated the political value in allowing Amery to broadcast his views to British radio listeners, he was sceptical of the Englishman's plan to recruit a British anti-Bolshevik legion:

> I gave it as my opinion that the whole plan was extremely difficult and that I thought it practically impossible to get British people to fight for Germany as long as war between Germany and Britain existed, even if these people were promised that they would only be used against the Russians.[1]

Before describing the setting up and running of this small band of British SS volunteers, it is necessary to explore the wider context in which the unit was established. As much of Western Europe was invaded by the German Army in 1940, committed fascists and National Socialists from the occupied territories offered their services to the German war machine. Although non-German nationals were barred from joining the regular German Army, individual foreigners were allowed to join the SS. After the German occupation of France, Belgium, Holland, Denmark and Norway SS recruiting offices were opened in major European cities. In The Hague 1,000 Dutchmen joined the Waffen-SS during May 1940. Foreign volunteers from Denmark and Norway were incorporated into the SS 'Nordland' Regiment and Dutchmen and Flemings joined the SS 'Westland' Regiment. During the war a total of 125,000 West Europeans served in the Waffen-SS, most of whom were volunteers.[2] Following the German invasion of Russia in 1941 individuals came forward from neutral countries such as Spain and Portugal. There were also ethnic German recruits (the so called '*Volksdeutsche*'), from Slovakia, Croatia, and Romania.

Men volunteered to fight for the Reich for various reasons. Fear of communism was a major factor. Many volunteers from territories occupied by the Germans, as well as recruits from neutral countries, regarded Hitler as a hero embarking on a crusade against Bolshevism. Ideological reasons apart, some joined because of the status associated with wearing an SS uniform. Others signed up out of boredom, for better food, or in the hope of adventure. At least some were petty criminals or juvenile delinquents who joined to avoid prosecution.[3]

By the end of the war, of the 900,000 men serving with the Waffen-SS more than half came from outside Germany. Their nationalities were as diverse as Latvians, Walloons, Italians, Crimeans, Frenchmen and even a detachment of Bosnian Muslims, who wore a red fez complete with SS eagle and skull insignia.[4] As fighters from this cosmopolitan mix of nations stepped forward to offer their services to the Third Reich, the German propaganda machine presented a picture of a genuinely international movement ready to rally behind Hitler in the fight against world communism.

Amery's idea for recruiting a British legion was closely influenced by Jacques Doriot, leader of the anti-communist Parti Populaire Français, whom he had met in Paris in 1936. In July 1941 the first all-party rally of fascists in France was held in Paris which led to the formation of the Légion des Volontaires Français, a volunteer force offering to fight alongside the Germans against the Soviets. Hitler welcomed the idea of the force, which attracted over five thousand members, and Doriot became one of the first collaborators to join the unit and set off for the Russian front.

Dr Fritz Hesse's doubts about the wisdom of Amery's grand plans were soon reinforced. Fired up by Doriot's belief in a Europe-wide anti-Bolshevik legion, Amery decided to test the water himself. On 21 April 1943, Amery and his German entourage arrived at the St Denis civilian internment camp on the outskirts of Paris. Through his contacts in the German Embassy in Paris, Amery persuaded the German commandant at St Denis to assemble a group of prisoners to listen to what he had to say. Fresh from his Berlin broadcasts Amery arrived at St Denis confident that he could help to raise a British 'volunteer army'. But the visit was a flop. Amery began by distributing a leaflet entitled: *British National Representation. Proclamation to all British subjects interned.* The leaflet explained how British subjects were being given the opportunity to join the Legion of St George, a military legion against Bolshevism. It stressed that hundreds of British soldiers had already volunteered to join the fight against 'Communism, American rapacity, and the dragon of Asiatic and Jewish bestiality'.[5] As an incentive, the leaflet promised that anyone signing up to the legion would be given 'a permanent well placed job in British administration or priority in any other employment they should desire once peace is signed, or the possibility to form the elite in the new British army'.[6] Amery suggested to his 'captive' audience that not everybody in England was actually in favour of continuing the war. He stated that a British plane had only a few days earlier defected from the RAF to join the legion. Signing up to the legion would mean instant release from the internment camp and although volunteers would be required to wear German uniform, they would never be asked to fight against British forces.

Amery's message was heard in stony silence. One internee named Wilfred Brinkman was already acquainted with Amery. Before the war he had been employed to look after British interests in the American consulate in Nice and had dealings with Amery, whom he suspected of being a German informer. He later recalled: 'I subsequently had considerable trouble with Amery over his relief allowance, as he expected to receive more than I was authorised to grant – the matter being adjusted after telephone communications with London.'[7]

Amery immediately recognised the elderly ex-official. Brinkman asked him where this supposed 'British legion' was expected to fight. Amery replied on the Russian front. Brinkman continued his questioning:

I asked him what would happen if they were confronted by British troops. He replied that they would be moved to another sector. I asked what would happen if they were taken prisoner. No reply was given. I then asked what would happen to them after we had won the war. No reply. I then asked, did these men realise that they would be traitors to their country, as he was. No reply.[8]

Sensing that his message was falling on deaf ears, Amery thanked the group of men for listening to him, promising them he would soon provide further literature explaining his views. Amery also tried the personal approach to recruit volunteers, but this too had little effect. Pte David Philp of the Black Watch was originally captured at St Valery following Dunkirk. He escaped from a POW column but was recaptured by the Gestapo and placed temporarily at St Denis. He later recalled his meeting with Amery:

He asked me if I would like to be free and I asked him what he meant. He then suggested that I go and work with him in Germany. I asked him what at and he went on to tell me that he wanted me to go with him to a camp in Germany to train young civilians in the use of British arms. I said 'What for?' He explained that he had hundreds of volunteers from other camps and was forming a battalion composed entirely of British troops to fight against the Russians in what he called the Anti-Bolshevik Legion. He promised me a rank in the new British Army when England was conquered. He told me he had interviewed General Fortune

Lt Baillie-Stewart, below in his Seaforth
Highlander uniform and right in civvies.
He was jailed for five years in 1933 for
supplying military secrets to the Germans,
and for a second time in 1945 for
broadcasting propaganda from Berlin.
(KV 2/184, KV 2/188)

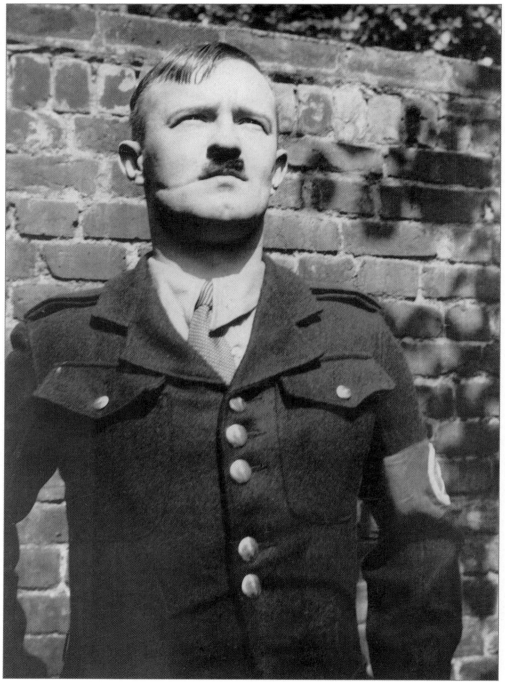

William Joyce, pictured in fascist Blackshirt uniform in his garden near the Dutch border in 1945 after American bombing raids had forced him to leave Berlin. (KV 2/346)

Joyce's *Kriegsverdienstkreuz* (war merit cross), signed by Hitler. The certificate says 'To chief commentator William Joyce'. (KV 2/250)

IM NAMEN
DES DEUTSCHEN VOLKES
VERLEIHE ICH

dem Hauptkommentator
William Joyce
in Berlin-Charlottenburg

DAS
KRIEGSVERDIENSTKREUZ
1. KLASSE

Führerhauptquartier, den 1. September 1944.

DER FÜHRER

Joyce's military passport issued when he joined the *Volkssturm*, the German version of the Home Guard. (KV 2/250)

John Amery (second from left), clearly in his element sitting among German officers and Belgian Nazi collaborators. (HO 45/25773)

Amery delivering a pro-Nazi speech in 1944 as part of his propaganda tour throughout occupied Europe. (WO 204/12856)

James Clarke, the seventeen-year-old who remained in Berlin with his mother and became a German newsreader. (WO 204/12856)

Frances Eckersley, a member of The Link, a pro-Nazi organisation based in England. She was in Berlin when war was declared and helped William Joyce to find employment on German radio. (WO 204/12856)

Pearl Vardon, a former schoolteacher from Jersey who followed her German boyfriend to Berlin, from where she made radio announcements reading out letters written by British POWs to their relatives. She later received a nine-month prison sentence for her treachery. (KV 2/256)

The passenger liner on which Susan Hilton was travelling was sunk by a German destroyer in the Indian Ocean, and she was transported to Berlin where she made radio broadcasts. She was once taken off the air for being intoxicated. She was sentenced to eighteen months' imprisonment in 1945. (HO 336/8)

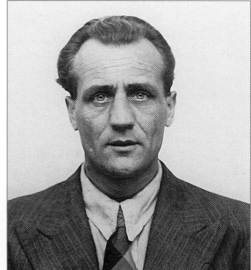

Roy Walter Purdy, a sub-lieutenant in the Royal Navy, volunteered to become a German stool pigeon at Colditz, where he betrayed an escape tunnel. When arrested by police in 1945 Purdy admitted to being 'a rat and a traitor' and was sentenced to death for his crimes, but this was commuted to life imprisonment. (HO 336/8)

Thomas Cooper was the only Englishman to receive a combat medal while serving in the German Army. He is pictured wearing a music hall outfit as part of the camp entertainment at Genshagen 'holiday camp', where he recruited potential British collaborators. Cooper served in the Waffen-SS, and took part in atrocities against Jews. He was sentenced to death after the war but reprieved on the grounds that he had divided loyalties, his mother being German. (KV 2/254)

Barrington Payne Jones, schoolteacher turned enemy broadcaster. He wrote to his brother in England during the war boasting of how much money he was earning while working for German radio. Amazingly he never faced criminal charges after the war. (KV 2/632)

Francis Maton, in Gestapo-like pose, complete with Nazi Party member's badge. He served with 50 Middle East Commando and was captured in Crete. During his time as a POW Maton learned German. (KV 2/264)

Reginald Humphries pretended to be a priest broadcasting on the Christian Peace Movement station under the name of 'Father Donovan'. (KV 2/258)

P.G. Wodehouse, the world famous writer and humorist, and creator of Jeeves and Wooster. Reports of his light-hearted radio talks broadcast from Berlin to America reached England. He was investigated by MI5 but never prosecuted after the war, but decided not to return to England. Because of his war-time activity, he was deprived of a knighthood until 1975. (WO 204/12856)

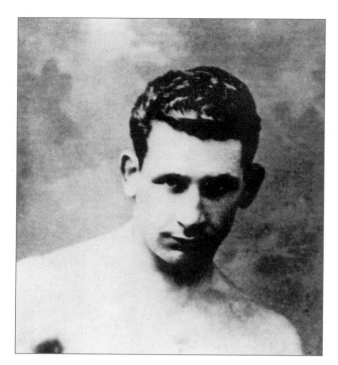

Eric Pleasants, a former professional wrestler and British Union of Fascists bodyguard. He joined the British Free Corps for adventure and better food, and was later imprisoned by the Russians, spending seven years in a Siberian labour camp before being exchanged for a Russian spy. He returned to England but was never prosecuted. (WO 204/12856)

Harold Cole, alias the serial seducer, nicknamed 'Sonny Boy'. Cole was the ex-army sergeant who infiltrated the Allied escape line in France for downed airmen. He betrayed over one hundred French agents and Allied escape line helpers. He even attempted to betray his pregnant wife to the Gestapo. Cole was killed in a shoot-out with French police in Paris in 1944. (WO 204/12856)

Kenneth Berry, the youngest British Free Corps recruit. He was taken prisoner aged thirteen in 1940 when his ship was torpedoed. He believed John Amery was the British Foreign Secretary. (WO 204/12856)

Gerald Hewitt agreed to broadcast on the German-controlled Paris radio in exchange for money and luxury goods. In a letter to his mother he described Hitler as 'the greatest man of our time'. (KV 2/427)

Alexander Fraser Grant made broadcasts on Radio Caledonia, urging Scotland to make a separate peace with Germany. (CRIM 1/1833)

Kenneth Lander was a former school teacher who read German radio announcements. He was never prosecuted after the war. (WO 204/12856)

Leonard Banning, a former member of Mosley's Blackshirts, joined the German-run New British Broadcasting Service, and told British listeners that they were being misled by the actions of the British government. (WO 204/12856)

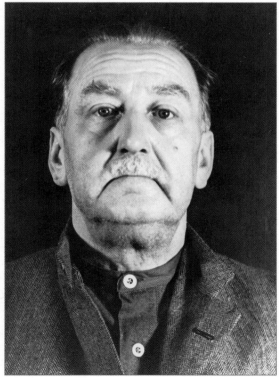

Oswald Job was hanged for treachery after police found secret ink crystals in his key ring. The Germans faked his escape from a French internment camp and sent him to England to assess the effects of bomb damage in London and the level of British morale. (KV 2/250)

Kenneth Berry (left) and Alfred Minchin (second right) in the British Free Corps German-style uniform, with a Union Jack shield worn on the left arm and a St George patch depicting three leopards. (HO 45/25817)

Duncan Scott-Ford, a merchant seaman, betrayed positions of British convoy routes to the Germans for £20. He was hanged for treachery in 1942. (KV 2/57)

Unterschrift des Inhabers

Margaret F. Bothamley —

Nr. 30249 B/43

Margaret Bothamley, a committed Nazi and member of The Link, was strongly pro-Hitler, but also furnished her flat with a portrait of the King and Queen of England. (CRIM 1/1763)

Frederick Rutland was awarded the Distinguished Service Cross for gallantry during the Battle of Jutland. He later passed on secrets to the Japanese. (KV 2/337)

Francis MacLardy, a qualified pharmacist and member of the British Union of Fascists, wrote propaganda leaflets and distributed them among British POWs. (KV 2/252)

and said that the General was willing to take command of this unit when formed. I told him I didn't believe his story and there was some high words between us. He told me I was making a big mistake in taking up this attitude, and I made an endeavour to have a go at him, but the other men stepped in and stopped me. Amery then went on to tell me if I was prepared to join him no one in England would know anything about it and that I would still receive my Red Cross parcels and letters from England, which would be addressed to a Stalag in Germany. As far as anyone in Britain was concerned I would still be an ordinary prisoner of war. That only upset me more and Amery sent for the German guard and I was taken out and put direct into cells.[9]

Clearly flustered and by now being booed and jeered by some prisoners, Amery abandoned the meeting though not the idea. He returned to St Denis a few days later to see if anyone had been swayed by the propaganda literature. Only four men showed an interest in Amery's ideas, two of whom were British citizens, Oswald Job, and Kenneth Berry, a seventeen-year-old merchant seaman from Cornwall. Berry had had an unhappy childhood. He did not get on with his father, a civilian policeman working at the Admiralty, and openly rebelled by being prosecuted for stealing from a car and taking items from a house. Aged only thirteen the young rebel ran away to sea and was captured in 1940 when his ship, the *Cymbeline*, was sunk. Berry had not had an easy time in captivity. He had already escaped once from St Denis and survived by working for a group of black-marketeers in Paris. Questioned by the Gestapo, Berry betrayed the names of those who had helped him escape, so it came as no surprise that on being returned to the camp Berry was sent to Coventry by the other inmates. Berry's young age and isolation made him an easy target for Amery's indoctrination. The gullible 'boy' merchant seaman explained in his own words what happened when the German commandant at St Denis, Captain Gillis, took him to see Amery:

Gillis introduced Amery to me as Mr John Amery, the Foreign Secretary of England. Amery then said, 'I suppose you are wondering what you are doing here. I expect you have heard what I came to the camp for.' I said I had heard about it from other people and Amery then said, 'Do you think you are doing right by staying in a prisoner of war camp? Your duty is to fight Russia.' I asked 'What makes you say that?' and Amery replied, 'I have been sent over specially from England to form this legion to fight against Russia. I have my orders to ask all prisoners of war if they are willing to join in order to fight Russia.' Amery then asked me if I would like to join, and I said I did not know. . . . So I spoke to the Camp Captain Gillis, a German who said it was good and that most of my friends had volunteered but he could not tell me their names, so I thought if he said it was good it must be so. I told him I would join too.[10]

Berry was in fact the first volunteer for the Legion of St George and the only British subject Amery succeeded in recruiting throughout the entire war. After his experiences in detention Berry was sent at Amery's request to a boarding house in Berlin. Amery sent the boy a selection of his own propaganda works, plus 300 Reichsmarks spending money. Berry spent the next few months alone in Berlin awaiting contact from his altruistic and important new English friend.

Despite Dr Hesse's misgivings about the recruitment of British nationals, Hitler realised the propaganda value of a British legion, and in May 1943 gave the plan the go-ahead. His only proviso was that the quality of recruits should take precedence over quantity. The legion should be restricted to former BUF members or those with a fascist or National Socialist outlook. But the St Denis fiasco only confirmed that Amery was not the right man to be involved in the recruitment of a military unit. He was subsequently kept well away from the project, possibly because the Germans discovered that he was partly Jewish. The Waffen-SS took control of the project. Amery was philosophical about this decision, explaining that

Eventually the SS took the whole affair over, apparently a certain Sturmbahnführer Vivian Stranders, an Englishman, had a good deal to do with this, and although I never met him, he had a very great dislike of my person, in consequence I handed over my 'baby' to the SS with my wishes of success.[11]

Although Amery had been removed from involvement in recruitment for the Legion of St George, his propaganda works were distributed among prisoners of war and civilian internees. These included *John Amery Speaks*, a booklet containing transcripts of his radio broadcasts. The Germans also distributed anti-Jewish and pro-German books and pamphlets (including 20,000 copies of the anti-Semitic pamphlet, *How Odd of God*) to British prisoners, but it is difficult to gauge what effect if any this had on recruitment for the anti-Bolshevik legion.[12]

Following the distribution of printed propaganda material among POWs, Dr Fritz Hesse focused his recruitment drive on those prisoners holding extreme right-wing political views or who had been active in pre-war British fascist groups. Conditions in prisoner of war camps in Germany and the occupied areas were pretty bleak with problems of chronic overcrowding, lack of heating, proper sanitation and decent food. To increase the recruitment potential of the legion, Berlin decided to improve conditions for British POWs by establishing two special 'holiday camps' for those men who had been held in captivity longest since the beginning of the war. During their stay inmates would enjoy better food, greater freedom and organised activities within the camps. While ordinary POWs had the chance to let their hair down, prisoners holding known fascist views would be filtered into the camps, and in this way those considered to be susceptible to indoctrination, threats or bribery, could be isolated from their fellow prisoners. Two 'holiday camps' were set up in the Berlin area to cater for those British prisoners wishing to enjoy a 'break'. The first camp was for officers: 'Special Detachment 999' was situated in a villa in the Zehlendorf district; while the soldiers' camp 'Special Detachment 517' was sited in a former state railways camp at Genshagen, south-west of Berlin. Although both camps were administered by the German Army High Command, they were actually run by the German Foreign Ministry via Hesse's England Committee. The man placed in charge of organising the project was Arnold Hillen-Ziegfeld, who became the special representative for British POWs.

Apart from English-speaking guards to monitor the prisoners at Genshagen, the Germans also recruited a British non-commissioned officer to meet and greet new arrivals at the 'holiday camp'. The man they chose was Battery Quartermaster John Brown of the Royal Artillery. Adrian Weale, the leading authority on the British Free Corps describes Brown as 'a very controversial figure'.[13] Brown was certainly resourceful. A member of Mosley's BUF before the war, he was captured near Dunkirk in May 1940 and placed in a prisoner of war camp at Lamsdorf. Brown soon found himself in charge of a work detail seconded from the camp to build a large industrial complex. As well as being an Oxford graduate (which was unusual, considering his NCO status), Brown was a deeply religious man and undoubtedly a persuasive talker. Through his contact on the building site with foreign workers and local civilians Brown set up a black-market scheme smuggling contraband goods into the camp for distribution to his cronies, and to bribe the prison guards. Playing on his fascist credentials, Brown ingratiated himself with his German captors, and a combination of entrepreneurial skills and eagerness to keep the Germans happy, led many fellow prisoners to believe that Brown was a collaborator or German stool pigeon.

But there was another side to Brown's personality, which he managed to conceal. Sometime during his military career he had learned to use a special code devised by MI9 the 'escape and evasion' organisation for prisoners of war, to conceal secret messages in letters sent home to England.[14] Brown later revealed that he had deliberately set out to co-operate with the Germans so that he could gather sensitive information to send disguised in letters to his wife. As a secret information gatherer for the British security services, Brown could not believe his luck when he was sent to Berlin to be interviewed for a potential job in the Free Corps. In Berlin Brown was allowed to roam freely through the city, and managed to identify details of artillery defences and camouflaged installations which he relayed to England in his coded letters. He also met William Joyce, who may have recognised Brown from their pre-war fascist links. On another visit to the German capital, Brown was told by MI9 through a message hidden in a letter from his wife to 'verify the identity of John Amery'.[15] By now a 'trusted' pro-German, Brown managed to get an introduction to Amery at Berlin's Adlon Hotel. He congratulated his fellow Englishman on the success of his book, which had been widely read in POW camps, but suggested that some prisoners, although not of course himself, believed that the book had actually been written by a German. His pride wounded, Amery brazenly thrust his passport on to a table to identify himself, and Brown managed to memorise the issue number, and to relay the information back to London. Whether Brown was simply an opportunist who used the secret code as an insurance policy against accusations of being a German collaborator after the war, while in the meantime filling his pockets on the black market, is difficult to gauge. Either way, he was pleased to accept the role of British camp leader at Genshagen without any hesitation.

In total, three hundred 'volunteers' were sent to the Genshagen camp for two or three weeks of indoctrination and education during the second half of 1943. Most had no idea about the true role of the camp. On the outside it seemed like a genuine holiday camp with a variety of performances by visiting German musicians and artistes. The local YMCA provided English and American films, and visiting celebrities included Max Schmeling, the world boxing champion, and the Wigan-born opera singer Margery Booth from the Berlin State Opera, the latter a great favourite of Goebbels. The camp also had a hospital and a tailoring and shoe repair service. John Brown was left alone by the Germans to run the camp and he brought in cronies from his former POW camp to help with its organisation. Brown knew the true purpose of Genshagen and says he set about monitoring the hard-core group of British collaborators who had been put in place by the Germans to encourage and 'recruit' prisoners as potential Free Corps members. Many of these 'persuaders' were former members of the BUF.

Francis Maton from Coventry had originally joined the Territorial Army in 1938 and later served as a regular soldier in Norway and North Africa until joining 50 Middle East Commando in 1941.

Captured during the battle for Crete, he was sent to a POW camp in Germany. Maton learned German in the camp and was approached by the Foreign Ministry chief renegade recruiter Peter Adami to work as a broadcaster on the Berlin propaganda station Radio National. Maton joined the recruiting team at Genshagen in June 1943. Along with other renegade broadcasters, he was allowed to live as a civilian in Berlin complete with a false name and German passport.

Another pro-German volunteer was Francis George MacLardy. Born in Liverpool in 1915, MacLardy originally trained as a pharmacist, but also found time to join the BUF where he became an active local district leader. On the outbreak of war, MacLardy joined the Royal Army Medical Corps, rose to the rank of sergeant and was captured in Belgium in May 1940. While in a POW camp in Poland, he wrote a letter, care of the commanding officer, to the Waffen-SS stressing that he wanted to take part in the struggle against Bolshevism. MacLardy was fiercely pro-Nazi, and was involved in writing propaganda leaflets for distribution among captured British POWs. While awaiting news of his application to join the SS, MacLardy did his bit for the German cause at Genshagen in the form of the recruiting propaganda leaflet written by him and distributed to Allied POW camps after the Legion of St George had officially changed its name to the British Free Corps:

As a result of repeated applications from British subjects from all parts of the world wishing to take part in the common European struggle against Bolshevism authorisation has recently been given for the creation of a British volunteer unit. The British Free Corps publishes herewith the following short statement of the aims and principles of the unit.

(1) The British Free Corps is a thoroughly British volunteer unit, conceived and created by British subjects from all parts of the Empire who have taken up arms and pledged their lives in the common European struggle against Soviet Russia.

(2) The British Free Corps condemns the war with Germany and the sacrifice of British blood in the interests of Jewry and

International Finance, and regards this conflict as a fundamental betrayal of the British people and British Imperial interests.

(3) The British Free Corps desires the establishment of peace in Europe, the development of close friendly relations between England and Germany, and the encouragement of mutual understandings and collaboration between the two great Germanic peoples.

(4) The British Free Corps will neither make war against Britain or the British Crown, nor support any action or policy detrimental to the interests of the British people.

Published by the British Free Corps

Roy Courlander was another member of the broadcasting staff at Radio National to volunteer to infiltrate newly arrived British POW contingents at Genshagen. Courlander had been sold the idea of the Legion of St George by John Amery, and was keen to help the Reich, and himself, by being paid two salaries, one to broadcast and the other to 'recruit'. Also enrolled in the new unit was Amery's one successful recruit from his disastrous visit to the St Denis internment camp, the teenager Kenneth Berry. Apart from attending a party for Amery's friends at the Kaiserhof hotel, the young boy had been kicking his heels alone in Berlin. He spoke hardly any German and spent his days at Berlin zoo. Some nights he stayed behind at the zoo to snare rabbits, but was arrested by the police and returned to his guest-house. On other occasions Berry was held for drunken behaviour. He later claimed to have been arrested no fewer than twenty-three times. On one occasion he was accused of signalling to Allied aircraft. The RAF was inflicting a lot of damage on Berlin and Berry's captors retaliated by giving him a severe beating. Receiving no replies from his letters to Amery, in desperation Berry went to see Dr Hesse at the Foreign Ministry to remind him why he had been sent to Berlin. Hesse despatched Berry to a requisitioned café in the Pankow area of Berlin where new volunteers for the Free Corps were being accommodated. Berry was never fully accepted or trusted by the other renegades because Amery had personally recruited him. All the others were given some rank, but Berry remained a 'Schutze' (a private).

Perhaps the most sinister character to emerge from the British Free Corps was Thomas Cooper. He had first been introduced to John Brown at Genshagen as a 'Sergeant Bottcher' and immediately aroused Brown's suspicions.[16] He had sustained a foot injury while on active service with the SS on the Russian Front and the Germans at Genshagen, particularly the camp commandant Oskar Lange, seemed very interested in spending time with this young SS NCO. Bottcher initially told Brown he spoke very little English. The next morning the British sergeant asked the German if he would care for a cup of English tea. Bottcher said that he would, and Brown (realising that Bottcher was German for 'Cooper'), suggested to Bottcher that now he was in Germany, he must miss his English tea and cigarettes. Bottcher replied to Brown in perfect Cockney that indeed he was English, and proceeded to tell him his life story.

Although he was born and brought up in Britain, Germany was in Thomas Cooper's blood from birth. His father Ashley was working as a photographer in Berlin before the First World War when he met Thomas's mother Anna-Marie. The couple married and returned to England where their only son, Thomas Haller Cooper, was born in 1919. Thomas won a place at the famous Latymer School in Hammersmith. He was a loner at school and made no real friends. Cooper was remembered by his old headmaster Frederick Wilkinson as someone in need of very careful handling, as the schoolboy strongly resented discipline. Thomas left school in 1936 but found it hard to find employment in a country still suffering from the Depression. He thought about entering the armed forces or the Foreign Office, but settled on the Metropolitan Police. However, his application to join the police was rejected at least twice, on the grounds of Thomas having a German mother. Following a year on the dole, Cooper found a job as a junior clerk in a small firm in Hackney. He looked for a scapegoat for his lowly status and bleak employment prospects and found it in the Jewish community where he worked in the East End of London. Cooper later told his fellow Free Corps members how he had joined Mosley's Blackshirts, had smashed up Jewish shops, and even boasted that he had killed a Jew in a street fight.

In 1939, as war loomed, the Cooper family decided that Thomas might be better off getting a job in Germany where he would also be able to visit his mother's family. The Coopers contacted the German Academic Exchange Organisation, which arranged visits to Germany by sympathetic foreigners under the auspices of the state-controlled German Labour Services. Two months before the outbreak of war, Thomas and his mother travelled to Stuttgart. Within a few weeks Cooper was offered a job teaching English at a school near Frankfurt. He had only just started at the school when Britain declared war on Germany. Cooper was sacked because of his British nationality and forced to report to the police and register as an enemy alien. An examination of the paperwork held at the German Academic Exchange verified that Cooper was considered an ethnic German (*volksdeutscher*), which meant he could not be interned as a foreign national. But Cooper had to find employment, and after doing labouring and other casual work in Berlin, he decided to join the German Army.

As a matter of policy the German Army did not accept recruits from foreign countries. But nationality was not a barrier when it came to membership of the SS, which is why the various collaborators in German occupied countries who had volunteered to fight alongside the Nazis had been placed under SS supervision. Following basic training Cooper was accepted into the Waffen-SS. The SS was the vanguard of both the German army and the Nazi Party. The Waffen-SS was a fanatical fighting unit whose members had to swear a personal oath of loyalty to Hitler. Cooper served in the SS Leibstandarte, which formed Hitler's personal bodyguard, and also in the Totenkopf or 'Death's Head' division, whose members manned the concentration camps. Cooper was soon promoted to the rank of sergeant and posted to the SS training base at Oranienburg near Berlin. He then travelled to Poland where in the course of his military 'career' he helped organise slave labour in the areas occupied by Germany in Eastern Europe, including the guarding of Slavs, Jews, communists and gypsies, and also spent time as a guard at Dachau concentration camp. Cooper was personally involved in genocide against Polish Jews. He proudly boasted to fellow BFC member Thomas Freeman that he had lined up 200 Poles and 80 Jews against a wall and shot them. Cooper told Francis Maton how he had led a unit of Ukrainian volunteers conducting a house to house purge of Jews in the Warsaw ghetto:

His attention was drawn to a house by reason of loud screams issuing from the back of it. On going inside the house he found in a top flat a bunch of these Ukrainians holding at bay with pistols some twenty Jews. On asking them what the noise was about they told him in broken German that they had found a new way of killing Jews. This was done simply by opening the window wide and two men each grabbing an arm and a leg and flinging the Jews through the open window. The small children and babies followed their parents because they said they would only grow into big Jews.[17]

In early 1943, Cooper was seriously wounded in both legs while fighting on the Eastern Front. He was evacuated back to Germany and received a medal for being wounded in action, the only Englishman to gain a German combat decoration during the war. After recovering from his wounds Cooper was seconded to the German Foreign Office and sent to Genshagen to help boost recruitment to the British Free Corps.

Despite the ideological fervour of Courlander, Cooper, MacLardy and the others, hardly any POWs were recruited at the Genshagen 'holiday camp'. One of the few who was won over in this way was Alfred Minchin, a merchant seaman from Kingston in Surrey. Minchin's ship, the SS *Empire Ranger* was sunk off Norway in 1943 while on Russian convoy duty. Interned initially at the Milag camp for captured merchant seamen, Minchin volunteered to go to Genshagen where he met Cooper. The fanatical Nazi showed Minchin recruitment posters for the new legion and persuaded him that many British soldiers were flocking to the new unit and were having a 'marvellous time'. Minchin later claimed: 'Cooper did not tell me what the aims of the Legion were and they were never laid down at any time. I thought it was just a propaganda unit in order to bring Germany and England together. I decided to join to find out what Germany was really like.'[18]

When an Allied air raid destroyed most of the Genshagen camp, the Germans devised a new plan to increase recruitment to the Free Corps. At the Luckenwalde detention centre, close to Genshagen, a small interrogation team was attempting to extract information from newly captured prisoners of war (as opposed to POWs who had been in captivity for some time), while they were still physically and psychologically vulnerable. The Germans believed they could use threats, intimidation and blackmail to encourage imprisoned British servicemen to co-operate with them. The captured men had no experience of captivity and no one to advise them about their rights as POWs under the Geneva Convention. Those snared in this trap included Pte John Welch of the Durham Light Infantry, who had been captured in Belgium. While deployed on a work detail, Welch was approached by a German woman who took her clothes off and proceeded to have sex with him. His guards explained to Welch that having unlawful sex with a German woman could result in a death sentence so the infantryman decided to co-operate with his captors.[19]

A more experienced soldier, John Eric Wilson, was also intimidated into joining the Free Corps. Wilson originally joined the Military Police in 1939 but then transferred to the Royal Army Service Corps, and subsequently volunteered for 3 Commando. Wilson was sent to Lukenwalde shortly after being captured in southern Italy. On arrival at the camp Wilson faced 'interrogation'. He was strip-searched and his uniform shredded before he was placed in solitary confinement for three days with only a blanket to wear. The Germans then used the recently recruited John Welch as a stool pigeon to pump the new arrival for military information. Introducing himself as 'Johnnie', Welch offered Wilson tea and sympathy but then left almost as soon as he had arrived. Some days later the Germans told the bewildered Wilson that because he had been captured while on a Commando mission he had the choice of either joining the Legion of St George or spending the rest of the war alone in a prison cell. He was also assured that 30,000 volunteers had already joined the Free Corps under the command of a British brigadier. After a further period spent alone in his cell, Wilson's spirit was broken and he agreed to co-operate with the Germans.

Other POWs seemed to collaborate willingly. Edwin Barnard Martin was a private in the Canadian Army's Essex Scottish Regiment who had been captured after the abortive raid on Dieppe in August 1942. Martin appeared to befriend new arrivals at Luckenwalde but was really a German stool pigeon. He was to form part of the main group of Free Corps renegades, who became known as the 'big six'. Others recruited through the indoctrination techniques at Luckenwalde included: Henry Alfred Symonds from Princess Louise's Kensington Regiment, Ronald Heighes of the Hampshire Regiment, and Robert Henry Lane and Norman Rose of the East Surreys.[20]

Many of the men who were recruited through the Luckenwalde system only agreed to co-operate because they believed they were to form part of a 30,000 strong force wearing British army uniforms under the command of a senior British officer. They soon realised that in reality the Free Corps was just a small bunch of misfits, cowards, malcontents and fanatical BUF members. Anyone protesting that they had been recruited under false pretences was threatened with a spell in an SS punishment camp. However, Thomas Cooper realised that although the indoctrination and intimidation methods employed at Luckenwalde had worked in the short term, disgruntled men who had been snared through deception were not likely to form an efficient fighting unit in the future. Cooper expressed this opinion to Arnold Hillen-Ziegfeld, an expert in British affairs from the England Committee of the German Foreign Office. Following consultations with Berlin, many of the recruits were allowed to leave. Rather than returning the men to ordinary POW camps, a move which might compromise the security of the entire British legion project, the 'drop outs' were sent to work as agricultural labourers on a farm in remote Mecklenburg. Meanwhile the recruitment of additional 'Legion' collaborators continued throughout the POW camp system.

The Germans gave much thought to planning and organising their embryonic British unit. The idea was to form a force which would both act as part of a frontline battalion and create sufficient propaganda to encourage others to defect. In November 1943 the German Foreign Ministry appointed SS-Hauptsturmführer Hans Werner Roepke as commander of the Corps. A highly experienced officer, Roepke also spoke excellent English having spent a year as an exchange student in America before the war. Berlin considered the title the Legion of St George too long-winded and reminiscent of the British Legion's ex-servicemen's association, so the unit was re-named the British Free Corps. The force was not to be used against British or Commonwealth forces but was to be dressed in the usual field-grey German uniform with an insignia which included a Union Jack shield worn on the left arm and a St George collar patch depicting three leopards. Pay and most working conditions were to be on a par with those of the regular German Army. The SS wanted members of the unit to be tattooed with their blood-group in the armpit. The men unanimously rejected this suggestion as such a tattoo would have been permanent and could later provide evidence of their treachery.

In early 1944 the Free Corps detachment set up camp at an old monastery requisitioned by the SS in the small town of Hildesheim located near Hanover. The town seemed an unlikely spot to base the renegades. With its narrow winding streets and little sugar-white houses, the place was like something out of a Brothers Grimm fairytale. When the BFC moved to Hildesheim it totalled only nine members plus its German support team. The group soon settled into the little German town, sampling its local bars and cafés and, in some cases, the local young women, who were keen to have British male company in the absence of their own menfolk. The spectacle of these men marching in formation through the streets singing 'Bless 'em All' must surely have startled some of the town's older residents.

The Germans wanted the BFC to assume a fighting strength of at least thirty men before being sent to the front line. This meant more man-power had to be found, so Cooper, Minchin, Berry and the others set off on a tour of POW camps in Germany and Austria in search of new recruits. Their travels took them to the Marlag/Milag POW camp which housed captured merchant seamen. The Milag camp was situated a few miles north of Bremen. Standing on the edge of the large, flat, inhospitable and sandy wasteland known as Luneburg Heath, the Milag compound also included the Marlag block which housed captured Royal Navy personnel. The two camps held a combined total of 4,000 interned seamen.

The inmates of Marlag/Milag knew that the Free Corps was recruiting British servicemen because the camp had been flooded with BFC propaganda leaflets intended to persuade prisoners to join the fight against Bolshevism. Captain Wilson, the senior British officer in Marlag, prevented the BFC from attempting to recruit his men by making an official complaint to the German commandant. The senior British officer at Milag, Captain Notman, also made objections and managed to restrict BFC 'interviews' to an area outside the camp perimeter. Capt. Notman also issued a warning to his men about the consequences of throwing in their lot with the enemy: 'The so-called British Free Corps is a traitorous organisation. Each man joining will be reported by me to the authorities at home, where action will be taken.'[21] On their first visit to Marlag/Milag, Minchin and Berry managed to persuade two merchant seamen to sign up. Herbert George Rowlands had been on the liner *Orama* when it was torpedoed in the North Sea in June 1940. Rowlands was a Londoner and BUF member who had fought with the International Brigade during the Spanish Civil War. He had been put in solitary confinement in Milag and did not need much persuasion by Minchin to see the benefits of joining the BFC. Ronald David Barker was an Australian who sometimes used the alias 'Vorsey' after the surname of the woman who adopted him. He had been a cabin boy on the *British Advocate*, which was captured by the German pocket battleship *Admiral Scheer* off the coast of Mozambique in 1941. After becoming friendly with a German girl who worked in the camp censorship office, the German security officers told Barker both he and the girl would be sent to a concentration camp unless he agreed to leave with Minchin and Berry. After the war Capt. Notman said he had spent four hours at the Milag camp trying to persuade Barker not to join the BFC, but the Australian seaman had simply told the senior British officer that he felt it his duty to join the Germans in their fight against communism.

The two BFC recruiters returned to Marlag/Milag in search of more recruits in June 1944. Alfred Minchin was already known to some of the camp inmates because of his previous internment in Milag following the sinking of his ship the *Empire Ranger*. Kenneth Berry was also recognised during the second visit to Milag. Some of the group from a working party at the nearby village of Westertimke had been members of the crew of Berry's former ship the *Cymbeline*. J. Williams, former second mate from Berry's crew, managed to speak to the young adult whom he had last seen as an impressionable fourteen-year-old boy in 1940. Berry was told how the Allies had Germany on the run and things were not as rosy as portrayed by the Nazi propaganda machine in Berlin. Clearly shaken, Berry requested to see Captain Notman, the much respected camp leader. The confused Berry, by now realising that he had made a major mistake in joining the BFC, wrote Notman a frank letter explaining his true predicament and feelings. The letter read:

It's not been for the last month that I have realised I am a traitor to England and by what I am doing I am causing my Mother the greatest agony she has ever felt so I implore you not for my sake but for my parents' sake to help me get out of the mess I am in. I'll face anything if I can get out, but if it is possible to see Brigade-Major Internee I think he will see that I don't get down the mines because I am scared for my health and I would (I have realised) like to come to Milag with real Englishmen, I thank you Sir.[22]

Minchin and Berry also added two more names to their list of recruits – Eric Pleasants and John Leister. Pleasants was raised in the grounds of a large estate in Norfolk where his father was the local gamekeeper. He took up boxing at fifteen and fought at fairgrounds for 5 shillings a fight. He had a professional boxing career for three years before his doctor diagnosed double vision, forcing Eric to switch to wrestling. He was also employed as a bodyguard by the Bowes-Lyon family, and often looked after the little princesses Elizabeth and Margaret. Pleasants put his strength to good effect when he joined the Norfolk branch of the BUF, acting as the local 'enforcer' and physical trainer to new Blackshirt recruits. Despite his physical powers, Pleasants was actually a committed pacifist. In his autobiography,[23] Pleasants described himself as being neither anti-British nor anti-German, neither anti-Semitic nor anti-Russian, but simply anti-war and anti-establishment. To avoid what he regarded as a senseless war, he fled to the Channel Islands and worked as a farm labourer. In Jersey Pleasants made friends with John Leister. A 19-year-old Londoner, Leister also regarded the war as a matter of conscience, but of a different kind. He came from an Anglo-German family and had frequently visited relatives in Germany before the war. In 1939 he was unsure where his loyalty lay, so he too decided to go to Jersey and find labouring work. When Germany invaded the Channel Islands in July 1940, Pleasants and Leister were determined to make the best of the situation. Leister became an interpreter for the Germans while, in the face of food shortages, Pleasants turned to thieving from local people. The pair decided to steal a boat and some petrol and make for England, but were caught red-handed by the Germans. Sentenced to six months' imprisonment for stealing, Pleasants and Leister were sent to prison in Dijon, but after making their escape they were recaptured in Paris and sent to a civilian internment camp in Germany and then to the Marlag/Milag camp. Both men needed little persuasion by Minchin and Berry to join the Free Corps. Pleasants admitted later that he was an opportunist, and saw the chance of getting better rations, more freedom and access to pretty girls. He also had no intention of fighting for the Germans on the Russian front, and regarded the Free Corps as a means of survival and ultimately as an escape route.

From his visit to Stalag XVIIIa in Austria, Roy Courlander recruited Cpls Lionel Wood and Albert Stokes and Pte Robert Chipchase, all of the Australian Army, and Pte Thomas Freeman from 7 Commando. Wood later asked to be returned to his POW camp, but Freeman stayed with the BFC. He claimed he had only volunteered to join the Hildesheim group so that he could attempt to reach the Russian lines. Like John Brown at Genshagen, Freeman played a game of double bluff, intending where possible to subvert the smooth running of the BFC. The MI5 file on the renegades later noted that 'Private Freeman was a member of the British Free Corps but has been cleared of suspicion as it is abundantly clear that he joined with the object of escaping and of sabotaging the movement.'[24]

After the initial enthusiasm of setting up base at Hildesheim things suddenly went very quiet. The handful of men amused themselves by practising German-style marching techniques and giving the Hitler salute. Some physical fitness classes and marching drill were organised but most men, when not engaged in drinking sessions in the town, simply stayed in their rooms awaiting the arrival of fresh recruits. Of the group only Courlander, MacLardy, Maton and Cooper could be described as committed Nazis. The rest of the men were on the whole a bunch of opportunists who simply craved an easier life with better food, improved living conditions and a ready supply of alcohol and prostitutes. There was a certain amount of jostling for position between the men and petty jealousies often led to fist fights and intrigues between the various factions in the group. One fight was provoked by men who objected to ardent fascist William Charles Britten having a swastika flag draped over a window and pictures of Hitler and Himmler on both sides of his bed. Britten, a lance-corporal in the Royal Warwickshire Regiment, had of course been one of the original recruiting 'persuaders' at Genshagen.

Another new arrival, Cpl William Cecil Perkins of the Royal Northumberland Fusiliers, sold a gun he had stolen from a German officer on the black market. This was considered a sign of insubordination by the staunch fascists in the group. Perkins was a popular figure so when Cooper and MacLardy had him removed to an isolation camp, others in the unit complained and threatened to abandon the BFC altogether and demanded a return to their POW camps. Then a quarrel broke out between Britons and Germans over the insignia on the unit's uniforms. The German standard issue field-grey uniform had three leopards and the words 'British Free Corps' written on the sleeves. Some of the men objected to the Union Jack badge being placed below the more prominent German eagle insignia on the volunteer's arm. They believed Britain was being slighted. Rather oddly, having effectively betrayed their country, the renegades made the uniform design an issue. Pleasants and Leister actually cut off the Union Jack badges and placed them above the eagles. This was just one of the many instances of insubordination among the BFC that the Germans would not tolerate. Captain Roepke made an example of the revolt's ring-leaders by expelling Pleasants and Leister from the unit and sentencing them to a spell of hard labour repairing bomb-damaged roads. One of the other men also punished was Roy Futcher, a private in the Durham Light Infantry. He had originally been recruited at Genshagen and told the other recruits he was an anti-communist and member of the BUF. He wrote Anglo-German poems and complained that recruitment to the Free Corps was not selective enough and that all potential candidates should be staunch fascists. Futcher later maintained he had only joined the Free Corps because he wanted to get back to England to sort out his troubled marriage. His wife had two children by different men and he had never seen his own baby daughter. He came up with the well-worn excuse that volunteering for the Free Corps was hopefully a means of escape.

Commando Thomas Freeman continued to undermine BFC morale by organising a petition, demanding that he and a group of other recruits be released from the unit and returned to their POW camps. He knew that if the company's manpower reached the round figure of thirty demanded by Berlin, then the unit would be sent into action. The petition came about because of Courlander's idea to broadcast a message to Winston Churchill on German radio, on behalf of the BFC, to urge the Prime Minister to stop the senseless war with Germany. The rest of the Free Corps members, egged on by Freeman, objected to the radio broadcast in case their identities were revealed to British listeners. The broadcast was never made and the Germans removed the disruptive Freeman by sending him to a concentration camp near Danzig.

Despite upheavals within the group, new arrivals continued to trickle into Hildesheim. The Hitler worshipper William Britten travelled to Stalag VIIIb at Lamsdorf, where he netted an NCO from the Military Police called William How. The next recruit to the unit was Pte Ernest Nicholls from the Royal Army Service Corps. Captured during the retreat towards Dunkirk, Nicholls had spent four years in captivity doing mainly labouring work. He agreed to join the unit after reading

BFC propaganda literature. Hugh Cowie of the Gordon Highlanders was taken prisoner near the Maginot Line in May 1940 and sent to Stalag XXa in Poland. While working as a tractor driver he made a bid for freedom but was recaptured just short of the Russian border. The Germans later discovered a short-wave wireless in his bunk and Cowie agreed to join the BFC to avoid punishment. Harry Dean Batchelor of the Royal Engineers was captured in Crete and recruited from a POW camp in Austria. Other new additions were effectively threatened and blackmailed into joining the unit by the German military. Frederick Croft of the Royal Artillery had made numerous escape bids, being punished with long bouts of solitary confinement which finally broke his spirit. Pte Edward Jackson of the King's Own Royal Regiment fell foul of the Gestapo after he went absent from a working party to visit his German girlfriend. Charlie Munns of the Durham Light Infantry was in a worse position having made his German girlfriend pregnant, an offence punishable by firing squad.

Perhaps the most bizarre attempt at recruiting was made by Roy Courlander. During his trawling of POW camps, Courlander came across Lt William Alan Watson Shearer of 4th Battalion, the Seaforth Highlanders. Originally from Bromley in Kent, Shearer was captured in France in 1940 and sent to various POW camps around Germany. In 1942 he began an accountancy course to reduce the monotony of camp life, but the studying led him to suffer a nervous breakdown and he was committed to the Ansbach mental asylum. In his depressed state of mind, Shearer, a strong anti-communist, made a request to join the German Army. He later described his reasons for doing so:

I had it in my mind that if I were allowed to join the German Army, I might be sent to the Eastern Front where I hoped I might be killed by the Russians. . . . The result of this was that at the insistence of the British doctors I was confined to the camp hospital. My behaviour was not quite normal in other directions.[25]

Shearer was correct in his self-assessment. Courlander took him to a local hotel where the officer asked to have a bath. He then proceeded deliberately to let the bath overflow, resulting in the hotel dining room being flooded. Then, while travelling with Courlander to Berlin in a crowded troop train, Shearer decided to pull the train's communication cord, occasioning further embarrassment. Shearer was the only officer to officially join the BFC. Courlander intended to use him as a figurehead whom he could easily control. However, the plan backfired because of Shearer's fragile state of mind. He was too disturbed to take part in the unit, refusing even to wear a BFC uniform. Frank MacLardy, the BUF agitator, believed Shearer was faking his illness but being of no further use to Courlander, the young officer was eventually sent back to the mental asylum at Ansbach for further treatment.

One officer who did make it to the front line was Capt. Douglas Berneville-Claye. His is one of the most bizarre stories to emerge from the renegade files. Born in Woolwich in south London, Berneville-Claye followed his father into the Army, via the Army Apprentice College at Chepstow. By the outbreak of war he had joined and left the RAF and managed to leave behind a string of failed relationships, including a cleaner he made pregnant while working in a pub. He subsequently found himself married to two women at the same time, but managed to conceal his bigamy by taking various jobs in different parts of the country. In 1940 he appeared in court for passing false cheques while on duty with the Home Guard, but managed to avoid going to prison, instead enlisting as a private in 11th Battalion, the West Yorkshire Regiment. Berneville-Claye succeeded in inventing a totally new persona. He claimed to have been educated at Charterhouse and Cambridge. Perhaps his double-barrelled name impressed the officer selection board because he was chosen to attend Sandhurst, gaining his commission in October 1941. He was posted to the Middle East and volunteered for the Special Air Service. By now he was calling himself 'Lord Charlesworth', but it is doubtful whether his brother officers, many of whom held real titles, were convinced by the eccentric fantasist.

Berneville-Claye's actual SAS duties were confined to driving a lorry, and it was while on patrol in the desert behind enemy lines that his unit was captured by the Germans. He was sent first to a

POW camp in Italy. He claims to have escaped before being recaptured on a train outside Florence, and transferred to Stalag VIIIb at Lamsdorf, and then to Oflag 79 in Brunswick where he ran a coffee stall in the camp. By this stage he was almost certainly working as an informer for the Germans. When a hidden camera and wireless set were mysteriously discovered by the German guards, the finger of suspicion pointed at Berneville-Claye and he was removed from the camp for his own protection. In a later statement to his commanding officer, he claimed to have escaped from his German escort and walked for several miles before coming across a German refugee woman and her two daughters who were cooking a meal at the roadside. The woman gave him the SS officer's uniform that had belonged to a dead relative. He put the uniform on, placing his own uniform in a rucksack. Challenged at a German roadblock he said he was a member of the 'British Free Will Army' engaged in the fight against Bolshevism. The Germans took him to the headquarters of III SS Panzer Corps, where he was questioned by *Obergruppenführer* Steiner, the corps commander. When Steiner suggested that he would provide guards to escort Berneville-Claye to the SS Kurt Eggers Regiment, the indignant Englishman claimed he replied that he could find his own way if a vehicle could be put at his disposal. It was shortly after this that the rogue officer literally stumbled across the bedraggled remnants of the BFC. When questioned by Thomas Cooper and the others, Berneville-Claye said that although he was wearing the uniform of a *Hauptsturmführer*, he was in fact a captain in the Coldstream Guards and had been sanctioned by the British authorities to fight against the Russians. He excitedly ordered the men to follow him into action against the advancing Soviet army. Meeting with a rather sceptical response, Berneville-Claye said he would fight on alone, and quickly left the scene in an armoured truck, taking a BFC man called Alexander Mackinnon with him. The pair subsequently became completely lost and after changing back into British uniform handed themselves over to the advancing Allied forces near the town of Bad Kleinen.

The D-Day landings in Normandy in June 1944 effectively put an end to organised recruitment for the BFC. The invasion of Europe lifted morale among Allied prisoners of war, while even the staunchest of the pro-Nazis in the BFC realised that England was probably going to win the war. Some just wanted to cover their tracks and conceal their treachery by removing all evidence of their membership of the BFC. MacLardy believed he actually stood less chance of detection by joining the Waffen-SS medical service. Others started to think about an escape route out of Germany or simply to blame their colleagues for their own predicament. Some of the group conspired against Cooper, and he was charged with anti-Nazi activities and transferred to the 'Leibstandarte Adolf Hitler' SS regiment to work as a military policeman. Courlander and Maton decided to volunteer for the Kurt Eggers propaganda regiment, then serving near the front line in Belgium. After travelling by train to Brussels the pair discarded their German uniforms, changed into civilian clothes and gave themselves up to a British army advance party. Courlander and Maton had made their escape just in time, for in early October 1944 the BFC was transferred to the Waffen-SS training pioneer school in Dresden. The chronic shortage of German manpower meant that the unit, however small, would be sent into action. The only remaining members of the hard group were Minchin, Wilson and Berry, plus the relative newcomers Heighes, Symonds and Cowie. The new additions were William Alexander from the Highland Light Infantry, a hard Glaswegian who later represented the unit in a boxing match against the SS, and Harry Nightingale of the Royal Artillery. Both men had been forced to join the BFC because of their sexual involvement with German girls. In the first few days of training the group was equipped with camouflaged SS field uniforms, drilled in weapons use and put through an extensive physical fitness routine. Meanwhile the rapid westward advance of the Russian forces made some of the men extremely uneasy. Reluctant to stay and fight, Cowie hatched a plan with Roy Futcher to forge travel documents and head towards the Russian lines where they could go to ground. Convincing the Germans they were embarking on another recruitment trip, Cowie, Futcher and four others travelled by train to Prague and on to Teschen where they became completely lost. After eventually being spotted by a local police patrol, word of the escaping men's presence was passed to the Gestapo who arrested the group and returned them under armed guard to Berlin. Cowie, Alexander and Futcher were all sent to a punishment camp while the others decided to stay with the unit.

The Allied blanket bombing of Dresden in February 1945 claimed over thirty thousand lives, mainly civilian. In the ensuing chaos, all BFC men were sent out to help extinguish fires and to search for survivors. Taking advantage of the general confusion, Ronald Heighes of the Hampshires and William How of the Military Police managed to successfully blend into a column of British POWs being evacuated west, and escaped. Acting on information received from the German girlfriend of one of the group, the entire remaining BFC force was arrested by the Gestapo on suspicion of prior knowledge of the Dresden bombing raid and of planning a mass escape. Taken to Berlin to await their fate, the group was joined by the last men to enlist in the BFC, Frank Axon and Douglas Mardon. Axon, a corporal in the Royal Army Service Corps, was taken prisoner in Greece in 1941 and spent most of his time employed as an agricultural labourer in work parties from Stalag XVIIIa in Austria. Bizarrely he was found guilty of 'cruelty to farm animals' and as an alternative to being punished by his German captors was offered the chance to join the BFC. Mardon was a South African who held classic anti-communist views and joined the group after reading one of MacLardy's propaganda leaflets in a POW camp.

Hardly any of the men recruited to the BFC saw any real action. The early 'recruiter' Minchin contracted scabies, Barker the Australian anti-communist merchant seaman smoked aspirins and took to his sick bed, and John Eric Wilson managed to avoid going to the front line by getting himself a desk job as the BFC–German Army liaison contact in Berlin. He subsequently helped himself to the unit's Red Cross parcels before deserting his post. The remains of the group were sent to join III SS Panzer Corps in Stettin. The unit came under Soviet mortar and artillery fire but sustained no injuries. What probably saved the lives of the last surviving BFC men was the reappearance of Thomas Cooper in the midst of battle. The fanatical

Cooper had spent the last six months in the Leibstandarte Adolf Hitler as a military policeman. He had received orders to join III SS Panzer Corps, finding himself close to the front line not far from the BFC's position. Summoned to a planning meeting with *Obergruppenführer* Felix Steiner, the corps commander, Cooper told the general that given the way the BFC had been organised and some of the characters involved, it would not be productive to use the small force as a combat unit. Steiner decided to meet and inspect the group for himself, taking Cooper with him. After talking to the men and shaking each member by the hand, Steiner decided that the BFC should not remain in the line and had them reassigned to his headquarters transportation unit based near Templin. There, they served as truck drivers, traffic marshals and generally helped civilian evacuations to the west.

Following Hitler's suicide General Steiner ordered Cooper to take the remnants of the BFC and make his way to a position at Schwerin in Mecklenburg. By this time most of the British group feared the consequences of being taken by the Russians and decided to get rid of their uniforms and to just keep heading west in order to surrender to the Americans. Gathering about thirty men, Cooper headed towards Schwerin to discover that the American Army forward base was only a few miles away. Cooper visited the American advance guard in Schwerin hoping to find a British presence. He discovered that Hugh Cowie and other BFC 'troublemakers' who had been sent to the punishment camp at Dronnewitz, had by coincidence also arrived in the town. All together about thirty men, formerly linked in some way with the BFC, were held for questioning.

Capt. Denys Hart of the British 1st GHQ Liaison Regiment carried out the initial interrogation of the renegades. Cooper told Denys Hart he was a British secret agent who had been passing on information to British Intelligence from Germany since 1939. The young British officer alerted the Second British Army that he had apprehended suspected members of the British Free Corps and other assorted misfits. He then awaited further orders.[26]

CHAPTER SIX

Harold Cole and Theodore Schurch

HAROLD COLE

'He was among the most selfish and callous traitors who ever served the enemy in time of war.'[1] This was how Airey Neave assessed the damage inflicted by Harold Cole, the Cockney 'con-man' who caused more damage and human suffering than any other British traitor of the Second World War. Cole delivered at least fifty and perhaps as many as a hundred and fifty Allied agents and civilian helpers into German hands. Yet for a time he was regarded as a hero, a resourceful and valued British agent in the dangerous business of guiding British and American servicemen along the hidden pathways out of occupied France.

Harold Cole was born in St Thomas's Hospital in London in 1906. His father Albert Cole was killed in the First World War, and his mother remarried. Harold did not get on with his stepfather. Despite his gaining a scholarship to the Stormont House school in London's Hackney Downs, Cole's stepfather wanted Harold to leave school as soon as possible to bring in a wage. Cole reluctantly took a job as a laboratory assistant at the Metropolitan Hospital in north London. Having spent his formative years in the tough East End areas of Hoxton and Dalston, places with strong links to London's East End criminal fraternity, and given his character, it was probably inevitable that Cole drifted into petty crime. After a succession of car thefts he was sentenced to a year's borstal detention. On his release he joined the Queen's Royal West Surrey Regiment and was posted to Hong Kong. For a while Cole was happy with his job of chauffeur to his commanding officer. But on being transferred to he stole a car and deserted, travelling for a time in China. Returning to Hong Kong he gave himself up and was given six months imprisonment and discharged from the Army.

Cole was desperate to escape from his working-class background. Giving himself the nickname 'Sonny Boy', he started to work on losing his pronounced East End accent. He tried to pretend he was middle-class by using expressions such as 'old man' or 'old boy' to ingratiate himself with those in authority. He even grew a military style moustache, acquired a military tie and told people he had served with famous British army regiments in Africa and the Far East. A neighbour remembered Cole as someone who was ashamed of his upbringing and had never done an honest day's work in his life. 'You never knew when he was in the nick or away somewhere else.'[2] The family friend added: 'To us he was a toff. He didn't speak like us. He was a six-footer, slim-built, and always well dressed, the type of person that can walk into clubs, attractive to gullible women.'[3] He may have had middle-class aspirations but Cole financed his flashy lifestyle by bouts of fraud, car trafficking and housebreaking. After being kicked out of the Army he spent the 1930s in and out of prison. While in prison Cole used his powers of deception to the full, gaining an early release from captivity on bogus medical grounds. He told the Prison governor he had suffered a long history of consumption, despite the fact that he had played trombone and trumpet in the prison band!

In early September 1939 the ex-convict decided to join the Royal Engineers. Almost immediately Cole's regiment was sent to France as part of the British Expeditionary Force. His silver tongue and sharp wits helped the Cockney wide boy to become a corporal within a week and by the time his regiment had made camp in northern France, Cole had been promoted to acting sergeant. But it did not take the unscrupulous NCO long to slip back into his criminal ways. Under cover of darkness Cole broke into the office containing the non-commissioned officers' mess funds. He attempted to frame a fellow NCO by planting some cash in his locker but immediately confirmed the suspicions of some his fellow soldiers who had already suspected that Cole had spent time behind bars prior to joining the

Army. Placed under surveillance by the military police, he was followed to a house in Lille where he had hidden the stolen money. As well as the cash the police also netted two prostitutes whom Cole had set up in business. He was immediately arrested and placed in a temporary army correction centre. Part of Cole's story is a long catalogue of escaping from military custody. On this particular occasion he managed to pick the lock of his cell and confidently stroll out of the prison declaring that he had been cleared of all charges. Having being recaptured he escaped again, this time by squeezing through a hole in his makeshift cell. He managed to steal an officer's uniform and go on a spending spree before being recaptured. To make sure the crafty Cockney could not launch yet another escape attempt, the authorities put Cole under guard at the Citadelle in Lille, an impressive seventeenth-century fortress. This time Cole did not have to think up a new escape plan; events in Europe conspired to enable him to walk free from the prison. On 10 May 1940 the German Army launched its blitzkrieg attack on the Netherlands, Belgium, Luxembourg and France. As the Germans advanced towards the French coast in an attempt to cut off the retreating British Expeditionary Force, Sgt Cole was told by the commander of the fortress prison guard: 'I don't care a bugger what you do, we're off.'

While the dejected British Army headed towards the port of Dunkirk, Cole simply kept his head down amid the chaos of the German onslaught. In the confusion of battle many British soldiers found themselves left behind in northern France. If the stragglers managed to avoid being captured by the Germans, they were often given shelter by sympathetic local people. Cole probably remained in the Lille area because he knew the terrain and sensed that he could benefit from the panic that accompanied the German advance and the Allied retreat at Dunkirk.

As the Germans consolidated their occupation of northern France, groups of local French and Belgian patriots looked for ways of thwarting them. They set up an escape line to co-ordinate the awkward and dangerous task of moving out of the country, overland, the British soldiers who had been left behind at Dunkirk. They also helped Allied airmen shot down over France who managed to evade immediate capture. In the summer of 1941, a tall, well-dressed Englishman made contact with the escape group based in the Lille area. He said he was a British Intelligence agent who had been ordered to remain after the Allied evacuation at Dunkirk to help co-ordinate the escape of stranded servicemen. The tall well-spoken Englishman introduced himself as Capt. Paul Cole of the Royal Engineers. In a meeting with members of the embryonic French Resistance, Cole said his assignment was to co-ordinate all the French escape networks into one cohesive group. Even though Cole was successful in keeping up the pretence of being an army intelligence officer, some of the Resistance men became uneasy when the conversation turned to money matters. Cole asked them if they could put up the initial finance for the escape network until official funds were sent from London. Although they had doubts about Cole's direct approach, the Frenchmen went along with his plans because they believed he was a British officer and therefore a gentleman. Men like Henri Duprez, a self-made factory owner from Lille, were keen to show their patriotic mettle by agreeing to help Cole in any way possible.

Why Cole became embroiled in the risky business of helping the Resistance to smuggle British servicemen out of France is unclear. With his track record of theft and fraud he could probably have feathered his own nest in the murky world of the French black market, or simply have made his escape to neutral Switzerland or Spain. In his classic study of Harold Cole, Brendan Murphy believes the corrupt Englishman yearned for the rank and respectability denied to him by his tough East End upbringing. Far from being a petty criminal he suddenly found himself a million miles away from his Cockney background in the role of a British army captain who commanded almost instant respect from his newly found French friends.

Cole perfected a clever way of covering up his poor French. He got one of the Resistance workers who had access to official forms to provide false identity papers for him in the name of 'Paul Delobel'. Cole also obtained a document in German certifying that he was deaf and dumb. If he was ever stopped for questioning by the Germans, 'Delobel' would behave like a deaf-mute, pretending to use a sort of sign language. As a result he managed to move around the Lille area meeting his contacts and moving British escapers to various safe houses without raising the suspicions of the local police or Gestapo. Cole soon established a network of trusted helpers in northern France. There is no doubt that during the latter part of 1940 he tirelessly recruited and motivated dozens of volunteers who in turn helped over two hundred Allied soldiers and airmen to flee occupied France. The escaping servicemen were escorted by train from northern France as far as the demarcation line between the German occupied and Vichy administered zones. Cole and his helpers would then guide them on foot into Vichy France to the port of Marseilles, where they were placed in safe houses before being led by local Basque guides over the Pyrenees into neutral Spain.

With the constant stream of soldiers and downed pilots being evacuated from the north through France to Marseilles it was only a matter of time before Cole came into contact with a genuine British officer associated with the escape line. He was Captain Ian Garrow, a powerfully built, intelligent Scotsman. Garrow had been with the 51st Highland Division when it was surrounded at St Valery near Dunkirk, but he managed with a few stragglers to avoid capture and headed south to Marseilles where they were interned by the Vichy authorities. Garrow and his men were placed in a strange dilemma. They were allowed to leave their camp, a former Foreign Legion sandstone fortress, and move freely around the city. However, the official Vichy French policy would not permit them actually to leave Marseilles or France. They were in effect in limbo. Garrow soon made contact with a Coldstream Guards officer named Jimmy Langley. Langley had been wounded at Dunkirk, losing an arm, but had managed to escape from hospital in Lille before reaching Marseilles. After working closely with Garrow on the escape line south, Langley was rescued from France and recalled to London to help run the escape and evasion service MI9. The War Office established MI9 to monitor all the escape lines out of Europe and the Far East. The plan was to facilitate the escape of British POWs, especially in Europe, as well as to return home Allied servicemen who had succeeded in evading capture in enemy-occupied territory.

The French end of the escape network was well organised in Marseilles largely because it had as its base a seamen's mission for destitute sailors. Funded by the American consulate, the mission was ostensibly a home for sailors of all nationalities who had fallen on hard times. It soon became a focal point for British escapers. The mission was run by a Church of Scotland minister named Donald Caskie, who had moved to Marseilles following the German occupation of Paris.

When Harold Cole was made known to Ian Garrow, the Londoner introduced himself as 'Sergeant' Cole. He had abandoned the officer rank he had previously assumed because he knew Garrow would see through that deception. Above all Cole wanted to make a good impression on somebody in Garrow's position. The act seemed to work because shortly after telling the Scottish officer a convincing story of how he had been left behind at Dunkirk, Garrow made Cole head of the escape line's operation in the north and gave him funding amounting to 10,000 francs. Garrow needed a reliable agent to run the vital link between Paris and the south, especially following Vichy's decision to transfer all interned British troops from Marseilles to an isolated barracks in Nîmes. This meant Garrow would have to stay behind and effectively go underground in Marseilles. The flow of RAF pilots transferred from the north to the south continued. In Garrow's eyes Cole was doing an excellent job. Other escape helpers in Marseilles did not agree. The clergyman Donald Caskie suspected Cole had a fertile imagination when the Cockney told of his various skirmishes and close run-ins with the Germans. Nancy Fiocca, a young Australian journalist was married to a local businessman and through his contacts many British soldiers were given money and safe shelter. Nancy took an instant dislike to Cole, regarding him as an ill-mannered rogue. She actually banned him from her apartment for helping himself from her drinks cabinet. The Australian girl proved to be very perceptive. Events in the south of France were to demonstrate her extreme courage and bravery because she subsequently became better known as Nancy Wake, the most highly decorated woman in France, earning the Croix de Guerre and the George Medal.

To Cole's brave French helpers in the north 'the Captain' was a hero. He had personally helped French families, split apart by the German occupation, to see their loved ones in the Vichy zone. His deaf-mute act always fooled the Germans. Once he actually stopped a German patrol in the street and after showing them the document proving he was deaf and dumb, gestured that he would appreciate their help in moving a large stove into a house. On another occasion a lorry containing British escapers broke down on its way to Lille railway station. Realising the importance of the escapers catching the scheduled train, Cole persuaded a detachment of German soldiers to tow the truck several miles to the station.

One man who found it difficult to accept that Cole was a traitor believed he owed his life to him. Flight Sergeant 'Taffy' Higginson was shot down over the Pas de Calais in June 1941. After being sheltered in a safe house, Cole arrived to collect the disoriented airman and on a hot sunny day the pair headed off south towards Marseilles. They were just approaching the town of Tours when a group of Germans sitting drinking in a café became suspicious of the two Englishmen. Higginson's forged identity documents identified him as a French soldier who had been discharged suffering from shell shock. The Germans persisted with their questioning of Cole, who persisted in telling them in poor pidgin French that his friend was mentally unfit. The RAF man was convinced they were about to be rumbled. Cole reacted by shouting at the soldiers and threatening to report them to their commanding officers for drinking on duty. When the Germans ordered Higginson to empty his briefcase, its contents were covered in thick sticky chocolate. The heat of the sun had caused a large bar of unwrapped French chocolate to melt. Cole gave an accusing look at the case and then, turning away in disgust, told the Germans that his deranged friend had relieved himself in the briefcase! The Germans had also formed that impression and angrily waved the two men on their way. Higginson was full of admiration for the way Cole had bluffed his way through and later found it difficult to accept that the smooth Londoner was in fact a traitor.

As Cole grew more confident and won the trust of British and Frenchmen alike, he gradually slipped back into his crooked ways. The port of Marseilles was a hot spot of intrigue, black-market trading and corruption. Harold Cole was easily and willingly sucked into the den of drug dealers, pimps and assorted international criminals. Cole was a serial womaniser with girlfriends scattered along the entire escape line. He drank and ate in the best bars, restaurants and nightclubs, and always seemed to have plenty of cash to pay for whatever he desired. Soon questions were being asked about his exotic lifestyle, and how he was paying for it. While the escape line guides escorted soldiers and airmen from the north into Marseilles, Cole often stayed in the city simply collecting the escapees and taking the credit from Capt. Garrow for the entire operation. Garrow's deputy, a Belgian doctor named Albert-Marie Guerisse, also had grave doubts about Cole. He later said of the Englishman: 'To me from the first moment I set eyes on him he was a nobody. No good at all. And most certainly not the sort of person for us to be in harness with.'[4] The minister from the seamen's mission, Donald Caskie, continued to regard Cole as a wide boy just out for a good time. Cole was actually rumbled by his close French helpers. Some members of the escape line were successful businessmen, happy to finance escaping British soldiers. But Cole had led them to believe they would be reimbursed by British Intelligence for their troubles. When no money was forthcoming and Cole continued to ask his French associates for more 'loans' they grew increasingly suspicious of the debonair Englishman. Cole was also taking foreign currency from escaping airmen on the basis that if they were travelling with him they would not need cash. The French doubters in the north alerted Capt. Garrow to their reservations about Cole, but before he could confront the slippery sergeant, Garrow was arrested in Marseilles by the Vichy secret police.

Before his confinement Garrow had already made some preliminary enquiries on Cole via his MI9 contact in Lisbon. For some reason British Intelligence did not inform Garrow about Cole's colourful criminal past, of which they were clearly aware because they had been sent Cole's criminal file by Scotland Yard. The authorities in London could easily have confirmed the identity of the ex-sergeant by showing his photograph to the many airmen he had assisted in escaping to England. The word on the intelligence grapevine was that Cole should be left alone, at least for the time being. Brendan Murphy suggests that Cole was recruited by British Intelligence (SIS), because through his contacts in northern France he had amassed important logistical information with a usefulness far beyond the escape line alone. It was not therefore in SIS's interest to notify Garrow that his main escape expert was in fact a confidence man, thief and army deserter.

Whatever use Cole may have been to the shadowy intelligence cliques in London, he was proving a serious liability to the men of the escape and evasion line on the ground in France. With Capt. Garrow in prison, Albert-Marie Guerisse, the Belgian doctor, took over control of the escape line under the code name of 'Pat O'Leary'. There was much more to the Belgian than his medical qualifications. Pat had served in the Belgian cavalry in 1940 and was evacuated from Dunkirk. He returned to active service as a lieutenant commander in the Royal Navy, based on one of the clandestine 'Q' ships, disguised merchant vessels equipped with hidden armaments. On a secret mission to rescue a group of Polish officers off the French coast, Pat's rowing boat capsized and he was picked up by the Vichy French coastguard and interned at the military fort at Nîmes. Pat O'Leary had recently been sent north by Garrow to investigate claims of Cole's extravagant spending, his unexplained absences from the organisation, and the rumours that some escapers entrusted to Cole never reached their final destination.

The escape line's funds in the north had been put in the care of a civil servant based in Lille named Francois Duprez. Pat O'Leary soon discovered from Duprez that as much as 300,000 francs were missing from MI9 funds and both men had a good idea where most of the money had gone. O'Leary's initial suspicions about Cole convinced him he would have to confront the Londoner, so he decided to spring a carefully laid trap. In late November 1941 Cole was lured to a flat in Marseilles where O'Leary and some other organisation members casually asked him about details of the escape line's finances. Cole said that he had given all the money for safe keeping to the trusted Francois Duprez. On a pre-arranged signal, the concealed Duprez jumped out of a cupboard and confronted the startled Cole. The angry Frenchmen told the assembled group that far from paying him, Cole had been borrowing from him. Seeing that the game was up Cole dropped his cocky façade, admitted he was a thief and begged for mercy. One of Pat O' Leary's men struck him in the face and the decision was taken to court martial the by now trembling Cole. While O'Leary and other escape line members debated whether to dispose of Cole or to await further orders from London, the crafty Cockney managed to get on to the roof of the building in which he was being held and escape across the skyline.

Cole was now a loose cannon, his fate very much in his own hands. But he was not entirely alone. A few months earlier he had met a nineteen-year-old French girl named Suzanne Warenghem who had arrived at the seamen's mission in Marseilles with two escaping Scottish soldiers. Suzanne had wanted to help the Allied cause in some way, particularly as her father was half English and she had spent long periods of her childhood staying with relatives in England. Suzanne started to visit British soldiers in Paris hospitals. She then acted as a lookout while two soldiers climbed over a hospital wall and helped to escort the two men on the journey into Vichy France and on to Marseilles. Her resourcefulness impressed Ian Garrow who offered her a job as a guide in the escape organisation. She met Cole and despite knowing about his reputation as a womaniser, she became intrigued by his glamorous daredevil exploits, and the pair became close. Working as a team they guided thirty-five British soldiers from Paris down to Marseilles. The trip, which took two days, included a midnight walk of some 20 miles across the border into unoccupied France, and half a dozen different train journeys.

After fleeing Marseilles in a hurry, Cole surfaced in Paris. He told Suzanne he had been in some trouble in the south but naturally did not go into details. Following Cole's escape from Marseilles, Pat O'Leary sought permission from London to kill him. But the deputy head of the security service, Colonel Claude Dansey, did not agree that Cole should be killed, possibly because Cole was unofficially working for his department (MI6), as well as for MI9. Cole headed back north to a safe house to plan his next move, aware he was still very popular with the helpers there, as well as being able to call on an impressive network of contacts on the Channel coast. The one factor he seemed to have pushed to the back of his mind was the Gestapo. They were lying in wait for him at the 'safe house', dragging him out into the street and bundling him into a car before speeding off towards German headquarters in Lille.

It is not entirely clear exactly when Harold Cole decided to betray his friends and colleagues in the escape line to the Gestapo. His dramatic arrest may have been stage-managed to protect his cover as a German informer. If he wasn't a German stooge from the beginning, with the threat of execution hanging over him, Cole soon decided to do everything he could to save his skin. His massive embezzlement of escape line funds, his black-market deals and unsavoury side-lines, were small fry compared to the damage he was later to inflict on Frenchmen who had risked their lives in the fight against the Nazis.

One of the first men to be betrayed by Cole was Francois Duprez, the escape line banker who had first exposed Cole as a swindler. Following his arrest and interrogation he subsequently died in a German concentration camp. Next came the German interrogation of a young priest, the Abbé Pierre Carpentier. The clergyman had worked closely with Cole in the early days, helping him hide escaping airmen and providing them with forged identification documents. While awaiting his fate in the prison at Loos, Pierre Carpentier got word to the escape line that Cole had betrayed him. Soon afterwards the priest was transferred to a Berlin jail and condemned to death by a Nazi tribunal. He, along with Bruce Dowding, another escape line helper, was decapitated by the Gestapo in June 1943.

After helping the Germans to round up many of his former helpers in Lille, Cole led the Gestapo to his contacts in Paris. Those who were unfortunate enough not to have heard about Cole's dramatic escape from Marseilles were snared in a trap. The usual routine involved Cole arriving at the door of a trusted escape courier with two or three supposedly English or Polish pilots. Once Cole and the pilots had entered the helper's house and begun discussing escape plans, the supposed downed airmen would reveal themselves as German agents and arrest the householder. About fifty escape line personnel met this fate and few survived interrogation at the hands of the Gestapo.

At first Cole managed to conceal his treachery from his girlfriend Suzanne Warenghem by sending her on fictitious errands to Brussels to collect escaping airmen, who of course never appeared. After being told of Cole's 'arrest' by the Germans Suzanne was surprised when he turned up at her apartment. He spun her an elaborate story of how he had barely escaped with his life. In fact after his betrayal of a batch of escape line workers the Germans allowed Cole some degree of freedom which gave him the chance to go on the run again. He asked Suzanne to marry him and after ingratiating himself with her family Cole helped himself to some jewellery belonging to Suzanne's two aunts. He even attempted to dispose of Suzanne (by now pregnant), by asking her to deliver a letter to a secret address. The letter contained detailed plans of a German airfield, and the address was the home of a known German agent. Suzanne would almost certainly have been arrested, charged with espionage and possibly executed. Cole never had the opportunity to give Suzanne the letter because in June 1942 the Vichy secret police, the Direction de la Surveillance du Territoire, arrested the couple at a Lyon hotel.

Although the Vichy government co-operated with the Germans there were many in the secret police who were actually sympathetic to the British and even went as far as arresting known German agents. The police inspector in charge of Cole's interrogation, Louis Triffe, was not only pro-British but also knew all about Cole's activities. He made sure that the man who had betrayed many French lives would pay for his treachery. Cole was put on trial charged with espionage. He was found guilty and condemned to death. The Vichy police decided, thanks to Louis Triffe's intervention, that Suzanne Warenghem was just a poor misguided girl who had fallen under Cole's spell. She was cleared of all charges of spying and released. During the police interrogation of Cole, Suzanne was allowed to see her husband. Triffe's men had given Cole a beating and he seemed a broken man. With tears in his eyes he openly admitted his treachery and begged Suzanne to forgive him. She finally saw for herself that the man she had loved and trusted had completely deceived her.

The Vichy court's death sentence on Cole was never carried out, probably due to his British citizenship. He languished in prison in Lyon until the German takeover of the Vichy unoccupied zone in the autumn of 1942. The Germans commuted his sentence to life imprisonment and moved Cole to Compiègne prison near Paris. Here the Gestapo used him as a prison stool pigeon, and also as an *agent provocateur* to gather intelligence on the escape and evasion networks in northern France. Once again it seemed that Cole had fallen on his feet. He was taken under the wing of SS-Sturmbannführer Hans Kieffer and based at Gestapo headquarters at 84 Avenue Foch in Paris. Cole's knowledge of Resistance activities helped Kieffer to track down SOE agents in France. Cole was also present at the interrogation of captured airmen and members of the French escape line who had formerly been friends of the renegade Englishman. The sight of Cole dressed in Gestapo uniform must have both amused and terrified his former colleagues. Many vowed to track him down and kill him after the war, although few actually survived their experience at the hands of the Paris Gestapo.

Cole realised that the game was up when the Allies landed in Normandy. He began to formulate an escape plan. As the British and American Armies converged on Paris, Kieffer and a handful of Gestapo men headed into Belgium and turned south towards the German–Austrian border. Cole tagged along too. As the group reached the Black Forest they came within range of the American Sixth Army Corps. A combination of intense American shelling, chaos on the roads and freezing weather conditions led Cole and his Gestapo associates to reconsider their position. After shedding their SS uniforms the group surrendered to the Americans. Cole concocted the story that he was a certain Robert Mason, a British secret agent captured in France earlier in the war. He introduced

Kieffer and the others as ordinary civilian policemen whom he had persuaded to help him escape from the Gestapo. Through one of the quirky coincidences of war Cole met an American officer who recognised him from the early days of the French escape line. Cole was issued with temporary US Counter Intelligence Corps identification documents plus an American uniform and established himself as a sort of roving war crimes investigator. He moved easily between the American and French controlled sectors of southern Germany. While known Nazi war criminals were being rounded up to be tried by a series of Allied courts, Cole was given the authority to decide who would be punished on a more local level. He gathered around him a bunch of mainly Frenchmen, who had been brought to Germany at the beginning of the war to work as forced labourers.

Based in a farmhouse in the village of Saulgau, near Stuttgart, Cole set to work ostensibly seeking out wanted Nazis. But he had his own agenda and hoped to make a quick profit before getting out of Germany and beginning a new life. Just before fleeing SS headquarters in Paris, Cole found out about a network of Gestapo agents in southern Germany whose orders were to hold and distribute secret Nazi cash funds and consignments of gold bullion to finance the Nazi 'Werewolf' resistance groups. With thoughts of getting rich quick uppermost in Cole's mind, he and his assorted cronies arrested Georg Hanft, a former SS officer whom Cole believed had access to the hidden loot. Hanft was bundled out of his house in front of his family and taken way to a local barn where he was brutally tortured and then shot by Cole and his gang. Cole conducted a reign of sadistic terror, arresting and assaulting many alleged Nazis in his quest to find the supposedly concealed funds. During this period of arrests and interrogations, Cole continued to fool the numerous American officers whom he met. They regarded him as a classic British spy, complete with military moustache, and seemed in awe of his supposed military credentials. That he conducted his investigations wearing an American uniform was never queried by anyone in authority. Within his own small corner of southern Germany, Cole effectively had a free hand to do as he wished. Then he made a mistake.

After D-Day the British security service intensified their search for any military personnel who had openly collaborated with the Germans. For the various MI9 contacts in London and France, Cole was top of the most-wanted list. It was assumed he had fled to the Gestapo headquarters in Berlin and would possibly slip away in the chaos of the collapsing Reich. In Paris MI9 put Cole's mistresses under surveillance. Then out of the blue came a postcard sent by Cole to one of his girlfriends. It was signed 'Much love Sonny Boy', one of Cole's known nicknames. British intelligence officers identified where the card was posted and immediately sent two agents to southern Germany to find out if Cole was still in Saulgau. When told of the true identity of 'Captain Mason' the senior British and American officers in Saulgau, who had been in almost daily contact with him, simply did not believe it. Cole too denied being a traitor and tried to talk his way out of the confrontation with the unit sent to apprehend him. But after being restrained by three men and firmly handcuffed, he was taken to Paris for questioning.

In a lengthy statement Cole admitted all his crimes including firing the first shots that killed George Hanft. While MI9 and other intelligence departments checked Cole's testimony, the ex-sergeant and 'Captain' was working on his next escape plan. He was being held in the American administered Paris Detention Barracks and soon managed to win the confidence of the guards through his smooth talking and supreme confidence. He said he was going to write his memoirs and persuaded them to give him a typewriter. It seemed unlikely to the guards that somebody about to write their life story was going to make an escape bid. One night during a friendly chat in the guardroom Cole asked to use a nearby toilet before being returned to his cell. He managed to take an overcoat from a chair belonging to an American sergeant, quickly put it on and promptly marched out of the barracks before vanishing into the Paris underground.

Going to ground in a city full of military and civilian police, Cole knew he would have to find secure shelter. Avoiding hotels, which might display his 'wanted' poster, he persuaded the landlady of a small bar to let him stay in her spare room. He said he was a soldier who wanted to spend some time enjoying himself in Paris while awaiting demobilisation and before going home to England. Cole charmed the landlady and her regular customers with stories of his wartime exploits. But in a city used to intrigue and awash with informers it was not long before news of the charming stranger reached the police. Cole probably gave himself away by only leaving the bar at night, never during the day. This must have seemed rather odd behaviour for a young soldier who said he wanted to 'see Paris' before returning to civilian life in London.

After the use of numerous identities, confidence tricks, persistent escape scams, plus a seemingly endless supply of believable smooth talking, Cole's final reckoning was an anticlimax. Fearing the Paris police would eventually get around to checking for possible deserters staying at the bar, Cole planned to leave that evening for Brussels. He left it too late. When two policemen knocked on his door, Cole picked up his pistol and fired off a full magazine of bullets, wounding one of the men. The other policeman also fired a volley of shots and Cole was killed instantly. The theory later emerged that MI6 had silenced Cole because he knew too much about their operation in Europe. If there was a hidden agenda surrounding the activities of this treacherous chameleon, it must have given Albert-Marie Guerisse, alias Pat O'Leary, great satisfaction to identify Cole's body in the Paris morgue.[5] Lying before him was the man responsible for the deaths of many of his fellow Resistance colleagues.

Reginald Spooner, a Scotland Yard detective who was seconded to MI5 to interrogate British renegades, described Cole as 'the worst traitor of the war'. Perhaps the final word on this prominent collaborator should go to his French wife. Speaking to Commander Spooner about Cole some ten years after the war, Suzanne Warenghem said:

We all liked and admired him. There are some people who have since said that they never trusted him, that they were always suspicious of him. But that's being wise after the event. It wasn't what they said at the time. None of us had any suspicions about Paul Cole.[6]

THEODORE SCHURCH

Theodore Schurch came from an ordinary working-class family in north London and was born during the last summer of the First World War. His mother was English and his father Swiss. Schurch left school at sixteen and his first job was as a cost accountant with the Lancegaye Safety Glass Company based in Wembley. He became friendly with an older woman named Irene Page who worked as a telephone operator at the firm. Every Saturday Page came to work dressed as a Blackshirt, and soon engaged the impressionable Londoner in discussions about Mosley's movement. She started to take Schurch to fascist party meetings at a house in Willesden. These were purely political, not subversive meetings. On one occasion young Theodore met the great Mosley. At one social gathering a man approached Schurch and told him that the young man's quick intelligence could be used to better advantage by the party. Schurch thought he was having his leg pulled, because he had only just turned seventeen and was neither university educated nor well connected. The mystery man told him not to worry about that because all that was required was to be in a position merely to give information, and that the rest was simple. Schurch was intrigued and when he expressed interest in the man's proposition he was told he would be contacted in due course. These events prove that certain members of the BUF were linked with Mussolini's fascist regime because the unidentified English BUF man passed Schurch's details to the Italian intelligence service, and soon afterwards a man named Mr Bianchi called at Schurch's home. He suggested that the boy join the British Army to elicit information for the fascist cause. No remuneration was mentioned, but Schurch was also told he would be 'looked after'. Schurch was told that following his enlistment the Italian security service would know of his movements and contact him when necessary. The next day he went to a recruiting centre in Whitehall and enlisted in the Royal Army Service Corps. Schurch had not even told his family that he was joining up, although shortly afterwards they were contacted by the CID at Scotland Yard to check documents regarding their son. This may have been simply police procedure given Theodore's foreign-sounding name.

Once Theodore Schurch started his basic training at Aldershot, he received a letter requesting that he meet Bianchi at a London restaurant called Frascati's. Over dinner, Bianchi told Theodore to volunteer as an army driver, as this would place him in an ideal position for gaining logistical information. Bianchi also gave Schurch a £5 note to purchase a regimental dress uniform. When he had finished initial army training Schurch was transferred to undergo an advanced driving course at Feltham in Middlesex. He notified Bianchi by writing to him care of an antique shop in Piccadilly Circus called Spinks. His Italian contact had told him to address the letter to the shop to a 'Mr King'. Schurch received a reply from King asking to meet him on a Saturday evening at Trafalgar Square Tube station. The pair went to Lyons Corner House for a drink and King asked the new recruit if he wanted any money. Schurch said he needed money to buy Christmas presents for his family because he had lost all his money playing cards. King gave him £15 and told him to let him know which country he was being posted to after finishing his driver-mechanic course.

Schurch remained in contact by post with King throughout 1937. Acting on his contact's orders, Schurch volunteered for overseas service, specifically requesting to be sent to the Middle East. His regiment left for Jerusalem where he was assigned as a driver for the General Staff. Shortly after arriving in Palestine Schurch was contacted by an Italian who said he was a friend of Bianchi's. He told the young soldier to go to the house of a Mr Homsi, an Arab living in Jaffa. The shadowy Homsi told Schurch he was primarily interested in any information regarding the movements of senior personnel such as Gen. Wavell and the High Commissioner Henry MacMichael. Homsi also requested information about troop movements and general unit strengths. Being an official driver, Schurch had access to the regiment's transport pool, and a combination of cunning and cheerful banter with his fellow drivers resulted in him being able to draw up a comprehensive schedule of all the regiment's arrivals and departures.

Schurch saw Homsi at least once a week from February 1938 until the end of 1940. He was given a steady supply of money whether information was forthcoming or not. When Schurch was transferred to Genefa in Eygpt in early 1941, all mail was censored by the commanding officer of the unit, making it impossible to contact Homsi. By this stage Schurch had become a reliable and conscientious spy and decided to risk visiting his Arab contact. He put in a request for some leave, which was turned down. Undaunted, Schurch withdrew a week's pay and obtained a pass form on which he forged the name of 'Captain John Richards' (the alias used on later occasions). In possession of his forged pass Schurch went AWOL, taking a train to Ismalia, before crossing the Suez Canal and heading for Palestine. He cleverly evaded the Military Police by offering to carry the luggage of an officer who was travelling on the same train. Schurch continued to Homsi's house and told him everything about his new unit and its location. In return the Arab gave him £30.

Schurch gave himself up to his old unit in Safafand and admitted being absent without leave. He was immediately put in the guardhouse and later returned to his regiment in Egypt. Facing disciplinary action Schurch told his commanding officer he had absconded because he was frustrated at not being promoted despite signing up as a regular soldier before the war. His sympathetic CO said he would give him more interesting work to do and he was assigned to a detail dealing with ship movements and the registration of military equipment coming into Egypt. When he received word that Bianchi wanted to meet him in Cairo, Schurch requested leave on the pretext of visiting the Swiss consulate in Cairo. Again he was refused leave but went anyway. In case his senior officer checked on his movements, Schurch did visit the Swiss consulate to request information on obtaining a passport (to which he was entitled, being half-Swiss). After meeting Bianchi at the Cairo Savoy Continental Hotel, Schurch returned to barracks where he was fined two days' pay for his 'visit' to the Swiss embassy. Two weeks later Italy entered the war.

In an effort to re-establish contact with his Italian spymasters, Schurch asked for a posting to the front line. He was attached to 432nd Company in Tobruk. When the Germans took Tobruk, Schurch allowed himself to be captured and asked to be put in touch with Italian Intelligence. He was contacted by a Lt Col. Mario Revetria, who sent Schurch back across the British lines to gather information. In September 1942 he was ordered to Tobruk where two British naval ships, the *Sikh* and the *Zulu* had been sunk while trying to land troops at Tobruk. Schurch infiltrated the ranks of the captured POWs, the first of many missions where he acted as an effective stool pigeon, under the name of Capt. John Richards. He was also sent to Benghazi and placed among captured members of the Long Range Desert Group and Special Air Service to discover the unit's strength and operational plans. On a later occasion he was placed in a prison cell next to the founder of the SAS, Colonel David Stirling. Stirling soon saw through Schurch's 'Captain Richards' routine. The SAS man described Schurch as a Cockney masquerading in a captain's uniform. He later admitted telling him that he was the commanding officer of the SAS but knew Schurch was already aware of this.[7] The suggestion that Stirling gave useful military information to Schurch, resulting in the capture of units of the Long Range Desert Group, has not been proven and is extremely unlikely.

When his Italian controller, Col. Revetria, was transferred to Rome Schurch went too. There he was employed in various guises. Operating in civilian clothes he was told to locate a British wireless operation within Vatican City. He was loaned to the Germans and sent to a British POW camp to discover information about Allied submarine activity in the Mediterranean. Posing as 'Captain Richards' he found out where 'S' squadron submarines were operating from and the names of various submarine commanders. His next assignment was Perugia where he attempted to infiltrate a British intelligence network. When Italy changed sides in 1943 Schurch worked for the SS, again in plain clothes, pretending to be an escaping British officer in search of the local Italian resistance movement. While operating from La Spezia, Schurch was caught up in the American Army advance and placed under arrest as a potential deserter.

After being handed over to the British for questioning Schurch gave a detailed statement of his activities before and during the war, listing all the Italian and German contacts he had made over the years. The MI5 report on Schurch said:

Subject is an individual gifted with an innate shrewdness and a natural intelligence which compensates for his obvious lack of education. His story plainly reveals his treacherous nature. He has been a traitor in the pay of foreign powers, although he claims that his actions were based on an ardent love for fascist ideals.[8]

Theodore Schurch was hanged at Pentonville Prison on 4 January 1946, the day after the execution of William Joyce at Wandsworth Prison.

CHAPTER SEVEN

Windsor and Wodehouse

THE DUKE OF WINDSOR

Much has already been written about the Duke of Windsor's sympathies with the Nazi regime. Although it is probably going too far to argue that he was a traitor who intentionally betrayed the Allies, the Duke was certainly a naïve, irresponsible fool. He played into German hands with his erratic behaviour. After his abdication Edward married Mrs Wallis Warfield Simpson in June 1937. The new King George VI made Edward the Duke of Windsor and his wife the Duchess of Windsor, but she was denied the title of Her Royal Highness. The refusal of the establishment to grant this royal title to the former Mrs Simpson irritated and angered Edward. He also believed that the financial settlement he had received following the abdication was insulting, and felt he should have been given an important role to play in matters of state, instead of being effectively sidelined. These problems all combined to explain much of the Duke's later public outspokenness and also his childish and irresponsible behaviour in private.

Long before his abdication, Edward had supported Hitler's rise to power in Germany. Like many from his background Edward applauded the Hitler-inspired German recovery from the Depression and economic catastrophe. In 1935 he made a speech to the Royal British Legion arguing for an alliance between Britain and Germany. Edward's father, George V, accused his son of unconstitutional behaviour by such public interference in foreign affairs. In the more private setting of a cocktail party, Edward repeated his support for Hitler. Sir Bruce Lockhart later wrote:

The Prince of Wales was quite pro-Hitler and said it was no business of ours to interfere in Germany's internal affairs either re Jews or re anything else, and added that dictators are very popular these days and that we might want one in England before now.[1]

Edward supported the sudden German remilitarising of the Rhineland, even going so far as sending for Prime Minister Stanley Baldwin and threatening to abdicate if Britain responded militarily to the German move. It is doubtful whether Britain and France would have gone to war anyway at that early stage, but the new King was clearly interfering in the political arena and continuing to behave unconstitutionally. King Edward's pro-Hitler views were probably encouraged by his wife. Mrs Simpson soon became a friend and confidante of the newly arrived German Ambassador to London, Joachim von Ribbentrop. Whether the King discussed with his wife the briefings he received from Prime Minister Baldwin is unknown, but given MI5's concerns about the couple's relationship with the top Nazi, for reasons of security, some Foreign Office documents were not shown to the King.

The abdication of Edward VIII was a complicated affair involving many vested interests. The idea that Baldwin wished to get rid of the King because of his pro-Nazi views played only a very minor part in the saga. The real problem was that Edward still believed he had some divine right to openly interfere in British policy even after he had given up the throne. There are many examples of this behaviour; the ex-king effectively became a loose cannon, forever putting his foot in it!

In October 1937 the Duke and Duchess of Windsor arrived in Berlin as Hitler's guests. They were given the red-carpet treatment, with hundreds of Germans lining the streets, greeting the couple with hysterical cries of 'Heil Windsor' and 'Heil Edward'. This orchestrated welcome was not surprising given the propaganda value such a visit was bound to generate for the Nazi regime. The visitors were shown the latest German showcase factory, and inspected the elite Nazi SS Totenkopf (Death's Head) division. The Duke twice proudly gave the Nazi salute.

As Martin Allen points out, the Duke was overwhelmed and flattered by the respect the Nazis gave him. It made him feel welcome and wanted, in contrast to the rejection he believed he had suffered at the hands of Downing Street politicians, as well as his own brother, now the King, in Buckingham Palace.[2] The Germans believed they had a good friend in the Duke. Rudolf Hess, who along with Martin Bormann had earlier met the Duke in Paris,[3] reported to Hitler that

The Duke is proud of his German blood . . . says he's more German than British . . . [and is] keenly interested in the development of the Reich. There is no need to lose a single German life in invading Britain. The Duke and his clever wife will deliver the goods.[4]

Rudolf Hess clearly anticipated that the Duke would retain or regain some influence despite no longer being king. It was the Duke's reluctance to forgo any such influence and simply keep a low profile after the abdication that led to a further embarrassing action. Just after King George VI and his wife left for a trip to Canada and America, in May 1939, the Duke broadcast an appeal on coast-to-coast American radio for 'world peace' to commemorate the anniversary of the First World War Battle of Verdun. While the King was on his way to seek American support for British policy against German aggression, his brother was effectively undermining him by calling for the appeasement of Hitler.

When the war started the Duke was appointed as a major-general to the British Military Mission in France. He went on a two-day tour of the French lines, observing the French First Army's equipment and strategic fortifications, including the Maginot Line. The Duke prepared two reports on the French defensive positions for the British Mission. In November 1995 a Channel 4 television documentary stated that the Duke leaked details of the French positions to his pro-German friend, the French millionaire businessman and leading socialite, Charles Bedaux. After a long day inspecting the battlefield the Duke would dine with Bedaux at the Paris Ritz. He had first met

Charles Bedaux when the Frenchman generously offered his chateau to the Duke and Duchess as a retreat following the abdication. He became a confidant of the Duke and usually paid the 'royal' couple's hotel bill when they stayed in France. Bedaux was not only pro-German. He was actually a Nazi spy. He acted as an adviser to the Germans in the Vichy government.[5] MI5 had Bedaux (as well as the Duke) under surveillance. They knew that on numerous occasions he had visited Count Julius von Zech-Burkersroda, the German Ambassador to Holland, by train via Cologne. Bedaux was also spotted in the Reich Chancellery in Berlin by a Dutch agent, who informed MI5.[6] British Military Intelligence also sent a note to Major General Howard-Vyse, the commander of the British Mission to France, warning him of the danger Bedaux posed to security:

I would recommend that you inform Major-General HRH the Duke of Windsor that it has come to our notice that his acquaintance, Mr C.E. Bedaux, is believed to be engaged in conduct incompatible with his status as a citizen of a neutral state. HRH is therefore requested to cease all activity and contact with this gentleman immediately.[7]

Although he ignored the security warning not to associate with Bedaux, there is no proof that the Duke of Windsor actively gave away French military secrets. Given his capacity to be indiscreet, he may have openly criticised the French military organisation but it is unlikely that he gave Bedaux – or anyone else – military information which subsequently played a part in Hitler's attack on the Low Countries in the summer of 1940. With the fall of France imminent the Duke left his military post and made his way with the Duchess to the South of France and then to Spain and Portugal. Whether or not the Duke actually deserted his post in wartime, itself an offence punishable by court-martial, has never been substantiated. What is certain is that Churchill initially wanted him removed from any pro-German influences and returned to England, where his loose talk would be curtailed. Churchill then had second thoughts. He was concerned about the extent of public support for the Duke in England. By appointing him Governor of the Bahamas, the Duke would be far removed from the public eye and any pro-German influences. Windsor was in no hurry to return to England or indeed anywhere else. A further example of his reckless behaviour was the request he made to the Germans to be allowed to send his wife's maid back to Paris to retrieve some personal belongings. While the British Expeditionary Force was being evacuated from the beaches at Dunkirk, documents were being prepared by the Gestapo to allow the Duchess of Windsor's maid to go to Paris to collect a few items of clothing!

The Duke was happy to sit in Spain waiting to be given a position 'worthy' of his status, and hoping that the government would grant the official recognition to the Duchess which had so far been denied to her. The suggestion that he simply wanted to keep his options open, to see if Hitler would prevail over Churchill, is simplistic and pure speculation. He could have taken the 50 million Swiss francs offered to him by the Germans in return for agreeing to live in Europe as a 'King in exile' Nazi puppet, but he eventually saw sense and accepted Churchill's job offer in the Bahamas. Before he departed, the Duke attended a reception at the British Embassy in Madrid at which he told the American Ambassador A.W. Weddell that the only important thing was to end the war before thousands more were killed or maimed.[8] When the couple had moved to Portugal, the German Ambassador in Lisbon, Baron Oswald von Hoynigen's report to Ribbentrop said:

> He is convinced that had he remained on the throne war could have been avoided and describes himself as a firm supporter of a peaceful compromise with Germany. The Duke believes with certainty that continual severe bombing will make England ready for peace.[9]

The Duke's belief that Britain would have avoided war with Germany had he still been on the throne is wishful thinking on his part. After Hitler had concluded the Nazi–Soviet Pact and then invaded Poland, the British cabinet was determined to go to war; they had no other choice.

Perhaps the last remaining controversy surrounding the Duke of Windsor centres on the mission to Germany in 1945 undertaken by art historian Anthony Blunt, then an MI6 officer, to retrieve letters and documents concerning the Duke. According to the Channel 4 documentary, Blunt's secret mission involved the removal of papers and documents that might damage the reputation of the Duke or indeed the royal family. The collection may have included letters from the Duke to both Hitler and Rudolf Hess. Blunt removed the documents by lorry and returned them for safe keeping to Windsor Castle. At the same time the Americans discovered in the Thuringia Forest a buried microfilm record of the German Foreign Ministry entitled 'German-British Relations', which included a section on the Duke of Windsor. This was later called the 'Marburg File'. The Americans were also persuaded to co-operate to prevent the file's contents from ever entering the public domain. During a post-war meeting between the British Foreign Secretary Ernest Bevin and his American opposite number Secretary of State General George Marshall, it was agreed that the 'Marburg File' would never see the light of day. Marshall sent an urgent 'Personal for your eyes only' note to Dean Acheson in the American State Department informing him that either his own department or the White House had in their possession a microfilm copy of a document about the Duke of Windsor. Marshall said the British had destroyed their copy and that the State Department should do likewise, so as not to embarrass the Duke of Windsor's brother George VI.[10] In his book Martin Allen reproduces a letter from the Duke to Hitler, which was given to Allen's father by Albert Speer. To test its authenticity, Allen subjected the letter to hand-writing analysis, and although the letter itself is pretty innocuous, Allen argues that added to the other documents, the letter proves that the Duke was giving information to Charles Bedaux. In 1999 Allen attempted to track down some of the Duke and Duchess of Windsor's private papers (relating to dossiers headed 'German Documents' and 'Correspondence of Sir Samuel Hoare'), at the Institut Pasteur in Paris where they had been lodged by the Windsors' lawyers in 1989. But he was too late. The papers had been removed to the Royal Archive in Britain. Perhaps not surprisingly, when Allen contacted the Keeper of the Royal Archive at Windsor, he was informed that the specific papers he was searching for, the 'German Documents' and 'Correspondence of Sir Samuel Hoare' had *not* apparently been transferred to the Royal Archives by the Institut Pasteur.

There is no doubt that the Duke of Windsor was a bitter, sad figure, who indulged in reckless loose talk with his inner group of cronies, politicians and foreign diplomats alike. Through some of his actions he undoubtedly 'let the side down'. We cannot get a complete picture of the Duke's actions because any evidence that may incriminate him in acts of treachery has either been destroyed or is secreted away in the Royal Archive. For the time being he must therefore be regarded as a fool rather than a traitor.

PG WODEHOUSE

Until recently the internationally famous British author P.G. Wodehouse was considered by many to have been at least a German sympathiser, and possibly a full-blown collaborator. This is completely untrue. Wodehouse was the literary genius whose comic creations include Bertie Wooster, Jeeves and Lord Emsworth of Blandings Castle. The author of almost one hundred books, Wodehouse also contributed to plays and musical comedies on both sides of the Atlantic, either as author or lyric writer. His books have sold in their millions around the globe, and the prolific writer also found time to pen three hundred short stories and write scripts for Hollywood movie giant Metro-Goldwyn-Mayer. In 1939 Oxford University awarded him an honorary degree in recognition of his services to literature. When war broke out Wodehouse and his wife Ethel were living semi-permanently at Le Touquet in France. Along with other British residents, Wodehouse was surprised by the rapid German advance across France and left it too late to make an escape. After Le Touquet was occupied by the German Army on 22 May, Wodehouse and other British men were imprisoned, first at Loos prison near Lille and then at an internment camp at Tost in Upper Silesia. In June 1941, Wodehouse was released from custody and taken to Berlin where he agreed to write and record five humorous talks for transmission by the German radio service. The light-hearted talks were intended to reassure and thank Wodehouse's many American friends and fans who had campaigned for his release. The talks were made for transmission to America, a country then at peace with Germany. Without consulting Wodehouse the Germans subsequently broadcast the radio speeches to England, and this led to accusations of collaboration and treason against the famous writer.

It is necessary to examine the nature of the charges against Wodehouse.[11] Firstly, it was assumed that Wodehouse and his wife Ethel had made no attempt to leave France even though the Germans were advancing towards their home in Le Touquet. British residents living in France were in fact informed by BBC radio broadcasts that the British Army would drive Germany out of France, and this is why many Britons remained in their homes. On 20 May, Ethel Wodehouse drove to the local British military hospital at Etaples to seek information about the German advance from the local British commander. He advised her that there was no panic to leave the area. A day later the Wodehouses did decide to pack up as many possessions as they could fit in their Lancia car and set off southwards. They had only got a few miles on a road congested with fleeing refugees when the car broke down. They returned home and used their other smaller car to restart the journey, but this time travelled in a convoy of cars with neighbours who had also decided to leave. A neighbour's car travelling behind the Wodehouses' also broke down, and as it was late afternoon both families decided to return home and set out the next day. But it was too late; the Germans had already occupied Le Touquet and the Wodehouses were trapped.

A further accusation against Wodehouse was that he became very friendly with the German occupying forces in his village. This was fuelled in part by a passage in one of Wodehouse's radio talks that read, 'There was scarcely an evening when two or three of them [German soldiers] did not drop in for a bath at my house, and a beaming party on the porch afterwards'. The fact that Wodehouse was being facetious about the way the Germans had taken over his bathroom was interpreted by some listeners as the writer actually welcoming the soldiers into his home.

Perhaps a more serious allegation against Wodehouse was that he collaborated with the Germans while he was imprisoned in the civilian holding camp. The statement of a repatriated British merchant seaman suggested in an interview with British Intelligence that while in the camp at Tost, Wodehouse had acted as editor of the pro-German magazine, *The Camp*. This was untrue. Wodehouse actually contributed to the internees' own paper, *The Tost*. After the war, Wodehouse's fellow British internees in Tost, including Arthur Green and Burt Haskins, told the intelligence service that the writer had voiced no pro-German sentiments, and was completely innocent of any charges of treason. Indeed, Wodehouse portrays his distaste for fascist influences in British society by parodying Oswald Mosley in his book *The Code of the Woosters*. In the novel, Wodehouse depicts 'Roderick Spode', the pretentious dictator and his half-wit followers who march around London in black shorts shouting 'Heil Spode!'[12]

A further charge levelled at the writer was that he had agreed to broadcast radio propaganda on behalf of the Germans, putting him on a level with Lord Haw-Haw (William Joyce). Altogether Wodehouse broadcast five talks from Berlin, each about ten minutes long. There was nothing in the speeches that could be interpreted as being pro-German or indeed anti-British. The idea for the talks seemed to originate from Buchelt, the Lager Führer (camp commandant), at the Tost camp. He had read an article Wodehouse had published in an American magazine describing his daily life in the internment camp. Whether Buchelt was acting on orders from Berlin to find out whether Wodehouse would be willing to broadcast has not been proved, though it is likely that the order had originated from either the German Foreign or Propaganda Ministry. Wodehouse later pointed out: 'The Lager Führer told me how much he had enjoyed the article and said, "Why don't you do some broadcasts on similar lines for your American readers?" I said I should love to or, "There's nothing I should like better" – or some similar phrase. These remarks were quite casual and made no impression on my mind.'[13] Wodehouse argued that the five talks he gave on German radio simply illustrated how a group of British internees could put up with the hardship of camp conditions while at the same time keeping up their spirits. He had certainly not done a deal with the Germans to make the broadcasts in exchange for his freedom. Wodehouse was almost sixty, the age at which internees were considered by the Germans to be past 'military service' and therefore eligible for release, so he was about to be set free anyway. His release was hastened by a petition organised by friends and loyal readers in America, and presented to the German authorities. Signatories to the protest included senior press figures, literary critics, senators and congressmen.

Wodehouse became involved in a propaganda-driven tug of war between Ribbentrop's German Foreign Ministry and Goebbels' Propaganda Ministry. The Foreign Ministry wanted to reinforce US neutrality by sending a signal to American public opinion that Berlin was acting reasonably in agreeing to the release on humanitarian grounds of the respected and independently minded writer. Goebbels, on the other hand, believed that it would be more advantageous for Germany to portray Wodehouse as a writer who had agreed to make the broadcasts because he actually sympathised with the Nazi cause. This is why Goebbels' henchmen surreptitiously obtained copies of Wodehouse's speeches from the Foreign Ministry and transmitted them to the United Kingdom. Very few people in Britain actually heard the broadcasts, which were monitored by the BBC listening station at Evesham, but the fact that they had been given by a British subject on German radio caused uproar in the press. The newspapers did not actually publish what Wodehouse had said in the speeches, but merely hinted that his words had been treasonous. The situation was not helped by a broadcast interview Wodehouse gave to Harry Flannery, an American radio corres-pondent with strong anti-German views who was based in Berlin. Flannery scripted the interview with Wodehouse, which the writer was happy to follow. But much was subsequently made in the British press of the phrase uttered by Wodehouse: 'I'm wondering whether the kind of people and the kind of England I write about will live after the war – whether England wins or not I mean.'[14]

Another accusation Wodehouse faced was the charge that he lived at the luxurious Adlon Hotel in Berlin at the expense of the German government. The German authorities insisted that Wodehouse and his wife Ethel stayed at the Adlon. To pay for this Wodehouse sold some of Ethel's jewels, receiving 40,000 Reichsmarks from the sale of a bracelet, 5,000 Reichsmarks for a wrist-watch and 40,000 Reichsmarks from a German film company for the right to make a film of one of his novels.[15] The Wodehouses also borrowed money from a German count with whom they had become friendly during their time in Hollywood in the 1930s. One of Wodehouse's German 'minders' later recalled that if there was any bread left at the table at the end of a meal, the married couple would take the food to their room to eat later.[16] He added that the couple hardly ever left the hotel and made no new friends while in Berlin.

There is no doubt that one of the most damaging acts against Wodehouse was engineered by British Cabinet Minister Alfred Duff Cooper. As Minister of Information Duff Cooper was given special powers to direct the war effort of the BBC. He encouraged the *Daily Mirror* journalist William Connor, author of the 'Cassandra' column in the paper, to broadcast a highly critical speech in response to Wodehouse's Berlin talks. The speech was transmitted on both the BBC Home and Overseas services and accused Wodehouse of selling his soul to Goebbels for thirty pieces of silver and the price of a soft bed in a luxury hotel, while fifty thousand British troops were enslaved in German prisoner of war camps.[17] The Director General and the Governors of the BBC objected to the government giving Connor's speech the green light. The BBC believed Wodehouse may have been ill advised in his actions but they also believed it was wrong to place him in the same category as the traitorous Lord Haw-Haw. The BBC also objected to being ordered by a government minister to allow such a personal, and possibly libellous, attack on an individual who was popular on both sides of the Atlantic, by a columnist from a tabloid newspaper. Although the newspaper letters pages were filled with correspondence attacking Wodehouse's actions, the fact that he had been called a traitor on the BBC was a severe blow. Wodehouse was devastated when he heard about the reaction to his talks back in Britain. He attempted to leave Germany and return to London to explain how his broadcasts had been misunderstood, but the Germans would not let him leave Berlin, ever aware of the propaganda value of keeping him there. Wodehouse wrote a letter to the British Foreign Office via the Swiss Embassy in Berlin. He admitted he had made a blunder in making the broadcasts, but had meant no offence to anyone, and was living in a Berlin hotel at his own expense partly on money borrowed from friends, rather than as a guest of the Germans.[18]

In 1943 the Germans did allow Wodehouse and Ethel to leave Berlin if they agreed to base themselves under German supervision in Paris. Wodehouse had hoped to be allowed to travel to neutral Sweden but finally agreed to go to France as it was safer than remaining in Berlin, which by that stage of the war was under constant attack from Allied bombing raids. The Wodehouses led a quiet life in Paris until the city was officially liberated in August 1944. Wodehouse then received a visit from a Major Cussens from British military intelligence. Cussens was part of an army team conducting enquiries into the activities of British citizens who were perceived as having collaborated with the Germans. Over a ten-day period Cussens questioned the Wodehouses about their time in captivity and in Berlin. His report was sent to the Director of Public Prosecutions in London who concluded that: 'Having considered Major Cussen's report, I have informed M.I.5. that I am satisfied, on the present material, that there is not sufficient evidence to justify a prosecution of this man.'[19] The statement went on to say that if further information came to light which showed there were more sinister motives behind Wodehouse's stay in Germany, such evidence would be looked at, but as far as Wodehouse's radio broadcasts were concerned, there were no grounds for prosecution.

Perhaps inevitably, given the long-running publicity surrounding Wodehouse, questions were asked in Parliament. On 6 December 1944, the Conservative MP Quentin Hogg suggested that the fact Wodehouse had spoken voluntarily on German radio should in itself be made a punishable offence. Hogg believed Wodehouse was as guilty as Lord Haw-Haw in that both men had broadcast from

Berlin, though he conceded that Wodehouse's punishment might be less severe than Haw-Haw's. The Attorney-General Sir Donald Sommervell replied that he had read the Director of Public Prosecutions' papers and had agreed with him that there was insufficient evidence to proceed against Wodehouse. Hogg's parliamentary questioning then turned to government failure to prosecute Wodehouse under the terms of the Trading with the Enemy Act of 1939. The Act laid down that any British citizen engaged in commercial dealings with the enemy was liable to prosecution, and Wodehouse's actions might have come within this category because he had accepted a token appearance payment (250 Reichsmarks), for his Berlin talks. Sir Donald Sommervell replied that the Trading with the Enemy Act referred specifically to someone based in Britain actually engaging in commercial activity with someone in Germany. Under a separate clause in the Act, any British subject finding himself, like Wodehouse, stranded in Germany, was entitled to buy food and clothes in order to survive.[20]

Just when it seemed that Wodehouse had been vindicated for his actions, a change of government in 1945 brought with it a new Attorney-General, Sir Hartley Shawcross, who put a different interpretation on the existing treason laws. Shawcross had led the case for the prosecution against William Joyce, and during the trial had put the government view that anyone broadcasting on the German radio system was in effect 'adhering to the King's enemies'. When asked in the House of Commons on 13 March 1946 if the new government intended to take any further action concerning Wodehouse, the Attorney-General replied: 'The question of instituting proceedings against this man will be reconsidered if and when he comes within the jurisdiction of our courts.' This legal bombshell meant in effect that Wodehouse was not technically in the clear, and indeed could be culpable. His lawyers advised that were he to return to Britain he could be prosecuted, not for treason, but for committing acts likely to assist the enemy; if found guilty by the jury he could have faced a token penalty of three months in prison. Perhaps not surprisingly Wodehouse decided not to go back to Britain but to return instead to America where he remained for the rest of his life. George Orwell commented: 'In the case of Wodehouse if we drive him to retire to the United States and renounce his British citizenship, we shall end up being horribly ashamed of ourselves.'[21]

But the die was cast. The British security service, the Home Office and the Director of Public Prosecutions were all closely involved in the Wodehouse case. Their investigations concluded that there was insufficient evidence against Wodehouse, which would prevent a successful prosecution. But the inference was that if fresh information ever came to light then the author might be dealt with. This meant that in the public mind there would always be lingering doubts concerning Wodehouse's sense of 'patriotism' and his activities in Berlin. The author Dorothy L. Sayers maintained that Wodehouse was simply not conscious of the propaganda value Germany was gaining through his actions. His fellow writer A.A. Milne considered Wodehouse to be politically naïve, while George Orwell offers perhaps the best observation of Wodehouse. Pointing out that Wodehouse was interned by the Germans before Dunkirk and the Blitz, Orwell concluded that '. . . it is important to realise that the events of 1941 do not convict Wodehouse of anything worse than stupidity'.[22]

The security files on Wodehouse were closed to public scrutiny for forty years. When they were finally opened the writer was cleared of collaborating with the Germans, the British government deciding that the speeches were prompted by naïvety rather than by malice. Wodehouse's so-called Nazi sympathies were again thrust into the public eye when recently released documents highlighted plans to award the writer a knighthood in 1971. A Whitehall civil servant wrote to the head of protocol at the Foreign Office, suggesting that it would be better to 'bury the wartime hatchet' against Wodehouse.[23] Sir Patrick Deane, then British Ambassador to Washington, noted to the Foreign Office in 1967 that an honour for Wodehouse would 'give currency to the Bertie Wooster image of the British character which we are doing our best to eradicate'.[24] Deane's remarks betrayed a lack of understanding of literature and comedy, especially given the popularity of 'Bertie Wooster' in the United States. The matter was finally settled when Harold Wilson came to power and decided to award Wodehouse his knighthood in 1975.

CHAPTER EIGHT

Collaboration in the Far East

FREDERICK JOSEPH RUTLAND

It may appear incongruous to suggest that a military hero from the First World War would later let his country down by working as a Japanese spy. It is necessary to go back to the 1920s to assess this particular case of collaboration. Frederick Rutland was a Navy flying officer during the First World War. He had originally joined the Navy as a fifteen-year-old 'second class boy' serving on a variety of ships, and gradually rising from the ranks to become a flight sub-lieutenant. Rutland had the distinction of being the first man to fly an aeroplane off a warship in action. At the Battle of Jutland in 1916 he was awarded the Distinguished Service Cross for gallantry for flying within close range of four enemy light cruisers in order to obtain accurate information. He also crashed his plane into the sea to save a drowning sailor, for which he was awarded the Albert Gold Medal. A year later he was awarded a bar to his DSC for submarine hunting in home waters. By the end of the war Rutland had developed an almost unique knowledge of aircraft carriers and deck landings. His aviation expertise was second to none and his wartime exploits had earned him the nickname 'Rutland of Jutland'. Then in 1923, at the relatively early age of thirty-seven, Rutland resigned his commission. He believed he had been passed over for promotion, but his specialised work of landing planes on decks meant he had not gained enough general experience to reach captain's rank. Rutland had also fallen in love with a married woman and wanted a fresh start away from Britain. He told the Navy he would be relocating to France for a while to consider his next move. In fact he had already approached the Japanese Navy while serving on HMS *Eagle*, to offer his services as a flying adviser. Naturally the Navy was disappointed to lose such a high-profile officer, but Rutland was a free agent. The rule that ex-officers could not serve with any foreign power for five years following retirement did not come into force until 1924, a year after Rutland had 'retired'.

The Rutland case was part of a wider issue affecting Anglo-Japanese relations. The alliance between the two countries established in the early part of the twentieth century meant that the British government allowed Japanese Naval Intelligence to open a navy centre near London's Victoria Station. Interestingly, Britain was not offered a similar facility in Tokyo. The alliance was formally terminated by the Washington Naval Conference of 1921–2. While it had suited Whitehall to have the support of the Japanese Navy in the Far East during the First World War, the British government regarded the alliance as a major obstacle to an improvement in relations with the United States. There was therefore an understandable concern in British military circles when Rutland agreed to work for the Japanese. Some believed his actions contravened the Official Secrets Act in spirit if not in letter.

After retiring from service, Rutland hired a large villa and took his family to live in France, ostensibly to act as Paris representative of various British automobile companies. In London the intelligence service had received a tip off that Rutland was about to tell the Japanese everything he knew about the strengths and weaknesses of the Royal Navy. MI6 contacted the French police who questioned Rutland's servants about his movements and who confirmed that the Westminster Bank had credited Rutland's London account with monies transferred by the Japanese Mitsubishi Bank. The MI6 case-notes from this period describing Rutland's behaviour state:

Everything goes to show that this individual has been heavily bribed to betray his secret knowledge of the foreign power whose service he is now entering. We know that he was in low water financially, while in this country; but he appears to suffer from no such disability at the present time.[1]

While in Paris Rutland mixed in Japanese social circles and held a series of meetings with Japanese businessmen. He left Marseilles with his wife and two children in the summer of 1924 on the liner *Kaisar-I-Hind* bound for Yokohama. Once in Japan he had a house built on the coast and took up employment at the Mitsubishi aircraft factory at Nagoya on a salary of £5,000 pounds a year. His main task involved the improving of aircraft landing carriages. He retained his British interests by joining the Tokyo branch of the Royal British Legion and took every opportunity to meet officers from visiting British warships.

Rutland remained an adviser to the Japanese Navy until 1932 when he returned to London. He started up a company in Regent Street called Marston Barrs Limited; the firm was registered as an importer of shipping freight and the chartering of steamships. Monitoring Rutland's activities MI6 intercepted a series of letters between him and the company secretary, a 'Miss Macdougal', that appeared to use coded messages, although this was not proved. However, the British authorities were able to eavesdrop on Japanese Navy cipher traffic and managed to pinpoint Rutland's dubious activities.

The decoding of Japanese diplomatic and naval telegrams was carried out by the British Government Code and Cypher School as a means of keeping an eye on what was interesting Japan's fast expanding Navy. Through the interception and decoding of messages sent between the Director of Naval Intelligence in Tokyo and the Japanese naval attaché in London, it was established that Rutland (code-name 'Shinkawa') had opened a business in London 'according to plan'. Shortly afterwards he was contacted in London by an old Japanese Navy colleague and a series of clandestine meetings was arranged including a bizarre rendezvous in the bushes on Ham Common in Surrey.

Rutland was under continual surveillance in England until his Japanese controller ordered him to travel to Los Angeles to set up a world-wide importation business. The object of Japanese Naval Intelligence was to employ an English businessman in America who would be of use in the event of a war between Japan and the United States. Rutland's firm was used as a 'post-box' for the forwarding of communications to and from the Japanese secret service. He was paid an annual retainer of £3,000, plus travelling expenses and an additional insurance policy of £10,000 for his wife should anything happen to him. The family lived in some style in swanky Beverly Hills, complete with large outdoor swimming pool, and the two children attended the most expensive and exclusive school in the neighbourhood. The Japanese told Rutland to open branches of his import company in New York, Peking, Vancouver and Sidney. These subsidiaries were intended to carry on genuine business activities while serving as a cloak for Rutland's spying activities. During a visit to Shanghai in 1937 he was in the process of setting up a new company as a cover for his spying activities, but had to leave the city following the outbreak of the Sino-Japanese War.

In 1941 Itaru Tachibana, a major Japanese spy operating in the United States, was arrested for espionage. Rutland's address was found in his pocket. At this stage Rutland offered his services to the American secret service probably because he knew he had been rumbled. He was in fact already under FBI surveillance, but at first the Americans thought he was probably a British agent. Under questioning he claimed that he did nothing to earn his money from the Japanese, had committed no crime, and was merely drawing his pay from Tokyo. He described how he would only become active as an agent under certain circumstances: 'If they sent me a telegram containing thirteen words, it would mean war is imminent and I should take steps from that date to get information to their attachés in Canada, Mexico, or some other South American country.'

He said he was just waiting for the right moment to tell the US authorities what he was doing. The Americans were already in a position to prefer serious charges against Rutland, but did not want to put him on trial because apart from the delicate matter of his being a retired British officer, evidence presented in court might have revealed that Washington had broken the Japanese 'Purple' code. 'Purple' was the Japanese diplomatic coded machine cipher. It was cracked by the US Signal Intelligence Service, which was able to eavesdrop on Japanese diplomatic activity around the world. Rutland was persuaded to return to England where he suggested offering his services to British

Intelligence. During his interrogation in Britain Rutland was less forthcoming about his dealings with the Japanese. He was unaware he had been under MI6 surveillance for a considerable period, and that the security services had access to intercepted Japanese cipher messages. His first lie was that he had originally gone to work in Japan in response to a newspaper advertisement. Then he claimed his affluent lifestyle was supported by a windfall he had received as a result of sponsoring a young Japanese aeronautical inventor. He maintained that in return for working for the Japanese, they would arrange to collect the money owed to him by the inventor. His biggest untruth was the suggestion that the Japanese intelligence service had first approached him to work for them in 1936. In 1935 Scotland Yard had found a despatch case containing various papers. Among the items recovered from the case was a letter Rutland had written in 1932 to the Japanese naval attaché in London, Shiro Takasu. When questioned Rutland said he had only met Takasu on one occasion in Japan, and had made no contact with him in London. The security service interrogator presented Rutland with the letter, which read:

My Dear Takasu
I was most agreeably surprised this morning when I came across your letter in the post to hear that you were in England. I would be awfully pleased to have lunch with you on Friday next and if you could make it one o'clock sharp it would be fine. I am writing this letter on my firm's notepaper so that you will see the telephone number and perhaps you would ring me up telling me where we can meet. I shall look forward to receiving a telephone call from you sometime tomorrow.[2]

Rutland reacted by claiming there was no question of it being either his letter or his handwriting. Despite being adamant that the Japanese had first made approaches to him in 1936, Rutland was confronted with evidence that he had met Takasu's replacement as naval attaché, Capt. Arata Oka, six times in London in 1935, including the meeting in the bushes on Ham Common. Rutland's loyalty was at the least suspect. He had not disclosed his role to the British authorities when

Japan became part of the Axis powers in 1936. Although there was not enough evidence to prove that Rutland had passed on British classified information, it was decided to intern him under Government Regulation 18B on the grounds that 'he is of hostile associations and it is necessary to exercise control over him'.[3]

Rutland was released from internment on health grounds in 1943. In an attempt to clear his name he had waged a campaign among his former Navy colleagues, including Admiral of the Fleet Sir Roger Keyes. Winston Churchill told Keyes to 'leave the case alone'. Rutland retired to Caernarvonshire. He refused to return to California because he believed the cloud of suspicion might prejudice the future of his children. In 1949 he gassed himself. There was fresh public interest in Rutland's case in the 1960s but the newly released documents confirm that although there is no conclusive evidence that he passed on British military secrets, his clandestine behaviour and spying activities for the Japanese were, to say the least, suspect.

WILLIAM FRANCIS FORBES-SEMPILL

This Scottish peer had his family home at Craigievar Castle in Aberdeenshire. He effectively had a foot in both the German and Japanese camps. A prominent member of The Link and of the Anglo-German Fellowship, Sempill served with distinction as an aeronautical engineer during the First World War with the Royal Flying Corps and fledgling RAF. He left the service in 1919 and went to Japan as head of a civilian mission engaged in the training of Japanese navy aviators, for which he was paid £5,000 a year.

In 1923 he returned from Japan but stayed in touch with his Japanese navy contacts. As a director of the International All Steel Aircraft Syndicate Sempill had close ties with various aircraft-manufacturing firms in the United Kingdom. Intelligence cipher intercepts revealed the friendship between Sempill and the Japanese naval attaché Cdr. Toyoda. The naval attaché was using Sempill for the purpose of securing confidential information, which the Japanese could not otherwise obtain. Writing to Toyoda, Sempill said he had received information from HMS *Argus* regarding the results of the trials of the Jaguar IV engine, which, he stated, had passed all practical flying and landing tests imposed on it. Sempill also provided information on the respective qualities of the Royal Navy's Flycatcher and Plover aircraft. By relaying military information to the Japanese Sempill had infringed Section 2 subsection 1A of the Official Secrets Act. For reasons not given the Attorney-General advised against prosecution, although Sempill was cautioned. He communicated his apprehensions in a further letter to Toyoda dated 10 December 1924:

My dear Commander
I meant to tell you to day, please be very careful how you use information you get and don't couple the name of any individual with it.

I will tell you when we meet again but I know just exactly how the wind blows, and the need for being super cautious.

Yours sincerely
W. Sempill [4]

Prior to Hitler's rise to power Sempill was director of the Anglo-German Club, an organisation designed to foster cultural relations between Britain and Germany. When war in Europe broke out Sempill was employed in the Naval Air Service and had access to all the latest technical information about aircraft and equipment. At the same time he maintained his Japanese contacts by acting as a paid adviser for Mitsubishi. In June 1940, MI5 intercepted a letter from Tokyo to the Mitsubishi Bank in London requesting it to make use of Sempill through military and naval attachés in London, and that regular payments to him should continue. This led to the Navy Board informing Sempill that his Japanese involvements were causing a conflict of interest and he was asked to give his word that as long as he was employed by the Admiralty he would sever links with Japan. Replying to the Admiralty in September 1940, Sempill agreed to limit his links with Japan to purely economic issues. But he continued his support for Japan. In August 1941 Mitsubishi's general manager in London, Satoru Makihara, was detained under the Defence Regulations. Tokyo asked Sempill for his assistance, resulting in Makihara's release. Sempill telegraphed to Tokyo: 'Delighted results – proud to help – working hard cause.'[5]

Sempill's telephone was tapped, and in one call he told the Japanese Ambassador he had important information for him. As the Ambassador was out Sempill arranged to call and see him. MI5 also searched Sempill's office and flat but found nothing incriminating. Word of Sempill's activities reached Churchill who scribbled on an intelligence minute: 'Clear him out while time remains'.[6] Sempill 'retired' from the Admiralty shortly afterwards.

THE FAR EAST BROADCASTERS

As well as the large group of Britons employed by the German radio organisation in Europe, a few renegades also volunteered to work for the German and Japanese propaganda machine in the Far East. Japan launched an attack on China in July 1937. By the autumn of 1938 the cities of Nanking, Hankow and Shanghai had all fallen to the Japanese Army. The port of Shanghai in particular was an important commercial centre, with a cosmopolitan mix of peoples from Asia and Europe. This led to the city becoming a hotbed of political intrigue with Britain, Japan, Germany, France, Russia and America all establishing intelligence gathering centres there in the 1930s. The major European powers were all drawn into the wider conflict in the Far East after the Japanese attack on Pearl Harbor in December 1941.

Shanghai had about fifty radio stations[7] broadcasting in a variety of languages to the city and the entire coastal region. All of the major powers had their own broadcasting stations but following the Japanese occupation of the city the two stations that dominated were those controlled by the Axis powers. The German propaganda station in Shanghai was Radio XGRS. It boasted a powerful transmitter, with its short-wave transmissions reaching much of East Asia.

One of the first British subjects to offer their services to Radio XGRS, was J.K. Gracie. Gracie had worked on oil tankers in the Far East before his ship was torpedoed in 1940. He was then employed as a Royal Fleet Auxiliary gunner but was paid off and so decided to try his luck in Shanghai. Finding it difficult to obtain work in the city, and with his funds exhausted, Gracie approached the local British Residents Association for help. They gave him £10 and sent him with his wife and son to stay in a shelter run by the Salvation Army. Gracie was appalled at his treatment, believing the residents association had fobbed him off. He described the hostel as 'A crummy broken-down old godown, wherein resides released gaolbirds, dope addicts, bums, sneak thieves, incurable drunks and in general the scum of the earth'.[8]

Gracie thought he deserved more respect, as someone who had served as a corporal in the British Army in the First World War (claiming to have won the DCM), and had more recently been in the Navy. He blamed his treatment on the fact he had a Japanese wife. He subsequently claimed that the Germans first approached him to work for them and he accepted their offer because he was poverty-stricken. His job at Radio XGRS was as an announcer, reading anti-British commentaries twice a day. He said he merely read out whatever script he was given. Some years later, at his trial, the German head of Radio XGRS, Carl Flick-Stager, testified that Gracie had made the first contact, willingly offering his services. He described Gracie as full of hatred for the British government, which he blamed for his own misfortunes. Furthermore, he also insisted on writing all his own radio scripts. The commentaries were full of venom, swearing and bad grammar and delivered in a Scottish accent, with Gracie being announced as 'Sergeant Alan McKenzie'. Flick-Stager added:

Gracie was a sincere Communist, and to my knowledge believed what he said. In the commentaries he did criticise and discredit the leaders and social conditions in Great Britain, and addressed himself to the poorer classes of the British peoples, such as the stevedores, mine workers and merchant seamen.[9]

In November 1942 Gracie was arrested by the Japanese as an enemy alien and interned in a local civilian camp. Gracie renounced his British citizenship (an illegal act in wartime), and was let out of the camp to continue his broadcasting activities. His wife and son were sent away to Japan and he never saw them again. When Germany capitulated in May 1945, the Japanese took over Radio XGRS, renaming it XGOO, and retaining the services of J.K. Gracie.

A second British collaborator (who claimed to be Irish) was Frank Johnston. Possessing a good broadcasting voice, Johnston was employed by a British radio station in Shanghai before the war. He broadcast news and magazine programmes on Radio XGRS in the name of 'Pat Kelly'. In addition he appeared in propaganda sketches usually playing the part of President Roosevelt. Like Gracie, Johnston was also arrested by the Japanese but was released after his German employers intervened. Carl Flick-Stager eventually dismissed him for being continually late for work. The Japanese soon signed Johnston up for Radio XGOO. One of his tasks was recording propaganda interviews with Allied prisoners of war held at the Kiangwan camp near Shanghai.

Another pro-Japanese collaborator was Robert Sandeman Lamb. A former officer in the Indian Army, Lamb ran an English language political magazine in Shanghai before the war. His German contacts led to his employment by Radio XGRS where he presented programmes under the pseudonym 'Bill Bailey'. He translated German press communiqués and propaganda articles into English. Lamb also dabbled in radio dramatics playing the part of Winston Churchill in the station's sketch programme. He was fired after turning up for work drunk. The switchboard operator had to be hastily drafted in to read the news bulletins.

There were many other instances of collaboration with the Axis powers in Shanghai. Apart from a handful of Australians tried for working for Japanese radio, up to thirty British subjects were initially detained in Shanghai, but all were released without charges being brought against them. Only Gracie, Johnston and Lamb remained in custody. The Chinese used the men as pawns in an effort to secure the unconditional surrender of alleged Chinese collaborators in British-held territory. Britain refused to capitulate on this issue and in February 1947, following eight months in prison, China allowed all three men to be transferred to Hong Kong to face trial under the Defence Regulations. Gracie was found guilty of giving aid to the enemy and sentenced to eight years' imprisonment. Johnston received ten years (despite claiming to be an Irish citizen). Lamb escaped prosecution on a legal technicality and was released. He took legal action against the Hong Kong government for wrongful imprisonment but having won his case, he was awarded only token damages.

One of the most bizarre cases of collaboration with the Japanese was that of Dr Thomas Baty. Born in Cumberland in 1869, Baty was educated at Oxford and Cambridge before being called to the Bar at the Inner Temple. He moved to Tokyo in 1916 to work in the legal department of the Japanese Foreign Office. Baty immersed himself in everything Japanese. A follower of Shintoism, he was also a theist and expert in heraldry, and often appeared in public dressed in the costume of a Geisha.

In 1938 Neville Chamberlain received a letter from a Japanese national named Sakae Katayama. The note asked the Prime Minister if he would send a message of congratulations on the occasion of Dr Baty's 70th birthday, stressing the respect Baty commanded within Japan. The letter said:

> Dr Baty has no enemy in the world. He loves humanity and knows not any difference to the colour, caste or creed. Dr Baty was instrumental and, initiative in many instances, for the prestige and popularity which Japan maintains and enjoys, at present, with all the foreign nations of the world.[10]

A rather puzzled Chamberlain asked his advisers for further information about Dr Baty. The Foreign Office reply was blunt. Regarding Baty's activities on behalf of the Japanese Foreign Ministry they concluded: 'Any service he has rendered has been to Japan and to Japan alone, and to us he may be regarded as having done disservice rather than otherwise.'[11]

The Foreign Office briefing accused Baty of defending Japanese aggression in Manchuria and reported that the British Ambassador Sir Robert Craigie would not be sorry to see Baty replaced by a less biased adviser. Chamberlain never sent a congratulatory telegram. Following the Japanese declaration of war in 1941 Baty continued to work at the Foreign Office in Tokyo, refusing all offers of repatriation to Britain. He never applied for Japanese naturalisation although he did at some stage during the war consider applying for Swedish citizenship, although he never followed up his initial enquiry. The British kept tabs on him during the war. A letter sent by Baty's sister Ann to a friend in England was passed to the British authorities by the Turkish Ambassador in Tokyo. The letter contained the line: 'Thomas goes to the office every day'.[12]

MI5 also knew that Baty had contributed to Japanese propaganda publications such as *Contemporary Japan* and the *Nippon Times*. The Japanese secret police eventually moved Baty out of his cottage into a Tokyo hotel. His work at the Foreign Ministry brought him a salary of 3,000 Japanese yen per month.

After the war the security services investigated Baty but concluded that he was a senile eccentric. According to Whitehall files the incoming Labour Foreign Minister Ernest Bevin believed Baty's conduct had amounted to treason. The Foreign Office concluded that Baty's wartime publications came from 'the pen of a man well known in international circles and must have done much to give comfort to the King's enemies'.[13] Whitehall instructed the United Kingdom Liaison Mission in Tokyo to refuse to grant Baty any protection as a British subject and to seize his passport. He escaped prosecution because of his age (he was almost eighty). He remained a virtual prisoner in Japan, even being refused leave to visit his cousin in India. In 1947 Baty approached the Foreign Office to test their reaction to the idea of a book of wartime reminiscences he hoped to publish. The British government took the view that if Baty was permitted to go ahead with the book, questions could be asked why he had not been prosecuted for his wartime activities. The book's potential publisher was warned off. Writing in a letter to a friend just before his death, Baty said he loved Japan but had never collaborated with the Japanese militarist regime which, he said, had virtually wrecked his cottage before forcing him to move into a Tokyo hotel. Baty died in Japan in 1954, aged eighty-five.

PATRICK HEENAN – THE SINGAPORE SPY

The fall of the supposedly impregnable fortress of Singapore in February 1942 was not only a crushing blow to Britain's war effort, but was also a symbol of the beginning of the end of the British Empire. The worst defeat in British military history was due to many factors. Britain, just as the United States before Pearl Harbor, seriously underestimated the capabilities of the Japanese fighting machine. A well-equipped British, Australian and Malayan force of some 130,000 troops was defeated by a poorly equipped Japanese Army consisting of only 35,000 men. Some of the military and intelligence assessments examining the reasons for the fall of Singapore have touched on the existence of a traitor within the British military. But there are no government files on the identity of the Japanese collaborator – they may have been destroyed in the chaos leading up to the fall of Singapore. Nonetheless, there has been enough evidence unearthed by military historians to provide at least a sketch of the Singapore spy.[14]

Patrick Vaughan Stanley (Stanley being his mother's surname) was born in New Zealand in 1910. He was illegitimate, something that was to plague him for the rest of his life. He also had dark skin, which was to make him sensitive to the racism of the time. Patrick was named Heenan after the mining engineer George Heenan whom his mother met in New Zealand, and Heenan was the name entered on Patrick's certificate of baptism. The family later travelled to Burma. Following the death of George Heenan, Patrick and his mother subsequently returned to England. Patrick entered Sevenoaks public school and later transferred to Cheltenham College. The young Heenan was an academic failure but excelled at sports, especially boxing. He was unpopular with his fellow students, which probably worsened the chip on his shoulder. Patrick joined the Officer Training Corps, but because of his dismal academic record admission to Sandhurst and a career in the Army seemed out of the question. Instead he left college and joined a commodities firm in the City of London with commercial links to the Far East. He hoped to return to Burma or perhaps Malaya but when the company refused to transfer him overseas Patrick once again considered a career in the Army.

Patrick actually got into the Army through the back door. There were only so many commissions available and Heenan of course had no academic qualifications and moreover would be competing with officer recruits from both Sandhurst and the Military Academy at Woolwich. He approached his old headmaster at Cheltenham for a letter of support, and backed this up with a character reference from his former Officer Training Corps commander who was pleased to help. These recommendations carried enough weight to get Heenan placed on the Army Supplementary Reserve List. In his application to join the Army, Patrick said his birth certificate had been 'lost' so instead he produced his certificate of baptism. In those intolerant days he would never have been granted a commission in the Army if it had been known he was illegitimate. He was eventually commissioned into the Army in 1935, and posted overseas.

He was earmarked for the Indian Army but first did a stint as a subaltern with the Royal Warwickshire Regiment based in Bombay. Heenan still wore the chip on his shoulder. He was a bad tempered maverick, a notorious womaniser and unpopular with his brother officers, often getting into fights to demonstrate his prowess as a boxer. With his dark complexion and lacking the required upper-class accent, Heenan did not fit the mould of a typical British officer. Nor did he do much better after being transferred to the 3/16th Punjab Regiment. One of his fellow officers commented: 'Heenan had a huge grudge against society and was out to get his revenge.'[15]

By the time Heenan took the leave due to him in 1938, he had been transferred to the Royal Indian Army Service Corps. He considered this a demotion, a career slide to an army backwater. Heenan certainly made the most of his army leave. He spent about four months in Japan, which is where he was recruited as a spy. The 6-foot tall, heavily built subaltern would easily have stood out in Japan. His idea of a good night out revolved around a large intake of alcohol and a pretty girl on his arm. Whether he approached the Japanese or simply responded to their overtures is not known. Either way, they must have made him welcome, and possibly even paid for his long stay in Japan. Soon after returning to India Heenan's regiment was posted to Malaya. South-East Asia was rife with spies among the Japanese community, so it would have been easy for Heenan to make contact with other 'sleeper' agents.

After Japan had joined the Tripartite Axis Pact with Germany and Italy in September 1940, Tokyo pushed ahead with its plan to attack much of South-East Asia. In a stroke of luck for the Japanese, Heenan was transferred to act as air intelligence liaison officer between the Army and RAF in Malaya. Through this post he gained access to British battle and logistical plans and, more importantly, to Allied contingency plans code-named 'Operation Matador'. He also made several unauthorised trips into Thailand, probably to make contact with his Japanese controller. Heenan persistently questioned RAF personnel about aircraft strength at the Alor Star base in northern Malaya. He wanted to know the deployment of a device for laying smoke-screens, and the capabilities of planes and their respective weapon loads. He made his biggest mistake by insisting to one station commander that he had permission from a senior officer to view highly secret papers locked away in a safe. Heenan's behaviour led to fellow officers viewing him with increasing suspicion. The fact that he was not popular with any of his colleagues in the first place only compounded their hostility.

When the Japanese invaded Malaya in December 1941, they performed successful bombing raids on RAF airfields, being guided to their targets by radio transmissions made by Heenan. He was searched, and found to possess unauthorised classified maps and code-books. More seriously, he had a two-way radio receiver and two transmitters, one which looked like a typewriter and the second concealed in a padre's field communion set. Heenan was taken to Singapore for court martial and during a three-day trial was found guilty of spying for the Japanese and condemned to death. On Friday 13 February, just two days before the beleaguered British forces surrendered to the Japanese, Patrick Heenan was escorted to Singapore harbour by a detachment of military policemen and shot in the head. His body was dumped in the sea.[16]

CHAPTER NINE

Collaboration in the Channel Islands

The Channel Islands was the only part of the British Isles to be occupied by the Germans during the Second World War. Recent studies of the occupation focus on the invasion as a testing ground for what might have happened had the British mainland also been overrun and occupied by the Nazis. In her book *The Occupation of the Channel Islands* Madeline Bunting argues that the fact some Channel Islanders collaborated with the Germans proves that Britons were no different in their behaviour from other European civilian populations under German occupation. How the wider British public might have behaved in the face of a German occupation compared to the Poles, Czechs and French, or indeed the Channel Islanders, is difficult to estimate, though it is fair to suggest that some collaboration would have been inevitable.

On the whole the collaborators and sympathisers covered in this book chose – for whatever reason – to collaborate with the enemies of the British state. The choice for those living in the Channel Islands was not as clear cut. The majority of Islanders had no option other than to walk a tightrope between opposition to the Germans and actively collaborating with them. Most did not or were not in a position to oppose the enemy although a few did choose to openly collaborate with them. Before looking at the cases of individuals who actively collaborated, it is necessary to look at the immediate background surrounding the German invasion. The Islands had no strategic importance for Britain and deploying additional manpower to the area could have had repercussions for the defence of the British mainland. The recommendation of the Imperial General Staff to demilitarise and evacuate the Islands in June 1940 meant that 30,000 inhabitants left before the German invasion, including all able-bodied men of military age. The 60,000 inhabitants who remained on the Islands were guarded by 37,000 Germans, a ratio of 2 to 1. It was therefore impractical to organise an armed uprising against the Germans. In fact the War Office in Whitehall had ordered the islanders to offer no resistance – in marked contrast with the situation in Britain where Churchill had vowed to fight the Germans 'on the beaches'.

As the war progressed the British government effectively forgot about the Channel Islands. In the wake of the D-Day landings the Islands were simply ignored. The Allies seemed in no hurry to liberate them until the war in Europe was over. No effort was made to supply the Islands, and a lack of food led to siege conditions and resulted in widespread malnutrition. Even the BBC, which broadcast morale-boosting messages to the various countries of occupied Europe, offered no specific service to the beleaguered Channel Islands. When the two Lieutenant-Governors left the Islands in June 1940 the function of administering the civilian population fell to the Bailiffs on Jersey and Guernsey, Alexander Coutanche and Victor Carey. In London the Home Office issued instructions to the Bailiffs to the effect that they should administer the government of the Islands to the best of their abilities in the interests of the inhabitants, whether or not they were in a position to receive instructions from His Majesty's Government. Jurat John Leale made the policy of the Guernsey administration very clear immediately prior to the invasion:

Should the Germans decide to occupy this island, we must accept the position. There must be no thought of any kind of resistance, we can only expect that the more dire punishment will be meted. I say this, the man who contemplates resistance should the Germans come is the most dangerous man in the island and its most bitter enemy. The military has gone. We are civilians.[1]

Once the Germans arrived they threatened to remove from office and punish or hold hostage any official who did not adhere to the orders of the military commander of the occupation forces, the 'Occupation Ordinances'. On one occasion Victor Carey, the bailiff on Guernsey, actively went out of his way to assist the enemy. This occurred when the Germans proposed to put their anti-Jewish measures into force. No protests were raised by any of the Guernsey state officials, and they hastened to give the Germans their total assistance. By contrast, when the Germans planned to take action against the Freemasons in Guernsey, Bailiff Carey protested strongly to the Germans and did everything in his power to protect the masons – mainly because he was the senior Freemason on the island!

The Germans passed a series of regulations covering every conceivable aspect of life on the Islands. A curfew was imposed from 2300 hours to 0600, alcohol was forbidden, petrol rationed and car use for private purposes banned. Berlin blackmailed the Channel Islanders with the threat of deporting all men between the ages of eighteen and forty-five. In fact over 2,000 were deported on the personal orders of Hitler, in retaliation for the internment of 500 German men in Iran by the British authorities. No one was shot for resisting German orders although people were imprisoned. People whom the Germans deported from the Islands were not so fortunate. Charles Machon, who ran the clandestine Guernsey Underground News Service (GUNS), which printed and distributed leaflets summarising BBC European broadcasts, was betrayed by an informer and sent to prison in Germany where he subsequently died. A Jerseywoman, Louisa Gould, was sent to Germany and died in Ravensbruck concentration camp for sheltering an escaped Russian slave labourer named Feodor Bourriy. Frederick Page, a farm labourer from Guernsey, defied Nazi orders by concealing a radio receiver at his home. He was arrested and sent to prison in Leipzig where he starved to death.

There were many facets to the collaboration on the Islands. Informers often acted for reasons of personal animosity and petty jealousies. People were denounced to the Germans for listening to the radio or hoarding food. Profiteers made considerable amounts of money at the expense of the more scrupulous Islanders by exploiting friendship with the Germans. Individual collaborators included the pub landlord who served nobody but Germans in his bar, and the barber who would only cut German hair. Sleeping with the enemy was another form of collaboration. According to British intelligence sources, out of the 320 illegal babies born in the Islands during the occupation, 180 were known to have had German fathers.[2] Cases of sexual collaboration mentioned in government files include that of a notorious Nazi sympathiser called Mrs Baudains, nicknamed 'Mimi the spy'. This 47-year-old had a German officer boyfriend and informed on fellow Islanders for £100 a time. On one occasion she had been thrown through a plate glass window in Jersey's Union Street. After the German surrender she went to the local police station and asked to be put in a prison cell for her own protection. Other pro-German women included a dancing instructor who gave special dance lessons for Germans and was allowed an extension through the curfew hours; a mother of a German child who informed against her own father; and a nineteen-year-old engaged to a German, who generally bad-mouthed the British and who swore and shook her fists at RAF planes flying over the Island. A well-known Jerseywoman in her early twenties had an affair with one of the senior German officers on the Island, Oberleutnant Zepernick. He organised 'parties' for willing local girls who found themselves drinking the best champagne and cognac provided by their genial host.[3]

It is of course easy to criticise the womenfolk of Jersey and Guernsey for this type of close co-operation with the invading forces. Many women were left alone while their husbands and boyfriends were away fighting with the British forces. The Germans helped to feed their girlfriend's families and acted as general protectors. Some genuine love affairs resulted in marriage after the war. In the wake of the Liberation, feelings were running high among Islanders who wanted to punish women who had 'fraternised'; there were instances of women (contemptuously nicknamed 'Jerrybags') being attacked in the street, stripped, smeared in oil and their heads shaved. In one case a woman thrown into the harbour in St Helier had to be rescued by British troops after the Jersey police failed to intervene.

After the war the British government ordered an investigation into possible cases of collaboration. But almost immediately the then Home Secretary James Chuter-Ede announced that there would be no prosecutions. The problem for the newly elected Labour government was how to define collaboration in the context of the Channel Islands. There were legal and practical difficulties. Under section 2a of the 1939 Defence Regulations Act, any person committing an act likely to assist an enemy could be liable to life in prison. In theory the various forms of collaboration committed by some Islanders seemed to fall within the jurisdiction of the Act. But because the Defence Regulations were revoked in Britain in 1941 by an Order in Council, the Act ceased to apply to the Channel Islands throughout the period of the occupation. The same view was applied to the Treachery Act of 1940 and the Trading with the Enemy Act. As a result, following the Liberation, the Director of Public Prosecutions Theobald Mathew decided that only cases of the greater crime of treason would be prosecuted. The punishment for acts of treason was the death penalty, and however distasteful acts of collaboration were, there was insufficient evidence to prosecute anybody specifically on the grounds of treason. The British government seemed to acknowledge that collaboration had existed on the Islands but decided to sweep it under the carpet. Whitehall had no wish to undermine the ruling bodies of Jersey and Guernsey by demanding that Channel Islanders be tried in British courts. They also realised that given the strength of popular feeling in the Islands, suspected collaborators would not be given a fair trial if tried in Jersey or Guernsey. The public image of civilian members of a part of the British Isles fraternising with the enemy (no doubt whipped up by the British press) may have harmed Britain's prestige abroad. There was probably a fear that further investigations and high-profile trials might reveal deeper levels of collaboration.

CHAPTER TEN

Closing in on the Collaborators

Shortly after the Second World War war broke out in 1939 the security services began collecting important information about the activities of those British citizens in enemy-occupied territory who were involved in collaboration. The information on the renegades came from various sources. MI9, the escape and evasion service, received coded letters from British servicemen imprisoned in German POW camps giving information about fellow POWs who had gone over to the enemy. John Brown's coded messages in letters to his wife revealed the Nazi Free Corps recruitment drive at Genshagen. The approximate strength of the British community working for the German broadcasting service was also identified. As early as 1940 William Shirer mentioned the broadcasting activities of Norman Baillie-Stewart. Anglo-Irish security co-operation paid off when John O'Reilly parachuted into southern Ireland in 1943. O'Reilly originally worked for the Rundsfunk Irish service in Berlin before being recruited into German naval intelligence. In Berlin the different nationalities worked in close proximity within the German broadcasting service, enabling O'Reilly to name suspects, although the use of pseudonyms acted as an initial smoke-screen for certain renegades. Another Irishman, William Murphy, had worked as a teacher at the Berlitz School in Berlin since 1943 and after being interned was contacted by German Intelligence, who planned to return him to Ireland as a spy. Murphy strung the Germans along and in the meantime was offered propaganda work in Luxembourg by William Joyce. Despite the Germans offering Murphy his own teaching school if he would agree to spy for them, he managed to stall them long enough to let him surrender to advancing American troops in Luxembourg in September 1944. Murphy volunteered to give information about his time in Berlin and was debriefed in London by MI5.

Following the D-Day invasion in June 1944, MI5 began drafting a central register of all known or suspected British collaborators. The document containing the names of those who should be apprehended was called the British Renegades Warning List, and was circulated to British army units in the field. An MI5 Liaison Section was set up to monitor renegades in conjunction with the British 21st Army Group. In September 1944, MI5 sent a memorandum to the Supreme Headquarters Allied Expeditionary Force Europe classifying the renegades into four main categories:

(1) Persons engaged primarily during the war in propaganda on behalf of the enemy.
(2) Persons who have joined the enemy forces.
(3) Persons, whether prisoners of war or not, who during the war have voluntarily engaged in activities deliberately intended to assist the enemy's operations.
(4) Persons who have voluntarily assumed or applied for enemy nationality during the war.

All evidence collected by the Allied Expeditionary Force was to be forwarded to MI5. This included the records of any branch of the German government; letters addressed by renegades to the enemy; official documents of enemy broadcasting stations, and the enemy radio programmes themselves.[1]

The apprehending and prosecution of known renegades was too much for army intelligence personnel to handle alone. A small group of Scotland Yard detectives had been loaned out to MI5 at the beginning of the war. The best known members of the police team were Leonard Burt, Reginald Spooner and William Scardon. In 1945 all were commissioned into the Intelligence Corps and immediately despatched to Paris to co-ordinate the arrest and interrogation of captured renegades. Prior to receiving his captain's commission

Reginald Spooner had concluded his investigation into the activities of 'Sergeant' Richard Styles, a private in the Gloucestershire Regiment. Having escaped from Germany to Sweden in 1944, Styles gave interviews to representatives of the British press in Stockholm telling of his capture at Dunkirk and a series of dramatic escape bids. He claimed to have escaped from a German coal mine before being apprehended at the Romanian border. After spending forty days in solitary confinement, he once again gave his guards the slip, and maintained he had entered France riding on the axle of a train, before being arrested at a goods yard in Amiens. Styles claimed to have been promoted to sergeant in the field just before Dunkirk. He also boasted of being awarded the Distinguished Conduct Medal for bravery under fire, proudly showing the telegram to the assembled press confirming the bestowal of the award. When British newspapers printed the story, MI5 sent Spooner to Stockholm to check out the would-be war hero. He discovered that Styles had set himself up as a professional magician, conveniently entertaining the children of British diplomats. Spooner put Styles under surveillance and within days the soldier turned magician paid a visit to the headquarters of the Abwehr in Stockholm. Styles admitted he had negotiated his freedom from captivity in exchange for infiltrating a British POW escape line into Sweden. At his trial in February 1945, he was given a seven-year sentence for aiding the Germans. It emerged he had paid someone in London to send the telegram confirming the award of his DCM.

Inspectors Burt, Spooner and Scardon, the three detectives turned army interrogators, spent most of the summer of 1945 interviewing renegades who had fallen into British hands in Germany and Italy. These included William Joyce, Norman Baillie-Stewart and John Amery. Other less known 'traitors' who had slipped through the net and returned to Britain were rounded up by MI5 and Special Branch.

Most of the British citizens who had traitorously worked for the enemy were brought to trial. Even where their offences seemed to be largely the same, the charges brought against the renegades fell into two categories. The first and most serious crime was high treason and offences against the Treachery Act of 1940, both of which carried the death penalty. The court had no power to pass a lesser sentence for treason, so a person found guilty would automatically be hanged if not granted a reprieve by the Home Secretary. Duncan Scott-Ford, Oswald Job and George Armstrong had all been convicted of treachery and executed during the course of the war. Sentences for offences against the Defence (General) Regulations 1939 ranged from being bound over, or serving a short prison term, to the possibility of life imprisonment. Section 2A of the Act was all encompassing, and included any act to 'assist an enemy or prejudice the public safety, the defence of the realm or the efficient prosecution of the war'. A number of BUF members and others deemed to have engaged in activities inconsistent with 'defending the realm' fell foul of the Defence Regulations.

WILLIAM JOYCE TRIED FOR TREASON

To suggest that the trial of William Joyce was controversial would be something of an understatement. Although he was hanged for committing treason against the British Crown, Joyce was not nor had ever been a British subject. As far as he was concerned his fascist philosophy and wartime activities did not amount to treason. Put simply, Joyce did not believe he had betrayed anyone or any country, as he explained to his MI5 interrogator William Scardon:

I know that I have been denounced as a traitor and I resent the accusation, as I conceive myself to have been guilty of no underhand or deceitful act against Great Britain, although I am also able to understand the resentment that my broadcasts have in many quarters aroused.[2]

The British authorities were determined that Joyce would be executed for his activities despite the fact that he was one of a group of many involved in broadcasting for the Nazis. MI5 did everything possible to ensure his conviction. In 1943 the security service enlisted the help of the BBC to make transcription discs of Joyce's broadcasts. MI5 officials scribbled down what Joyce had said in readiness for a future prosecution. After his arrest and imprisonment at Brixton jail, MI5 put all of Joyce's friends, family members and former associates under surveillance. Further, the prison governor at Brixton ordered that notes be taken on subjects discussed by Joyce and his visitors. These minutes were passed to MI5 and Special Branch.[3] William Joyce's brother Quentin had his telephone tapped and his mail intercepted. Letters exchanged between Quentin Joyce and his brother's lawyers, Ludlow & Company of Covent Garden, were also intercepted by MI5.[4] This gave the security service information about the working strategy of Joyce's defence team.

Joyce's trial commenced on 17 September at the Old Bailey. He was indicted on the following counts:

(1) Between 18 September 1939 and 29 May 1945 giving aid and comfort to the said enemies in parts beyond the seas . . . by broadcasting to the subjects of our Lord the King propaganda on behalf of the said enemies.

(2) Becoming naturalised as a subject of the Realm of Germany.

(3) This part of the indictment was identical to the first except the dates, which were between 18 September 1939 and 2 July 1940 (the period when Joyce held a valid British passport).[5]

Although Joyce had said on his passport application that he was born in Britain, his defence lawyers produced conclusive evidence (including a copy of his birth certificate), that he had in fact been born in America. His father had become a naturalised American in 1894 and so William was a US citizen by birth.

Selwyn neatly sums up the situation Joyce found himself in during this stage of the trial:

Had he been British, it would have been treason to take German citizenship while the two countries were at war. Since he was American he committed no crime (America had not yet entered the Second World War). After 26 September 1940, it was impossible for him to commit treason against any country but Germany.[6]

In these circumstances the Attorney-General announced that the Crown no longer wished to pursue counts one and two of the indictment. The trial judge subsequently directed the jury to acquit Joyce of the first two of the three charges of treason. This meant that most of the surveillance information and eye-witness accounts MI5 had collected against Joyce (including the BBC monitoring of his speeches, and of his efforts to recruit British POWs on behalf of Germany), was disregarded. A successful prosecution rested entirely on the third count, namely that Joyce had been in possession of a valid British passport during the first period of his broadcasts on behalf of the enemy, between 18 September 1939 and 2 July 1940. Surprisingly, Joyce's defence team did not ask the judge to discharge the jury, and for a new jury to be put in place to consider the remaining third count.[7]

The main prosecution witness for the vital third count was Special Branch inspector Albert Hunt. He told the court that he was stationed at Folkestone from 3 September until 10 December 1939 and that he heard Joyce broadcasting on the radio either in September or early October. Hunt said he recognised Joyce's voice from having heard him address British Union of Fascist meetings before the war. When challenged, Hunt was unable to recall what day, at what time, or even the month in which he had heard Joyce's voice on the radio. Finally when Hunt was asked on what station he heard the broadcast he replied: 'I do not know . . . I was just tuning in my receiver round the wavelengths when I heard the voice'.[8]

Inspector Hunt was actually making history as a prosecution witness. Two days after William Joyce was arrested a new treason bill was introduced, receiving the royal assent on 15 June 1945. The new Act was supposedly passed to simplify procedure, but it abolished the requirement under the Treason Act of 1695 calling for a minimum of two people to witness that an act of treason had been carried out. The amended Act meant that Inspector Hunt was the only witness at the trial to identify Joyce's voice from a radio broadcast, the only direct evidence that Joyce had committed an act of treason. If Hunt's rather hazy testimony had not been believed by the jury, the third count in the indictment would have failed because the prosecution offered no further evidence of Joyce's early broadcasts to the court.

Despite dropping the first two counts of the indictment, the prosecution based its case on the grounds that by holding a British passport until July 1940 Joyce owed an 'allegiance' to the British Crown. The prosecution set out to prove that British subjects were not the only ones who might owe a duty of allegiance. The prosecuting Attorney-General Sir Hartley Shawcross quoted a legal precedent to argue that anyone, regardless of nationality, if under the King's protection, owed such an oath of 'allegiance' to the British Crown. Shawcross maintained that by renewing his British passport shortly before embarking for Germany, Joyce had obtained the protection of the Crown, and therefore he owed it a reciprocal duty of allegiance. In the famous phrase used by Shawcross during the course of the trial, 'Joyce had clothed himself in the Union Jack whatever his nationality might be'. Joyce's defence also used a legal precedent to argue that such allegiance applied only when an 'alien' passport holder was resident in Britain, but that once he had left the country, the allegiance ceased. Joyce, the defence contended, had only used his passport to leave Britain. He had no intention of seeking the 'protection of the Crown' after that. After a lunchtime adjournment the trial judge Justice Tucker ruled that when Joyce applied for his British passport on 24 August 1939 he owed allegiance to the Crown and that nothing had happened to put an end to that allegiance in the period when the passport was valid. He added, 'It will remain for the jury and for the jury alone [to decide] as to whether or not at the relevant dates he adhered to the King's enemies with intent to assist the King's enemies.'[9]

The author Rebecca West, who was reporting on the trial for the *New Yorker* magazine, commented on the judge's direction: 'This ruling meant that Joyce was going to die, and his death would be recorded in legal history as the most completely unnecessary death that any criminal has ever died on the gallows'.[10] West's assessment was correct. The jury took only twenty-three minutes of deliberations to return a guilty verdict. The judge then pronounced the death sentence. Joyce appealed against the sentence but this was dismissed on 7 November. The case then went before the House of

Lords, where it was dismissed following a three-day hearing. There were letters and appeals and petitions to the British government not to hang Joyce but these protests had no impact. A sizeable crowd of about three hundred had gathered outside Wandsworth prison when William Joyce was hanged in the early hours of 3 January 1946.

SOME REFLECTIONS ON JOYCE

During his trial there was very little public sympathy for William Joyce. His boastful and vindictive radio broadcasts had made him public enemy number one during the war and his notoriety earned him massive press coverage in the period leading up to his trial and conviction. Although most people hated Joyce what stuck in their minds after the trial was the fact that he was not a British subject, but an American. For this reason many believed that Joyce could not be guilty of treason against the British Crown. There is no doubting Joyce's moral 'guilt'. He had defined himself as being English. In his preface to *Twilight over England* he wrote that from his earliest days he was taught to love England and her Empire. In the statement to Police Inspector Scardon at Luneburg Joyce stated that 'we were generally counted as British subjects during our stay in Ireland and England – we were always treated as British during the period of my stay in England whether we were or not'.[11] Joyce clearly believed he was an Englishman. But according to British law, Joyce was not and never had been a British citizen. The issues raised by his trial suggest that the law was 'stretched' specifically to ensure his execution. Even Hartley Shawcross, the chief prosecutor at Joyce's trial, writing some years later, expressed reservations:

Why then, as a lawyer, do I now say that this legal success is one of which I am not particularly proud? It is because I fear the prosecution – which in this context means me – failed to give the public a simple, straightforward legal basis on which to rest a capital charge. It was all too subtle and technical, not calculated to convince non-legal minds of the reality of Joyce's guilt in law and his moral culpability.[12]

Following Joyce's arrest the hastily improvised Treason Act was rushed through Parliament. It abolished safeguards that had been traditionally regarded as protecting defendants in cases of treason. This led to Joyce being convicted on the evidence of just one witness, Police Inspector Albert Hunt. His identification of Joyce's voice from just one radio broadcast was far from conclusive. Although Joyce's voice was distinctive it was not the only English voice heard on German radio during this period. Radio broadcasts from the continent were prone to distortion and interference. Inspector Hunt could not recall the time, the day, month or station on which he had recognised Joyce's voice.

Another possible reason for updating the Treason Act was the limited legal scope covered by the 1940 Treachery Act. This legislation covered British subjects and acts carried out by 'aliens' within British jurisdiction. It did not cover acts committed by aliens outside the realm so it could not have been used to prosecute Joyce. All the more reason for the Director of Public Prosecutions and MI5 to push for a more modified version of the 1351 Treason Act. The trial judge Justice Tucker had earlier presided over the Anna Wolkoff trial in 1940. At that trial he described Joyce as '. . . a traitor who broadcasts from Germany for the purposes of weakening the war efforts of this country'.[13] The Law Lords rejected Joyce's appeal but announced that they would give the reasons for the decision at a later date. They eventually explained the reasons for dismissing the appeal a month after Joyce had been hanged.

A further unsettling aspect of the Joyce case was the punishment he received compared with fellow renegade Edward Bowlby. Like Joyce, the pro-German Bowlby travelled to Germany on a British passport which he had acquired in April 1937. It could be argued that Bowlby, like Joyce, had therefore placed himself under the 'protection of the Crown' and in return owed a reciprocal 'allegiance', The Germans interned him at the civilian internment camp at Tost in Silesia, where he claimed Irish nationality. In 1944, while working as a translator in the German Foreign Office, Bowlby applied for an Irish passport but his application was turned down. The MI5 file on Bowlby revealed that two days after the Allied

landings in Normandy he suggested in a radio broadcast that British
soldiers were 'pawns of the Jewish money game'. In June 1943
Bowlby had visited the Berlin home of a German woman whose
British husband Ben Owens he had met during his internment. Mrs
Ernestine Owens recalled Bowlby telling her that many Englishman
including himself were employed by German radio:

> When he asked me why my husband did not get his release and do
> broadcasting work I said, 'most certainly not.' I asked him why he
> as an Englishman did that type of work, when he replied, 'I'm
> Irish. I hate England and never want to go back.' He also
> expressed great admiration for the Führer.[14]

Despite delivering outstanding service to the German cause, the
Director of Public Prosecutions decided that Bowlby could return to
Eire. He escaped punishment, being regarded by officials as 'scarcely
a public figure like Haw-Haw'.[15]

The relationship between William Joyce and MI5 agent Maxwell
Knight has never been fully explored. The two men had known each
other since 1924 when they had both been members of a British
fascist party named the British Fascisti Limited. Knight had been
Director of Intelligence for the group between 1924 and 1927.
During his later MI5 days Knight conducted a 'dirty tricks'
campaign against fascists by using moles to penetrate the
organisation. In 1940 he had infiltrated agents into the pro-Nazi
Right Club culminating in the arrest of Anna Wolkoff for sending a
letter addressed to William Joyce in Berlin. She was egged on by
Knight's MI5 plants. Her only contribution to the letter was a short
postscript, but she had incriminated herself.

Knight had made the telephone call on 24 August 1939 alerting
Joyce that he was on the list of those about to be detained under
Regulation 18B of the Emergency Powers (Defence) Act, and
suggesting that he leave the country. Knight probably wanted Joyce
out of the way because he could no longer afford to be associated
with him given the imminent clampdown on prominent British
fascists. Joyce may also have possessed sensitive information about

Knight's fascist past. Having penetrated her circle, MI5 almost certainly wrote the letter that Anna Wolkoff sent to Joyce in Berlin. The letter was a tactic used by the security service to discover how Wolkoff was communicating with Germany.[16]

The British government set out to make an example of Joyce. He broadcast propaganda directly into people's living rooms and in doing so committed a treason previously unheard of in Britain. The government feared Joyce's influence even though the war had ended. In a way, Joyce was Britain's very own 'Nazi' war criminal, a victim of the postwar climate of retribution. It was no surprise that his prosecution at the Old Bailey was conducted by Sir Hartley Shawcross who had recently acted as the British chief prosecutor at the trial of German war criminals at Nuremberg. Did Joyce have to die for speaking on the radio? It is significant that the United States never executed any of its citizens who had broadcast from Germany. Like John Amery, Joyce's more serious crime was his attempt to recruit British POWs on behalf of the German war effort. By that stage of the war Joyce was a German citizen and outside the jurisdiction of the British courts. Perhaps a more fitting punishment would have been a prison sentence followed by deportation, as was the case with Baillie-Stewart.

MARGARET JOYCE

After her husband was transferred to Britain to stand trial Margaret Joyce awaited her fate in a Brussels prison. She told MI5 that she had made her first radio broadcasts to Britain in September 1939. This put her in the same category as other British renegades who had broadcast from Berlin. Although it could be argued that she colluded with her husband in committing high treason, the British authorities decided not to prosecute her. The decision was made partly for compassionate reasons, and partly because the Director of Public Prosecutions, fearing a trial might collapse on grounds of her nationality, preferred to argue that Margaret was a German citizen (even though she had been born in Britain), when she made her 1939 broadcasts from Berlin.

After her husband was condemned to death Margaret Joyce was brought to London to visit him during the six-week period leading up to his execution. She was forced to go through the charade of being classified as an 'enemy alien' and interned in Holloway women's prison from where she made frequent visits to see her husband. The couple also maintained a regular correspondence. Following William Joyce's execution Margaret was quickly returned to prison in Brussels but after a press campaign in Belgium and America she was released. When she argued that she still held British nationality the authorities denied her entry to the United Kingdom because of an upswing in fascist political activity. The Home Office was also concerned that if Margaret returned to London on the basis that she had never lost her British nationality, she might seek damages for wrongful imprisonment during her period of detention in Brussels and Holloway prison. Clearly she was considered an embarrassment to Whitehall. After settling in Hamburg, Margaret did return to Britain some years later where she died in 1972, aged sixty-one.

JOHN AMERY

Amery's trial was rather tame in comparison with that of William Joyce. After his arrest Amery was placed in a civilian internment camp in northern Italy. On 22 May 1945 he was interviewed by Major Leonard Burt from Scotland Yard. In an eleven-page document Amery described his role as an enemy broadcaster, propagandist and recruiter for the British Free Corps. He was brought to England in July 1945 and remanded pending further enquiries.

On 28 November 1945 John Amery appeared at the Old Bailey to face eight counts of treason. To everyone's astonishment Amery pleaded 'guilty' to all eight counts. The judge Mr Justice Humphreys told Amery's defence counsel:

I never accept a plea of guilty on a capital charge without assuring myself that the accused throughly understands what he is doing and what the immediate result must be, and that he is in accord with his legal advisers in the course he has taken.

Mr Gerald Slade (who had also acted as Defence Counsel for William Joyce) replied: 'I can assure you of that, my Lord. I have explained the position to my client and I am satisfied he understands it.' The judge then pronounced sentence of death. The trial lasted eight minutes. During the proceedings Amery appeared to have a slight smile on his face. When the judge passed sentence Amery showed no emotion. He simply bowed with some dignity towards the bench and turned to walk down the steps to the cells. By pleading guilty Amery spared his family, and particularly his father, the pain and publicity of a long drawn out trial. There were delays in the actual trial date because when the defence was preparing its case the question of Amery's nationality arose. It was suggested that Amery had acquired Spanish nationality during his service in the Spanish Civil War, and therefore could not be tried for high treason. In an effort to save his brother from the gallows, Julian Amery travelled to Spain in a bid to unearth some evidence of a Spanish link but nothing conclusive was found. In fact John had signed a certificate confirming he was a British citizen in July 1940 in order to claim his relief grant from the consulate in Nice. Stranded in the unoccupied zone of France, Amery qualified for the grant as 'a British subject in distress'.

Because Amery had pleaded guilty to treason there could be no appeal. The only hope his family had was to seek clemency on the grounds of Amery's personality disorder. His father Leo Amery asked a psychiatrist, Lord Horder, for advice on his son's mental state. Because Horder was not allowed to see John Amery, his team of psychiatrists compiled a dossier based on the eye-witness accounts of people who had come into close contact with Amery, such as teachers and tutors and even his first wife Una Wing. Dr Edward Glover, one of the investigating psychiatrists, believed in his professional opinion that Amery could not understand the moral difference between right and wrong. His report on Amery therefore concluded:

That whatever may be his existing mental state, as regards sanity, he is certainly a severe and long-standing case of psychopathic disorder of the type at one time called 'moral insanity' or 'moral imbecility' . . . he is incapable of a normal appreciation of consequences and is devoid of the moral sense by which normal people control their actions and utterances.[17]

The Home Office responded by appointing two eminent psychiatrists to carry out a further mental examination of Amery. With few days remaining before Amery's execution, the doctors notified the Home Office that Amery should be reprieved on the grounds that he was not of sound mind and was unable to form moral judgments about his own behaviour. Sir Frank Newsam, Permanent Secretary at the Home Office, did not believe that Amery was insane. In his report to the Home Secretary, Newsam argued that the evidence showed that Amery knew and was often told he was a traitor yet carried on his treasonable activities. Referring to the prosecution notes, Newsam recalled Amery's visit to the St Denis internment camp when he took the British businessman Wilfred Brinkman to one side and pleaded with him not to say anything incriminating about his previous activities in Vichy France. This was sufficient for Newsam to conclude that Amery had enough moral perception to realise that he was committing wrongful acts. J. Chuter Ede, the Home Secretary, clearly had sufficient medical evidence to save Amery's life with the option of committing him to a mental institution. What helped to tip the balance against the traitor was Newsam's assessment of the politics of the case:

There is the further consideration of the effect of a reprieve on public opinion. Capital punishment in this country is tolerated as a deterrent because the man in the street believes that the law is administered without fear or favour. If Amery were reprieved it would be difficult to convince the ordinary man that Amery had not received exceptional and privileged treatment.[18]

Amery was hanged at Wandsworth prison on 19 December 1945. Albert Pierrepoint, Amery's executioner, later described him as the bravest man that he had ever had to execute. When the two men met, Amery remarked: 'I've often wanted to meet you Mr Pierrepoint – although not under these circumstances.'[19]

THOMAS COOPER AND WALTER PURDY

Due to his membership of the Waffen-SS, Cooper was the only member of the British Free Corps to face a charge of high treason. During the course of his Nazi allegiance he had persuaded British soldiers to join the BFC, fought on the Eastern Front near Leningrad, guarded Soviet POWs and murdered Polish Jews. Cooper was never court-martialled by the British military authorities because he had never actually joined the British Army. He spoke fluent German and was probably more Teutonic than Cockney. This no doubt helped his case because after being condemned to death he was reprieved in February 1946 on the grounds that his mother was German and his loyalties had been divided. Instead, he was given life imprisonment. Thomas Cooper served seven years of his life sentence. He was set free in 1953. Cooper had always been fascinated by the East and in particular Japan, so it was perhaps no surprise that he settled in Tokyo, converted to Buddhism and became a language teacher. He died sometime in the early 1980s.

Walter Purdy was renegade number 80 on the list of wanted collaborators. The merchant seaman and former member of the Ilford branch of the British Union of Fascists faced trial for treason at the Old Bailey in December 1945. He had originally made it back to England undetected but was eventually arrested by police in a London pub. At his trial Purdy claimed that he had tried to sabotage the German war effort by sending messages from Berlin, via his mother in Barking, with coded instructions for the RAF. He also claimed that he had tried to assassinate William Joyce by placing three hand grenades beside Joyce in a train. The grenades failed to explode. Purdy was convicted of treason. The accusation that he revealed a hidden escape tunnel from Colditz was dismissed on the grounds of insufficient evidence. Purdy was reprieved from the death sentence on the dubious grounds that he was a follower in treason rather than a ringleader. His sentence was commuted to life imprisonment. Walter Purdy spent only nine years in jail. He emerged from Wandsworth Prison under the assumed name of Robert Wallace Pointer. Instead of trying to trace his German wife

Margarete and his son, Purdy married his childhood sweetheart, never revealing his wartime past to his wife. For many years he worked as a quality control inspector in an Essex car factory. He died from lung cancer in 1982.

THE BERLIN BROADCASTERS

There were inconsistencies in the severity of the punishments meted out to the other renegade broadcasters. All were tried under article 2A of the Defence Regulations. Leonard Banning, the former BUF member and language teacher from Dusseldorf who worked for the Concordia New British Broadcasting Service, was given a ten-year prison sentence. Kenneth James Gilbert, the pacifist who fled to the Channel Islands in May 1940, volunteered to travel to Berlin where he was interviewed by William Joyce. Gilbert also accepted work on the New British Broadcasting Service using the alias 'Kenneth James'. He was paid a salary of 600 Reichsmarks per month. At his trial in September 1946 Gilbert received a nine months' prison sentence. Donald Alexander Fraser Grant, an enthusiastic pro-Nazi, read and wrote scripts for Radio Caledonia the pseudo-Scottish Concordia station which urged its listeners in Scotland to campaign for a separate peace with Germany. Grant received a mere six months' imprisonment. Kenneth Vincent Lander, a former teacher, who had lived in Germany since 1930 and also willingly broadcast his own material for the New British Broadcasting Service, was never prosecuted. Reginald Arthur Humphries, who played the part of 'Father Donovan' on the Christian Peace Movement Concordia station, was sent for trial at the Old Bailey. Sentencing him to five years' imprisonment the judge said, 'You were one of those people who, finding themselves in an internment camp, were ready to do anything to get out of it. You were ready to betray your country, and you did it.'[20] Anthony Cedric Sebastian Steane, alias Jack Trevor, the British actor who appeared in German propaganda films and read the news for German radio's English-language service, was sentenced to three years' imprisonment for aiding the enemy. After serving only three months he was paroled, supposedly because he had been forced to collaborate with the Germans against his will. It seems rather strange then that the distinguished American broadcaster William L. Shirer recalls Trevor standing outside the offices of the German radio station berating SS guards for not doing enough to kill Jews. Lewis Barrington (Barry) Payne Jones was another to escape any punishment. The Nazi sympathiser, who left England for Germany in May 1939, was interned by the British authorities in 1945 pending investigations. He claimed to have married a girl from Cologne and become a naturalised German. Mr Edward Jones wrote a series of letters to the Foreign Office insisting on his son's innocence. He wrote in one letter, 'my son has never been politically minded, and certainly never shared Nazi views'.[21] Mr Jones was apparently unaware of the letter his son had written to Germany in 1938 offering his services to the Reich.

The trial of Norman Baillie-Stewart was perhaps the strangest of those of all the renegades brought to justice. The former Seaforth Highlander officer had first gained notoriety in the early 1930s for selling military secrets to Germany. Following his arrest in Austria he was brought back to England and indicted on charges of treason and of being in breach of the Defence Regulations by broadcasting for the Nazis. The problem for the court was that Baillie-Stewart had ceased to be a British citizen when he had applied for German naturalisation in 1938. His application for German citizenship was delayed until 1940, making him still technically a British citizen, but the Attorney-General Hartley Shawcross agreed that morally Baillie-Stewart had ceased to be British in 1938. The trial judge was about to order Baillie-Stewart to be deported back to Germany, when the prosecution announced that the Allied Control Commission in Germany would not accept him back into the country as he was too closely associated with the Nazi regime. A secret behind the scenes deal had actually been struck between MI5 and Baillie-Stewart. Realising that they could not achieve a successful prosecution for treason, MI5 persuaded the disgraced army officer to plead guilty under the Defence Regulations to aiding the enemy. Failure to do so would result in his likely deportation to the Soviet occupation zone in Germany, where he would have faced certain death. Reluctantly he agreed to the prosecution's condition. Following a day's adjournment the judge sentenced Baillie-Stewart to five years' imprisonment. As with the cases of Amery and Joyce described above, there were some political rather than judicial reasons behind Baillie-Stewart's punishment. He was released from prison in 1949, but was barred from returning to Germany. A Quaker lady who had befriended him while he was in prison arranged for Baillie-Stewart to start a new life in Dublin. At first he lived in Quaker guest-houses using the name James Scott. He became a stationery salesman, married a Dublin girl and had two children. He died in 1966.

Compared to their male counterparts the female broadcasters all received light prison sentences. Pearl Vardon, the Jersey-born schoolteacher who accompanied her German boyfriend to Berlin and worked enthusiastically for numerous Nazi-run stations, pleaded guilty to six counts of assisting the enemy and received a sentence of nine months' imprisonment. The 67-year-old eccentric Margaret Bothamley, who hung pictures of the King and Queen in her German apartment before taking to the microphone to present women's programmes on Radio Bremen, was sentenced to a year's imprisonment. Frances Eckersley, the staunch fascist who had remained in Berlin when war broke out, taking a job as a radio announcer as well as providing William Joyce with useful contacts when he arrived in the city, received a one-year sentence. Her young son James Clark was also charged with aiding the enemy, but the trial judge believed that the impressionable James had been 'hypnotised' by Nazi propaganda, and he was bound over for two years. The case of Susan Hilton was not as straightforward as it seemed. Twice shipwrecked, and finding herself transported to France possessing neither money nor passport, Hilton ended up an alcoholic working on the Büro Concordia station, for the Christian Peace Movement. At her trial at the Old Bailey Hilton faced ten counts including the accusation that she had belonged to the Gestapo. She pleaded guilty to broadcasting on behalf of the enemy but denied most of the other charges including membership of the Nazi security service, which the prosecution quickly dropped. This meant that only the minimum evidence was publicly revealed in court. She was sentenced to eighteen months in prison.

MI5 retained an interest in Hilton even after she had completed her prison sentence, stopping the publication of a book about her life. She thought she was the victim of mistaken identity and may have been confused with an MI6 agent who had also embarked on the *Kemmendine* from Glasgow before leaving the ship at Gibraltar. When the *Kemmendine* was sunk and Hilton transported to France, she believed the Gestapo suspected her of being the 'missing' British agent and swiftly arrested and imprisoned her.[22] Hilton was to some extent a victim of circumstances beyond her control. She agreed to work for the Germans while trying if possible to leave Germany. Given her dependence on alcohol and game of cat and mouse with the Gestapo, Hilton should probably have escaped prosecution altogether. On her release she worked as an international courier. In the 1960s she returned to Germany to thank people who had helped her during her internment. She eventually opened a pet shop business in England, and died in 1983. Hilton's case highlights the inconsistencies in the punishments handed out to the renegade radio announcers. Many of the other broadcasters escaped prosecution, either through insufficient evidence or because the Director of Public Prosecutions accepted that they had worked for the Germans under duress. Ralph Powell, nephew of Lord Baden-Powell, came under the latter category. He claimed that he was forced to work for the Nazis by threats of reprisals against his German wife's family.

THE BRITISH FREE CORPS IN COURT

Members of the British Free Corps were court-martialled under Section 4 (5) of the Army Act of 1881, which prescribed the death penalty or some lesser punishment for prisoners of war convicted of serving with or voluntarily aiding the enemy. A general court martial consisted of a panel of five serving officers supported by a judge advocate to counsel the court in their deliberations.

The motley band of BFC members apprehended by Captain Denys Hart in the German town of Schwerin were transported back to

Britain to face trial. They were joined by Nicholas Courlander and Francis Maton, who surrendered to the military police in Brussels in early September 1944.

Most of the British Free Corps chief recruiters received stern prison sentences. Francis MacLardy, qualified pharmacist and the author of the BFC's fascist literature, was sentenced to life imprisonment at his court martial although this was later remitted to fifteen years. L/Cpl Nicholas Courlander, perhaps the most ruthlessly opportunistic of BFC members (he had been promised high office by John Amery following a German invasion of Britain), denied he was a traitor. In an MI5 statement he asserted:

I am anxious to point out that I had no interest in politics whatever before the war and that during my imprisonment my politics were purely a camouflage for my attempts to escape. I do not share the views of the ex-BUF men who formed the foundation of the BFC.[23]

His pleadings cut no ice with the court, who sentenced Courlander to fifteen years' imprisonment.

Hugh Wilson Cowie, originally from the Gordon Highlanders, was also sentenced to fifteen years. Cowie had used in his defence the well-worn excuse that he only joined the BFC with the patriotic intention of sabotaging it. He was not believed. Francis Maton was sentenced to ten years' imprisonment. Former commando John Eric Wilson was sentenced to ten years' imprisonment, and Henry Symonds, an early BFC recruit from the Luckenwalde indoctrination camp received a fifteen-year jail sentence – one year for every month he had served with the BFC. Edwin Martin from the Essex Scottish Regiment of the Canadian Army, who collaborated with the Germans shortly after his capture, became another chief BFC recruiter. He was sentenced to twenty-five years' imprisonment at his court martial.

Other BFC members were given lighter prison sentences and cautions while some escaped punishment entirely. Carl Britten, another key BFC henchman who had portraits of Hitler and Himmler beside his bed, was not prosecuted because he had advanced stomach cancer, and Roy Futcher, another committed fascist and anti-Semite, was not considered to be a major player in the unit. How Douglas Berneville-Claye, the SAS officer turned SS officer, remained in the clear is a mystery. He was definitively recognised by other renegades, but consistently denied all involvement with the BFC. The army prosecution service asked the captured German SS General Steiner to identify Berneville-Claye from a photograph but he seemed to suffer a temporary memory loss. Shortly after the renegade trials had finished Berneville-Claye was cashiered from the Army for theft. After the war he returned to Yorkshire where he worked as a salesman for Rank Xerox. He remarried and emigrated to Australia, where he became a pillar of the local community in Campbelltown, New South Wales. He stood for local election and taught English at a boys' school. He died in 1975 and was mourned by many who were unaware of his wartime role. Vivian Stranders, the academic and Waffen-SS expert on British affairs, was detained by the American military near Munich but could not be tried for treason because MI5 investigations confirmed he was a naturalised German.

Another not to be prosecuted was Eric Pleasants, the former enforcer for Mosley's Blackshirts who originally volunteered for the BFC to improve his diet, preserve his impressive physique and enhance his sex life. While undergoing military training at the Waffen-SS Pioneer School in Dresden, Pleasants met and married a German secretary Annaliese Nietschner. With the German collapse and the Russians moving into Berlin, Pleasants and his bride were forced to take refuge in the city's sewers. While trying to escape into the countryside Pleasants was forced to kill two Russian soldiers who attempted to rape his wife. The couple stayed with Annaliese's parents for a while but then found themselves in the Russian-controlled sector of Germany. When the war ended Pleasants made a living as a circus strongman, entertaining the Russian troops. Then in 1948 he was arrested by the Russians on an espionage charge, separated from Annaliese, and sent to a labour camp in Siberia where he remained for seven years before being released in a British–Soviet exchange. The British authorities no doubt believed he had suffered enough and brought no charges against him for his part in the BFC. It is also possible that British Intelligence recruited Pleasants as a spy while he was living in the Soviet-occupied part of Germany. On returning from Russia, Eric Pleasants returned to his native Norfolk, where he taught martial arts and practised the wood-carving skills he had learned in Siberia. He died in the 1990s. Pleasants' friend from the Channel Islands, John Leister, fled from Berlin to Italy, where he was eventually arrested by the Americans. He was tried for his BFC activities at the Old Bailey and jailed for three years.

The merchant navy personnel who were largely recruited from the Marlag/Milag prison camp all appeared at Bow Street court charged under the Defence Regulations Act. Alfred Minchin, who had always claimed the credit for changing the name of John Amery's proposed 'Legion of St George' to the British Free Corps, was jailed for seven years. The Spanish Civil War veteran Herbert George Rowlands received two years, and John Amery's one and only BFC recruit, Kenneth Berry, was sentenced to nine months.

The few RAF men who collaborated all faced justice. Benson Railton Freeman, a former BUF member who joined the Waffen-SS, and later described the other renegade broadcasters as 'the finest collection of poor-type Englishmen one could hope to meet', was handed a ten-year sentence. He then told his lawyer, 'this just shows how rotten this democracy is. The Germans would have had the honesty to shoot me.' Air Gunner Raymond Davies Hughes, who made broadcasts in Welsh on Radio Metropole, was given a five-year sentence. RAF Flt Sgt Jack Alcock received a two-year prison sentence at his court martial at Uxbridge. Alcock had been forced to bail out over Mannheim and voluntarily gave the Germans information about RAF aircraft, and tried to persuade fellow prisoners to do the same.

Like many young Irishmen, James Brady enlisted in the British Army on the eve of the war. He joined the Royal Irish Fusiliers and was immediately posted to the Channel Islands. After smashing up a pub Brady was given eighteen months' hard labour. When war was declared Brady asked to be returned to his regiment but was refused. When the Germans took control of the Channel Islands Brady was sent first to a camp at Cherbourg and then on to Lamsdorff POW camp in Germany. On learning of his Irish nationality the Germans moved him to a camp with other Irish POWs.

The Germans hoped to recruit an Irish legion to fight against Britain and assumed that all captured Irishmen were members of the IRA. In fact thousands of Irishmen volunteered to fight against Hitler. A small group of Irishmen with Republican sympathies did offer their services to the Germans. Brady later claimed he had collaborated with the Germans on the orders of the senior British officer Major McGrath, who hoped Brady would be able to gather useful intelligence information. At Christmas 1941 Brady left the camp for Berlin. He and some other men were taken to a house and given training in bomb-making, including how to place explosives between railway lines. Brady was taught to assemble wireless sets and how to send Morse code. The Abwehr wanted to parachute Brady into Northern Ireland to report on American troop movements. He was given false identity papers and a large amount of cash in sterling and American dollars. However, the mission was abandoned at the last minute because the Germans doubted Brady's loyalty. He was locked up for three weeks in a Berlin jail. Offered the chance to broadcast radio propaganda, he proved to be a flop and instead found himself volunteering for the Waffen-SS. After three weeks' training Brady was issued with his SS uniform and posted to Romania on active service. His next mission was extracting the Hungarian fascist dictator Adm. Horthy from Budapest. Brady later said of the task, 'we had a scrap with some Hungarians and lost a few men before we got Horthy out'.[24] Brady then saw service holding a bridgehead over the River Oder against advancing Russian troops. He was shot in the head and sent to Berlin to recuperate. After being discharged from hospital he wandered around the American zone and was eventually arrested and sent to a camp for captured German POWs in the Rhineland. There he purported to be an Irishman who had been living in Germany since the war started. On his release he returned to Berlin but eventually gave himself up to the British POW interrogation department. At his court martial in December 1946 Brady was jailed for twelve years. It was only his requests to leave jail in Guernsey when war broke out and return to join his unit in Britain that spared Brady a life sentence.

CHAPTER ELEVEN

Conclusion

'Traitors are usually sad men; always there is something wrong with them, some defect in their character or some lack in their personal lives, failure in their jobs or in their social adjustments.'[1] John Bulloch's description of a typical traitor would cover many of the people described in this book. Most of the collaborators discussed were motivated by pro-German and in some instances anti-Semitic ideology. William Joyce is perhaps the ideal example of this. Veteran Berlin correspondent William L. Shirer once said of Joyce: 'He had failed to become much of anything in Britain, where he grew up, and he was a man who obviously craved recognition.'[2] It is true Joyce was to some extent an outsider. Although highly educated he never quite fitted in. He was cast out of Ireland, his application to join the Foreign Office was rejected, he was disregarded by Mosley, and forced to flee Britain for another country. Joyce could only find fulfilment in pursuit of an extreme political philosophy. Thomas Cooper was also an outsider, driven by a sense of rejection in Britain and instead finding his identity through the depraved activities of the Waffen-SS. The Singapore spy Patrick Heenan was another who felt insecure about his birth, nationality and career prospects. He felt unable to assimilate to his brother army officers and eventually to any other Englishmen, instead finding solace with the Japanese.

There were of course many people with similar backgrounds to Joyce and the others who did not become traitors. The difference is that these people did not have the complex set of personal, political or social circumstances that drove the collaborators to do their work. Many of the traitors combined their ideological beliefs with a desire for personal influence or gain. John Amery was something of a social outcast in Britain but his pedigree combined with his anti-Semitic beliefs meant he was initially accepted with open arms in Berlin. He was also motivated by financial gain and a voracious sexual appetite. Eric Pleasants began the war as a pacifist but he willingly collaborated to improve his own position as a prisoner of war and to use any power possible to preserve a degree of physical control over his fellow BFC members. The group of schoolteachers who for some reason found themselves stranded in Germany in 1939 collaborated because they wanted a more comfortable existence. However they were also mainly pro-Nazi, as shown by the letters 'Barry' Barrington Jones wrote to his parents. Pearl Vardon fell in love with a German officer and accompanied him to Berlin. But romantic images apart, eye-witness accounts testified that Vardon hated 'all things British'. The Duke of Windsor and P.G. Wodehouse both allowed their egos to be massaged by the Nazis. The Duke received a warm reception on his visit to Germany and willingly gave the Hitler salute. He felt wanted and accepted, circumstances he felt himself deprived of in Britain. P.G. Wodehouse agreed to deliver speeches on German radio because he too was flattered. Both men were fools and unwitting collaborators.

E.M. Forster said in 1937 that, faced with a choice between betraying his friend and betraying his country, he hoped he would have the guts to betray his country. Collaborators in the mould of Roy Walter Purdy and Harold Cole succeeded in doing both. The BFC members who acted as German stool pigeons also betrayed friends and colleagues. They might not have believed that wearing a German uniform amounted to being anti-British, but by doing so they enjoyed far better living conditions and perks than the POWs who did not volunteer.

Perhaps the most interesting conclusion to be drawn from this study is the reaction of the British state to the collaborators. Many of the renegades were simply let off or given light prison sentences, or obtained early release, on the grounds that they were followers in collaboration rather than leaders. Joyce and Amery were made examples of and executed because the state wished to demonstrate the maximum retribution against anybody who seriously challenged it. Future purveyors of treason beware!

Notes

Chapter One

1. Martin Gilbert (1973). *Sir Horace Rumbold – Portrait of a Diplomat 1869–1941*, London, William Heineman, p. 381
2. Ibid., p. 379
3. The National Archives (PRO), hereafter TNA CAB 16/109
4. G.W. Price (1937). *I Know These Dictators*, London, p. 21
5. Lord Londonderry (1938). *Ourselves and Germany*
6. Barry Domville (1947). *From Admiral to Cabin Boy*, London, p. 43
7. TNA (PRO), KV 2/834
8. *Daily Express*, 9 August 1939
9. TNA (PRO) KV 2/834
10. Richard Griffiths (1998). *Patriotism Perverted, Captain Ramsay and the Right Club and British Anti-Semitism 1939–40*, p. 87
11. TNA (PRO), HO 144/22454
12. For best account of activities of these groups see Griffiths, *Patriotism Perverted*
13. For more on Mosley's vision of a corporate state, see chapter 5 in Colin Cross (1961). *The Fascists in Britain*, London, Barrie & Rockliffe, p. 72
14. Richard Thurlow (1998). *Fascism in Britain*, p. 107
15. TNA (PRO), HO 144/20141
16. TNA (PRO), HO 144/20143
17. David Pryce-Jones (1978). *Unity Mitford: A Quest*, London, W.H. Allen, p. 143
18. David Rosenberg (1985). *Facing up to Anti-Semitism*, London, Jewish Cultural and Anti-Racist Group
19. Ibid., p. 27
20. Paul W. Doerr (1998). *British Foreign Policy, 1919–1939*, Manchester University Press, p. 160
21. Ernest W.D. Tennant (1957). *True Account*, London, p. 215
22. TNA (PRO), KV 2/193
23. TNA (PRO), KV 2/292

24. TNA (PRO), KV 2/359
25. See *Camp 020, MI5 and the Nazi Spies*, Public Record Office, 2000, and J.C. Masterman (1972). *The Double-Cross System, 1939–1945*, London
26. TNA (PRO), FO 371/21176
27. TNA (PRO), FO 371/21780
28. TNA (PRO), KV 2/882

Chapter Two

1. TNA (PRO) KV 2/843
2. A.W. Brian Simpson (1992). *In the Highest Degree Odious. Detention without Crime in Wartime Britain*, p. 269
3. Nigel West (1981). *MI5 British Security Service Operations 1909–1945*, p. 120
4. Christopher Andrew (1985). *The Making of the British Intelligence Community*, London, Heinemann, p. 480
5. For full account of Tyler Kent affair see R. Bearse and A. Read (1991). *Conspirator: The Untold Story of Churchill, Roosevelt and Tyler Kent, Spy*, London; see also Nigel West, *The Times*, 10 December 1983, on the possiblity that Kent was a Soviet spy
6. Simpson, *In the Highest Degree Odious*, p. 161
7. TNA (PRO), KV 4/140
8. Robert Skidelsky (1975). *Oswald Mosley*, p. 454
9. Richard Thurlow (1998). *Fascism in Britain*, p. 153
10. TNA (PRO), HO 45/24891
11. Thurlow, *Fascism in Britain*, p. 168
12. The Friends of Oswald Mosley website: Oswaldmosley.com
13. Thomas P. Linehan (1996). *East London for Mosley*, London, Frank Cass, p. 183
14. Simpson, *In the Highest Degree Odious*, p. 169
15. Simpson, *In the Highest Degree Odious*, p. 170
16. TNA (PRO), KV 2/486
17. Ibid.
18. Richard Griffiths (1998). *Patriotism Perverted. Captain Ramsay and the Right Club and British Anti-Semitism 1939–40*, p. 252
19. TNA (PRO), KV2/617.
20. TNA (PRO), KV2/618.
21. Ibid.
22. Ibid.
23. *Sunday Telegraph*, 7 April 2000
24. TNA (PRO), KV 2/257
25. Ibid.
26. TNA (PRO), CRIM 1/1300

27. Ibid.
28. TNA (PRO), KV 2/51

Chapter Three

1. Horst J.P. Bergmeier and Rainer E. Lotz (1997). *Hitler's Airwaves, The Inside Story of Nazi Radio Broadcasting and Propaganda Swing*, p. 3
2. Ibid., p. 4
3. Martin Doherty (2000). *Nazi Wireless Propaganda, Lord Haw-Haw and British Public Opinion in the Second World War*, p. 8
4. TNA (PRO), KV2/174
5. Nigel West (1981). *MI5 British Security Service Operations 1909–1945*, p. 81
6. Norman Baillie-Stewart (1967). *The Officer in the Tower*, p. 137
7. Ibid., p. 139
8. J.A. Cole (1964). *Lord Haw-Haw and William Joyce, The Full Story*, p. 113
9. Baillie-Stewart, *The Officer in the Tower*, p. 151.
10. Ibid, p. 180
11. TNA (PRO), HO144/22823
12. Ibid.
13. Ibid.
14. Ibid.
15. TNA (PRO), KV2/81
16. TNA (PRO), KV2/79
17. Ibid.
18. TNA (PRO), HO45/25773
19. Ibid.
20. Francis Selwyn (1987). *Hitler's Englishman: The Crime of Lord Haw-Haw*, 1987, p. 126
21. TNA (PRO), HO45/25773
22. TNA (PRO), KV2/81
23. W.D. Rubinstein (February 1999). 'The Secret of Leopold Amery', *History Today*, Vol. 49, no. 2
24. Reinhard Spitzy (1999). *How We Squandered the Reich*, Norwich, Michael Russell, p. 355
25. Adrian Weale (2001). *Patriotic Traitors, Roger Casement, John Amery and the Real Meaning of Treason*, p. 197.
26. TNA (PRO), KV2/81
27. Ibid.
28. TNA (PRO), HO45/25776
29. Ibid.
30. William L. Shirer (1941). *Berlin Diary, The Journal of a Foreign Correspondent, 1934–41*, p. 412
31. N. West, *MI5 British Security Service Operations*, pp. 78–9

32. TNA (PRO), CRIM 1/1763
33. BBC Monitoring Service Reports, *Weekly Talks for Women*, Hamburg, 19 December 1939, 22.25 GMT, courtesy of the Forman Archive
34. Doherty, *Nazi Wireless Propaganda*, p. 22
35. TNA (PRO), HO45/25806 (1998)
36. David O'Donoghue (1998). *Hitler's Irish Voices, The Story of German Radio's Wartime Irish Service*, Dublin, Beyond the Pale, p. 194
37. TNA (PRO), KV2/426
38. Ibid.
39. Bergmeier and Lotz, *Hitler's Airwaves*, chapter 7
40. TNA (PRO), HO45/25827
41. TNA (PRO), KV2/632
42. Ibid.
43. Ibid.
44. TNA (PRO), WO71/1112
45. TNA (PRO), HO45/25833
46. Ibid.
47. Bergmeier and Lotz, *Hitler's Airwaves*, p. 207
48. TNA (PRO), WO71/1131
49. TNA (PRO), WO71/1112
50. BBC Monitoring Service Reports, Worker's Challenge station medium wave: 20.14. BST: 11 July 1940
51. Doherty, *Nazi Wireless Propaganda*, p. 24
52. Rebecca West (1982). *The Meaning of Treason*, p. 108.
53. BBC Monitoring Service, Reports, Christian Peace Movement: 19.45 BST: 21 August 1940
54. TNA (PRO), KV 2/258
55. TNA (PRO), KV 2/421
56. Ibid.
57. TNA (PRO), HO 45/25798
58. Ibid.
59. Ibid.
60. Bergmeier and Lotz, *Hitler's Airwaves*, p. 111
61. TNA (PRO), Air 18/28
62. Bergmeier and Lotz, *Hitler's Airwaves*, p. 111
63. Ibid.

Chapter Four

1. TNA (PRO), KV 2/245. See also Helen Newman (1998) 'The Influence of Lord Haw-Haw (William Joyce) in Britain 1939–1941', unpublished BA dissertation, Monash University, Australia

2. J.A. Cole (1964). *Lord Haw-Haw, The Full Story*, p. 29
3. Francis Selwyn (1987). *Hitler's Englishman: The Crime of Lord Haw-Haw*, p. 29
4. Cecil Roberts (1946). *And so to America*, London, Hodder & Stoughton, p. 22
5. Sir Oswald Mosley (1968). *My Life*, p. 311
6. TNA (PRO), KV 4/118
7. Cole, *Lord Haw-Haw*, p. 75
8. TNA (PRO), KV 2/245
9. TNA (PRO), KV 2/248
10. Cited in E.S. Turner (1982). *The Phoney War on the Home Front*, London, Michael Joseph, p. 110
11. Joseph Goebbels (1982). *The Goebbels Diaries, 1939–41*, trans. and ed. Fred Taylor, London, Hamish Hamilton, p. 87
12. BBC Monitoring Service Reports, 2 August 1940, courtesy of the Forman Archive
13. Imperial War Museum Sound Archive, accession number: 10591/1, 1 June 1940
14. Ibid.
15. TNA (PRO), KV 2/245, courtesy of the Forman Archive
16. Cole, *Lord Haw-Haw*, p. 155
17. Angus Calder (1965). *The People's War*, London, Jonathan Cape, p. 135
18. TNA (PRO), INF 1/265
19. TNA (PRO), INF 1/292
20. Ibid.
21. Shirer, *Berlin Diary*, p. 411
22. William Joyce (1940). *Twilight over England*, p. 52
23. TNA (PRO), KV 2/246
24. Cole, *Lord Haw-Haw*, p. 227
25. TNA (PRO), KV 2/250, courtesy of the Forman Archive
26. Ibid.
27. Leonard Burt (1959). *Commander of Scotland Yard*, London, Pan, p. 11

Chapter Five

1. TNA (PRO), KV 2/81
2. George H. Stein (1966). *Waffen-SS, Hitler's Elite Guard at War*, Ithaca, NY, Cornell University Press, p. 138
3. Ibid. p. 141
4. Adrian Weale (2002). *Renegades: Hitler's Englishmen*, p. 88
5. TNA (PRO), KV 2/81
6. Ibid.
7. Ibid.
8. Ibid.

9.   TNA (PRO), KV 2/79
10. TNA (PRO), CRIM 1/485
11. TNA (PRO), KV 2/81
12. Max Weinrich (1999). *Hitler's Professors*, New Haven and London, Yale University Press, p. 213
13. Weale, *Renegades*, p. 92
14. See Airey Neave (1952). *Saturday at MI9*, London, Hodder & Stoughton, for background to MI9 operations
15. John Brown (1981). *In Durance Vile*
16. Ibid., p. 92
17. TNA (PRO), WO 71/1117
18. TNA (PRO), HO 45/25817
19. Weale, *Renegades*, p. 105
20. See Weale, *Renegades*, p. 10 and Appendix, p. 202, for fuller list
21. TNA (PRO), CRIM 1/485
22. R. West, *The Meaning of Treason*, p. 158
23. Eric Pleasants' unpublished memoir, Imperial War Museum, London, Department of Documents
24. TNA (PRO), HO 45/25805
25. TNA (PRO), KV 2/251
26. Weale, *Renegades*, p. 170

Chapter Six

1.   Airey Neave (1952). *Saturday at MI9*, London, Hodder & Stoughton, p. 311
2.   Brendan Murphy (1987). *Turncoat: The Strange Case of Sergeant Harold Cole*, p. 26
3.   Ibid., p. 27
4.   Helen Long (1985). *Safe Houses Are Dangerous*, London, William Kimber, p. 24
5.   Sherri Greene Ottis (2001). *Silent Heroes, Downed Airmen and the French Underground*, University of Kentucky Press
6.   Iain Adamson (1966). *The Great Detective*, London, Frederick Muller, p. 143
7.   TNA (PRO), KV 2/76
8.   Ibid.

Chapter Seven

1.   Sir Robert Hamilton Bruce Lockhart (1973). *The Lockhart Diaries*, London, Macmillan, p. 263
2.   Martin Allen (2000). *Hidden Agenda, How the Duke of Windsor Betrayed the Allies*

3. Gwynne Thomas (1995). *King Pawn, or Black Knight*, London, Mainstream Publishing
4. Documents on German Foreign Policy Series D, Volume X, HMSO
5. See Allen, *Hidden Agenda*, for best account of life of Charles Bedaux
6. TNA (PRO), FO 371/28741
7. TNA (PRO), WO 208/609
8. Allen, *Hidden Agenda*, p.252
9. Documents on German Foreign Policy
10. Allen, *Hidden Agenda*, p.15
11. For full account of charges against Wodehouse see Iain Sproat (1981). *Wodehouse at War*
12. P.G. Wodehouse (1938). *The Code of the Woosters*
13. Frances Donaldson (2001). *P.G. Wodehouse, A Biography*, p. 210
14. Sproat, *Wodehouse at War*, p. 56
15. Donaldson, *P.G. Wodehouse*, p. 256
16. Sproat, *Wodehouse at War*, p. 272
17. Donaldson, *P.G. Wodehouse*, p. 244
18. For full details of Wodehouse's letter to the Foreign Office, see Sproat, *Wodehouse at War*, p. 70
19. Donaldson, *P.G. Wodehouse*, p. 263
20. Ibid., p. 269
21. George Orwell, eds Sonia Orwell and Ian Angus (1968). '*In defence of P.G. Wodehouse.' The Collected Essays, Journalism and Letters of George Orwell, Vol. 3, 1943–1945*, London, Secker & Warburg
22. Ibid.
23. TNA (PRO), FCO 57/278
24. *The Times*, 16 August 2002

Chapter Eight

1. TNA (PRO), KV 2/328, and KV 2/331
2. TNA (PRO), HO 45/25105
3. Ibid.
4. TNA (PRO), KV 2/871
5. TNA (PRO), KV 2/872
6. Ibid.
7. For most detailed account of collaboration in Shanghai, see Bernard Wasserstein (1989). *Secret War in Shanghai, Treachery, Subversion and Collaboration in the Second World War*
8. TNA (PRO), FO 369/3790
9. TNA (PRO), FO 369/3791
10. TNA (PRO), FO 371/22193

11. Ibid.
12. TNA (PRO), FO 371/35966
13. TNA (PRO), FO 369/3175
14. Peter Elphick and Michael Smith (1993). *Odd Man Out, The Story of the Singapore Spy*
15. Ibid., p. 104
16. John Hughes-Wilson (1999). *Military Intelligence Blunders*, London, Robinson, p. 132

Chapter Nine

1. TNA (PRO), KV 4/478
2. Ibid.
3. Madeline Bunting (1995), *The Model Occupation, The Channel Islands under German Rule, 1940–1946*, p. 62

Chapter Ten

1. For MI5 memo in full see TNA (PRO), HO 45/25512
2. TNA (PRO), KV 2/250
3. Peter Martland (2003). *Lord Haw-Haw, The English Voice of Nazi Germany*, p. 85
4. TNA (PRO), KV 2/246
5. Martland, *Lord Haw-Haw*, p. 83
6. Francis Selwyn (1987). *HItler's Englishman, The Crime of Lord Haw-Haw*, p. 194
7. See Alan Wharam (1995). *Treason, Famous English Treason Trials*, Stroud, Sutton Publishing
8. Selwyn, *Hitler's Englishman*, p. 187
9. TNA (PRO), KV 2/250
10. Rebecca West, 'The Crown Versus William Joyce', *New Yorker*, 29 September 1945
11. TNA (PRO), KV 2/246
12. Hartley Shawcross (1995). *Life Sentence, The Memoirs of Lord Shawcross*, London, Constable, p. 83
13. John Cole (1964). *Lord Haw-Haw and William Joyce: The Full Story*, p. 181
14. TNA (PRO), HO 45/25789
15. Ibid.
16. Adrian Weale (2002). *Renegades: Hitler's Englishmen*, p. 30
17. TNA (PRO), HO 144/22823
18. Ibid.
19. Weale, *Renegades*, p. 180
20. J.W. Hall (ed.) (1946). *The Trial of William Joyce*, Notable British Trials Series, London, William Hodge, p. 187

21. TNA (PRO), FO 369/3547
22. David O'Donoghue (1998). *Hitler's Irish Voices, The Story of German Radio's Wartime Irish Service*, Dublin, Beyond the Pale, Appendix, p. 194
23. TNA (PRO), KV 2/79
24. TNA (PRO), WO 71/1149

Conclusion

1. John Bulloch (1966). *Akin to Treason*, p. 151
2. William L. Shirer (1984). *The Nightmare Years*, Vol. 2, *1930–1940*, New York, Little Brown, p. 601

Select Bibliography

Allen, Martin, *Hidden Agenda, How the Duke of Windsor Betrayed the Allies*, London, Macmillan, 2000

Baillie-Stewart, Norman, *The Officer in the Tower*, London, Leslie Frewin, 1967

Ben-Yehuda, Nachman, *Betrayals and Treason, Violations of Trust and Loyalty*, Boulder, Col., Westview Press, 2001

Bergmeier, Horst J.P. and Lotz, Rainer E., *Hitler's Airwaves, the Inside Story of Nazi Radio. Broadcasting and Propaganda Swing*, New Haven and London, Yale University Press, 1997

Brown, J.H.O., *In Durance Vile*, London, Robert Hale, 1981

Bulloch, John, *Akin to Treason*, London, 1966

Bunting, Madeline, *The Model Occupation, The Channel Islands under German Rule, 1940–1946*, London, HarperCollins, 1995

Cole, J.A., *Lord Haw-Haw and William Joyce: The Full Story*, London, Faber & Faber, 1964

Currie, John, *The Security Service, 1908–1945*, with an introduction by Christopher Andrew, London, Public Record Office, 1999

Doherty, Martin, *Nazi Wireless Propaganda. Lord Haw-Haw and British Public Opinion in the Second World War*, Edinburgh University Press, 2000

Donaldson, Frances, *P.G. Wodehouse, A Biography*, London, Prion, 2001

Elphick, Peter and Smith, Michael, *Odd Man Out, The Story of the Singapore Spy*, London, Hodder & Stoughton, 1993

Foot, M.R.D. and Langley, J.M., *MI9*, London, Book Club Associates, 1979

Griffiths, Richard, *Fellow Travellers of the Right: British Enthusiasts for Nazi Germany, 1933–39*, London, Constable, 1980

——, *Patriotism Perverted, Captain Ramsay, the Right Club, and British Anti-Semitism, 1939–40*, London, Constable, 1998

Hinsley, F.H. and Simkins, C.A.G., *British Intelligence in the Second World War, Vol. Four*, London, HMSO, 1990

Joyce, William, *Twilight over England*, Berlin, Internationaler Verlag, 1940

Martland, Peter, *Lord Haw-Haw, The English Voice of Nazi Germany*, London, National Archives, 2003

Mosley, Nicholas, *Rules of the Game*, London, Secker & Warburg, 1981

——, *Beyond the Pale*, London, 1983

Mosley, Oswald, *My Life*, London, 1968

Murphy, Brendan, *Turncoat, The Strange Case of Traitor Sergeant Harold Cole*, London, Macdonald, 1987

Overy, Richard, with Andrew Wheatcroft, *The Road to War*, London, Penguin, 1999

Roberts, Bechhofer, C.E. *The Trial of William Joyce*, London, 1946

Selwyn, Francis, *Hitler's Englishman, The Crime of Lord Haw-Haw*, London, Routledge & Kegan Paul, 1987

Seth, Ronald, *Jackals of the Reich*, London, New English Library, 1972

Shirer, William, L., *Berlin Diary, The Journal of a Foreign Correspondent, 1934–1941*, New York, 1941

Simpson, A.W. Brian, *In the Highest Degree Odious, Detention Without Trial in Wartime Britain*, Oxford, Clarendon Press, 1992

Skidelsky, Robert, *Oswald Mosley*, London, Macmillan, 1975

Slade, Marquis de, *The Yeoman of Valhalla*, privately published, 1970

——, *The Frustrated Axis*, privately published, 1978

Sproat, Iain, *Wodehouse at War*, London, Milner, 1981

Stammers, Neil, *Civil Liberties in Britain during the Second World War*, London, 1983

Thurlow, Richard, *Fascism in Britain*, London, I.B. Tauris, 1998

——, *The Secret State, British Internal Security in the Twentieth Century*, London, Blackwell, 1994

Wasserstein, Bernard, *Secret War in Shanghai, Treachery, Subversion and Collaboration in the Second World War*, London, Profile, 1998

Weale, Adrian, *Renegades: Hitler's Englishmen*, London, Pimlico, 2002

——, *Patriot Traitors, Roger Casement, John Amery and the Real Meaning of Treason*, London, Viking, 2001

West, Nigel, *MI5, British Security Service Operations, 1909–1945*, London, Bodley Head, 1981

West, Rebecca, *The Meaning of Treason*, London, Virago, 1949

West, W.J., *Truth Betrayed*, London, Duckworth, 1987

Young, Gordon, *In Trust and Treason, the Strange Case of Suzanne Warren*, London, Edward Hulton, 1957

Index